# YOUN

# Vulnerabilities, Boundaries, Protection and Integration

# YOUNG MIGRANTS

## Vulnerabilities, Boundaries, Protection and Integration

**Editors:**

Ana VILA-FREYER
Mehmet Gökay ÖZERİM

TRANSNATIONAL PRESS LONDON
2020

YOUNG MIGRANTS: Vulnerabilities, Boundaries, Protection and Integration
Edited by Ana VILA-FREYER and Mehmet Gökay ÖZERİM



First Published in 2020 by TRANSNATIONAL PRESS LONDON in the United Kingdom, 12 Ridgeway Gardens, London, N6 5XR, UK.
www.tplondon.com



Paperback
ISBN: 978-1-912997-40-4

Cover Design: Gizem Çakır
Cover Photo: "Running through the Trees" by Jed Villejo, @jmvillejo,
https://unsplash.com/photos/bEcC0nyIp2g

www.tplondon.com

# CONTENT

# ABOUT AUTHORS

**Tanja DEJANOVA** is currently completing a Postgraduate Award in Cognitive Behavioral Therapy at the University of Liverpool. Having earned an MA in Forensic Psychology from John Jay College of Criminal Justice in New York City, she has worked with and studied at-risk and in-need populations both in and outside of the criminal justice systems in Europe, the United States, and Mexico. In addition to her background in the social and behavioural realms of criminal justice, Ms Dejanova's work is informed by a strong belief in equality and the power of crossing cultural and educational barriers.

**Halina GRZYMAŁA-MOSZCZYŃSKA** is a full professor in Psychology of Culture and Religion at the Institute of Psychology at Jesuit University Ignatianum in Cracow. She has earned her degree in clinical psychology and psychology of culture and religion. She is also visiting professor at the research centre at Innlanded Sykehuset at Hamar ( Norway). Since 1990 she conducts research in Poland among refugees and in local communities in which refugees camps are located. Since 2019 she is a President of the International Association for the Psychology of Religion. She serves on the editorial boards of several professional journals and has taught courses in various European US and Asian universities.

**Sara JORDENÖ** is a documentary filmmaker, visual artist, researcher and an Assistant Professor at the Rhode Island School of Design (RISD). Jordenö's cross-disciplinary and longitudinal projects study social movements with a focus on communities facing different forms of marginalisation, such as unaccompanied minor refugees in Sweden and LGBTQ youth of colour in NYC. Jordenö's video installations and films have been shown internationally. Her documentary film KIKI has been featured in over 200 festivals around the world and was released in theatres in the US, Sweden and the UK. Jordenö is the recipient of prestigious awards such as the Art Matters award, the Teddy Award for Best Documentary Film and the Kathleen Bryan Edwards Award for Human Rights.

**Weronika KAŁWAK**, PhD, from Jagiellonian University, Institute of Psychology, Kraków, in 2018. Her thesis concerned epistemological, institutional and methodological aspects of pain diagnosis, as well as the experience and practices of medical doctors. Her scientific interests include the use of qualitative methods in various research areas of psychology, theoretical dimensions, ethical aspects and philosophical origins of qualitative methodology. In her research, she has adopted phenomenology and hermeneutics in cognitive science and experimental philosophy, critical health and social psychology, or research and development. Now she starts a new critical ecopsychological project on the problem of climate depression.

**Sirkka KOMULAINEN** has a background in social research since the early 2000s. She obtained her PhD in Sociology at the University of Surrey, Guildford in 2004 in Childhood Studies field with critical work on children's voices and minority group rights. She is currently based at South Eastern Finland University of Applied Sciences as a Senior Research Manager. She has published internationally on childhood/youth and immigrant integration matters.

**Chiara MASSARONI** is a Doctoral Student in Sociology at the University of Innsbruck, Austria, and member of the Doctoral School "Dynamics of Inequality and Difference in the Age of Globalization". Her work focuses on the identity negotiation of young migrant children living in Morocco. She also works as a consultant and is currently collaborating with UNODC and UNESCO on a project related to children's education. Prior to her PhD she completed a Master in International Relations in Rome, Italy, and worked for ten years with NGOs in Europe, Africa and Latin America in the field of children's education and inclusion

**Liliana MEZA GONZÁLEZ** graduated with honours from the Technological Institute Autonomous of Mexico (ITAM) from the Economics Master and Undergraduate. She also studied a Masters and a PhD in Labor Economics at the University of Houston. Dr Meza has published more than 40 articles, book chapters and policy briefs in topics related to the Mexican labour market and Mexican International Migration. Currently, she is a Researcher at the National Institute for Statistics and Geography (INEGI) and a part-time professor at the Universidad Iberoamericana. She has been part of the National Research System (S.N.I.) since 1999.

**Irasema MORA-PABLO** is a full-time teacher at the University of Guanajuato, Mexico, in the Language Department. She currently teaches courses in the area of English teaching and applied linguistics. She holds a PhD in Applied Linguistics by the University of Kent, UK. Her teaching experience at the university level and her own learning experience have shaped her areas of interest: Bilingualism, Identity formation, Second-language Acquisition and native and non-native teachers

**Marisol NAVAS** is Professor of Social Psychology at the Faculty of Psychology and research member and Secretary of the Centre of Migratory Studies and Intercultural Relations, at the University of Almeria. Her areas of expertise include intergroup relationships, prejudice, stereotypes and discrimination, as well as acculturation and adjustment processes of immigrant populations (adult and adolescents) from different ethno-cultural origins. Professor Navas has published widely in scientific national and international journals (JCR indexed) and books and has extensive experience in leading and managing national and international research projects about these topics.

**Pedro Paulo ORRACA ROMANO** holds a PhD in Economics from the University of Sussex. He worked as Project Support Assistant at the London School of Economics, as Deputy Director at Mexico's City Ministry of Finance, and as Professor of Economics at the Universidad Autónoma de Baja California. His work has been published in Oxford Development Studies, Review of Development Economics, Latin American Economic Review, Social Science Journal and Journal of Borderlands Studies. His main research interests are labour economics, development economics and international migration. He is currently Professor at the Department of Economics Studies at El Colegio de la Frontera Norte

**Mehmet Gökay ÖZERİM** is a member of the International Relations Department, and the Director of the European Union Research Center at Yaşar University, Turkey. His main study fields are international migration, youth, security and European integration process. Dr Özerim was awarded the Chevening Scholarship of UK Government in 2010 and carried out a part of his researches in the University of Oxford. In 2014, he was at the Institute of European Studies in University of California, Berkeley as a visiting scholar. He has also been working in several European Union funded projects and delivering training on youth participation and project management since 2006. In 2019, Dr Özerim was awarded a Jean Monnet Chair on migration by the European Commission.

**Amber HORNING** is an Assistant Professor in the School of Criminology and Justice Studies at the University of Massachusetts, Lowell. For the last nine years, she has researched commercial sex markets, human trafficking and forced migration. She has extensive fieldwork experience with hidden populations and conducting qualitative studies. Additionally, she has led research studies in international settings, such as South Africa and Sweden. She has published in journals such as Deviant Behavior, Sociological Perspectives, and Dialectical Anthropology. Dr Horning has an interdisciplinary background, and she uses innovative mixed-methods approaches, and she publishes her work both nationally and internationally.

**Omar SERNA-GUTIÉRREZ** holds a bachelor's in TESOL, and a master's in applied linguistics for ELT, both from the University of Guanajuato. His research interest includes transnationalism, return migration, and funds of linguistic knowledge.

**Paulina SZYDŁOWSKA** is a PhD candidate at the Institute of Psychology at Jagiellonian University in Cracow. Her research interests are related to cultural, social and developmental psychology. She conducts the research using qualitative approach about the acculturation of Polish adolescents and their parents living in Spain, but she also worked in a project related to returning child migrants situation. Beside the academical context, she works as a clinical child psychologist.

**Victoria TSE** is a PhD Candidate at the University of Cambridge, pursuing her doctorate in Development Studies, focusing on government policies and programs related to migrants abroad in the cases of Mexico and the Philippines. She holds an MPhil in Development Studies from the University of Cambridge, and a bachelor's degree in International Affairs and Economics from the George Washington University in Washington, D.C.

**Ana VILA-FREYER** holds a PhD in political science from Université de Montréal and is professor-researcher at Universidad Latina de México. Her research focuses on composed identities and multiple belongings developed by young Mexicans settled regularly or irregularly in the US or returning to Guanajuato, central Mexico. She has been part of the National Research System (S.N.I.) since 2017.

**Francesca VIOLA** is a development economist and an expert in children's rights and child migration. She deals with research and advocacy for children's rights in Italy (where she co-founded the organisation Articolo12) and supports the work of international NGOs and international organisations, such as the World Bank and UNICEF. Her main research interests focus on children's rights, adolescence, migration and social protection, both from a qualitative and a quantitative perspective.

# FOREWORD

## Víctor Zúñiga[1]

This book is the product of a fascinating conference held in Bari, Italy, in June 2019. Viewing the content of the collection of chapters included in the book, one can discover that, in that conference, presenters and organisers implicitly heed Dobson's invitation (2009) to *unpack children* [and youth] *in migration research*. Doing this, contributors successfully overcame two kinds of "adultist constructions" (Holt & Holloway 2006) that are typical in the literature about international migrant children. First, the perspective that overlooks children in migration research simply because they are not "migrants", they are "things", "objects" or "suitcases" carried by their parents or other adults. In the collection of contributions gathered by Ana Vila-Freyer and Mehmet Gökay Özerim, readers will discover exactly the opposite: children and youth are migrants. Instead of being "objects", children and youth circulate, produce mental maps, have educational purposes while moving from one country to another. They build their own forms of understanding about the role and the duties of their legal guardians when they move unaccompanied and separated from their parents; they also talk about their own experiences. These children produce their narrative about what international mobility means for them; they even create their identities referring to different heritages, languages and feelings. In some cases, they are proud of their origins while accommodating the changes for acquiring new nationalities.

As Dobson stated, one founds the second kind of *adult-centrism* in migration studies when researchers take into account children and teenagers in migration studies just when, and only when, they are sources of anxiety -for adults- because minors are victims and need protection. That literature depicts children and youth as not participants, but as handicapped, human beings deprived of knowledge and agency. In other words, this second kind of adult-centrism finds migrant children interesting because of their vulnerability, not because they are migrants, like their parents and other adults. In this book, children and youth are migrants even in the study of Afghani unaccompanied refugee minors in Sweden, the most vulnerable group included in this collection of works. Certainly, that chapter focus on psychological distress, sexual exploitation or homelessness – circumstances that are real for refugee minors in several countries. However, the chapter on Afghani refugee minors is not a mere description of the undesirable consequences of minors' displacement. Still, also

[1] Tecnologico de Monterrey, Mexico.

it presents a valuable critique of the current regulations and laws about refugee status in Sweden, where recent legislation changes maintain and reproduce the conditions of vulnerability. So, what one can learn from this work is that refugee minors are also victims of legal frameworks that produce victimisation.

Contributions in the volume also allow us to overcome different forms of myopic dominant perspectives which I discuss elsewhere (See: Zúñiga, 2017). The first form of myopia comes from an inability to see that wellbeing of sons and daughters very often are the most important purposes for adult migration (men and women) (Willis and Yeoh, 2000; Drebby, 2010). The success or failure in the decision and process of migrating to another country is inseparable from children's wellbeing even when they stay at home in their countries of origin. If you listen to the Dreamers who return to Mexico and are thankful for the generosity of their parents, you can observe this:

> "My parents dreamed of a better life. They dreamed of a life for their children that they didn't have" (p. 28);
>
> "A DREAMer is someone (...) who seeks wisdom and strength in her/his ancestors. Someone who values and feels great respect and honour to have such strong parents who gave up a life in their home countries to be able to provide a better life for their children" (p. 28);
>
> "The decision was made (to return to Mexico) due to her mother's concern. This represents the role of her mother in the family as an active decision maker" (p. 152);
>
> "Samuel's mother was a pivotal factor to encourage him to study the BA (in Mexico)" (p. 117).

The second form of myopia is the inability to recognise the agency of children and youth in the process of migration; leaving, residing, settling, adapting, integrating, circulating, and/or returning (Ní Laoire *et al.*, 2012). Several chapters in this book show us how these children are active participants, who are also builders of their own lives in the middle of uncertainties, anxieties, and fears. They build even defensive strategies like Patrick (14-year-old boy refugee from Ivory Coast living Ashua, Morocco):

> "I think (...) that Moroccans don't have a good image of us they don't like me much, that's why (...) every time I walk along the street, if there is a guy who passes me or I pass someone else, they call me like 'nigger', they start insulting me, but don't care, I pass, me, I didn't have any problems, they can say whatever they want." (p. 78).

Finally, the third form of myopia one can find in migratory studies is the inability to observe the roles played by children and youth in the process of migration. Recent research has overcome this kind of short-sightedness by showing how children become translators, interpreters, sponsors, and intermediaries, helping their parents and siblings (Orellana *et al.*, 2001; Valdés, 2003). In *Young Migrants: vulnerabilities, boundaries, protection and integration* one can discover how often youth become or try to become supporters of their families and friends: "In various informal conversations the children (minor refugees in Morocco) mentioned their role as language-brokers, especially helping their mothers shop in the local souk". (p. 81)

In sum, contributors in this volume are researchers who are unpacking the place of children and youth in migration studies. They are signifying that migrant is not a synonym of *working-age-men.*

## References

Dobson, M. E. (2009). "Unpacking Children in Migration Research." *Children's Geographies,* 7 (3): 355–360.

Dreby, J. (2010). *Divided by Borders. Mexican Migrants and their Children*, Berkeley, University of California Press.

Holt, L. and S. L. Holloway (2006). "Editorial: Theorising other Childhoods in a Globalised World." Children's Geographies 4 (2): 135-142.

Ní Laoire, C., A. White, N. Tyrrel and F. Carpena-Méndez (2012). "Children and Young People on the Move: Geographies of Child and Youth Migration", *Geography*, 97 (3):. 129–134.

Orellana Faulstich, M., B. Thorne, A. Chee and W. Shun Eva Lam (2001). "Transnational Childhoods, the Participation of Children in Processes of Family Migration", Social Problems, vol. 48 (4): 572–591.

Valdés, G. (2003). Expanding Definitions of Giftedness. The case of young interpreters from immigrant communities. Mahwah, NJ, Laurence Erlbaum Associates Publishers.

Willis, K. and S. A. B. Yeoh (2000). "Gender and transnational household strategies: Singaporean migration to China", *Regional Studies*, 34 (3): 253–264.

Zúñiga, V. (2017). "Los niños y las niñas migrantes en escena". *Sinéctica Revista Electrónica de Educación* 48, https://sinectica.iteso.mx/index.php/SINECTICA/article/view/700.

# INTRODUCTION

Ana Vila-Freyer and Mehmet Gökay Özerim

"The Global Migration Crisis" has become a buzzword of the international community that describes the increased human flow by the 2000s, which emerged mostly due to the conflicts and other forced reasons in the periphery and as a result of their outcomes in the core countries. It is not surprising when it is considered that 70.8 million people around the world were forced to flee their homes by 2020. However, although there are a growing academic literature and increasing policy level debates about the issue, one thing is still not adequately discussed: The centrality of youth for the contemporary migration flows.

Overall, the young population represents almost two-thirds of the immigrant and refugee population. Moreover, children below the age of 18 have been constantly increasing and currently, it constitutes half of the refugee population while it was 41% in 2009 (Global Trends in Forced Displacement Report, 2017). When only the refugees are analysed within the displaced population, again half of 25.4 million refugees are under the age of 18 (UNHCR, 2018). For the case of international migrants, the young population between the ages of 18 and 29 represents an extensive group while in almost every immigrant-receiving country children from 2 to 17 and young adults aged from 18 to 35 years constitute the majority of the immigrant community.

In spite of its' prominent role in human mobility, the young population is still mostly discussed and analysed as the passive actors/subjects of the migratory movements and post-migration processes rather than a focus. Youth is inadequately visible either in global policies or in theories on international migration. This is evident both at the academic level and also at the policy level. For instance, although youth forms an essential part of UNHCR's "Persons of Concern" (UNHCR, 2013), there is still a lack of adequate data on the global displaced young population. On the other hand, academia is used to studying migrants as the male bread-winner and, in general, as labour migrants who mainly go from south to north to improve their material conditions (Sandoval y Zúñiga, 2016; Zúñiga, 2018). Therefore, young migrants who moved borders with their parents socialising in the north and creating a different profile of the mobile population are mostly ignored. This volume maintains that young migrants face particular experiences and problematics underestimated both in political communities and migration theories.

When we analyse how the young people are recognised in migration theories, it has been mostly assessed as an additive and underestimated as a central actor of the discussions. The "youth as a variable" approach is still not adequately integrated into the migration theories, and youth is not visible in macro-level, micro-level, and meso-level migration theories. Neither the neoclassical economics nor the push-pull demographic models of the 1970s and 1980s, for example, have youth-specific explanations. The roles of young people were thought of as dependent on the parents', and mostly male labour migration. Classical theoretical debates in migration studies underestimate youth, although it can possibly act as an underlying element of conflict, unemployment, or other root causes of migratory flows. So, they lack concrete references to youth-specific migration experiences in both sending and receiving contexts.

While youth migration, in qualitative and quantitative terms, has been becoming increasingly important in migratory flows, migration scholarship focuses on youth by three definitive perspectives, which can be grouped as decision-making, integration, and marginalisation. Studies focusing on the decision-making process of young immigrants and refugees challenges the traditional idea which generally presumes that migrants are the first and foremost adults since they are considered as the ones making the decisions to initiate migration process (Bloch et al., 2013; Van Blerk, 2007; Tacoli, 1996; White, 2011; Ryan, 2011; Cairns, 2010; Adams, 2009). Therefore these studies tend to acknowledge youth as primary decision-makers and independently responsible for their own migration as young persons. Those decisions, as some of the chapters on the Mexican-USA migration corridor presented in this book suggest, may mostly be guided by anti-immigrant environment, pulled by a desire to continue higher education, or as a result of deportation of members of the immediate family. A personal or negotiated decision to return to Mexico, the formal country of origin, underscore new challenges arising from the difficulties faced by youth to re-integrate in their country of nationality, while their roots may seem to stay in the country-lived.

Studies on migrant integration and identity among young migrants analyse different domains of integration such as education, employment, health, rural youth, urban youth, poverty, the transition to adulthood, and the role of gender (Fangen et al., 2011, Fangen et al., 2016; Limage, 1984; Pfarrwaller and Joan-Carles, 2012; Berry et al., 2006; Hirschman, 2001; Gilroy and Lawrence, 1988; Gilroy, 1993; Gilroy, 1981; Kaya, 1997; Kayaoğlu and Kaya, 2011). Among these studies, some of them analyse young immigrants' integration in linkage with the "youth sector." The term youth sector mainly refers to public bodies, non-government organisations (NGOs), academia and the private sector, which develops and implements local, regional, national and international-level services for young people. For instance, Geddes analysed the roles of NGOs in the development of EU's anti-discrimination policy paradigm as a step to integration, Fangen, Fossan, and Mohn studied social exclusion and inclusion of young immigrants in Europe; Bello analysed the role of non-formal education for the empowerment of young migrants in Italy; Holton studied the relationship between public policy and young refugees and immigrant support systems; Caselli studied how to measure young immigrants' integration into local societies; Penninx analysed structural factors of integration in Europe based on the case of NGOs; Acconcia, Chiappero-Martinetti and Graziano studied the role of "third sector" for young population's integration policies.

As some of the chapters presented in our book demonstrate, moving in or out of the country of origin can be included in this perspective. Francesca Viola shows that young people moving out as refugees might face all sorts of risks in receiving society, and they are increasingly dependent on organised support by the host societies. Italy's organisation of legal tutors may have a positive impact on young refugees' integration, affecting negatively those unable to enjoy such support. On the other hand, Amber Horning, Sara Jordenö and Tanja Dejanova show that in Sweden, refugees face growing vulnerabilities even while being supported by voluntary organisations. They interviewed 19 members of a voluntary network of Swedish citizens who help young refugees. The network accounts how the Swedish state has reduced and changed the options granting asylum to unaccompanied minor refugees, including social welfare benefits, making them vulnerable to stress, homelessness, labour and sexual exploitation. Many are returned to the dangerous and uncertain conditions existing in their countries of origin. These native social networks are crucial to guide youngers in their integration or rejection in host countries.

Other chapters show that the negotiation of boundaries and self-definition are constantly challenging young migrants. Chiara Massaroni explores the importance of the street as a place of socialisation and identity negotiation for children and young migrants moving through Morocco. The street helps them to set boundaries and negotiate inclusion through the legal frames to facilitate the integration of migrants. Contrary to this case, the liminal situation lived by young persons of Mexican origin in the USA, as Ana Vila-Freyer shows, has created a different set of identification. There a Dreamer is independent of the country of residence. While the majority accepts to belong to the temporary condition of being a Dreamer as a DACA recipient, some others define themselves according to their own mental maps and boundary constructions. It is important to highlight different acculturation processes lived within the immigrant's family or as individuals. Paulina Szydłowska and her co-authors explain different, and sometimes, parallel processes of acculturation of children of Polish origin in Spain. While a mother's and her teenager child's perceptions and preferences may differ in peripheral domains of their lives, and the identification with mother's country of origin may seem forced to her child, there are similarities in the central areas of life.

The Mexican cases discussed in this book can help us to explain some of the visions in the receiving country. In some cases, return migrants are youngsters of Mexican origin socialised in the USA who returned or were forced to go back home; in others, there were children born in the USA to Mexican parents migrating to Mexico. Victoria Tse's chapter underscores the paradox that while social protection for Mexicans abroad has expanded in the last 25 years, there is no institutional framework or social programs to facilitate the integration of young Mexicans coming back home. Omar Serna Gutiérrez and Irasema Mora-Pablo present interesting empirical evidence on how students re-adapt and discover their linguistic ability and transform it into a cultural capital to facilitate their integration to Guanajuato, in central Mexico, where children and youth have arrived since 2008 as immigrants or as first-time residents of their parents' hometowns. Both chapters explore the experiences and interpretations of their lives that go beyond borders and feelings of belonging. On the other hand, Liliana Meza and Pedro Orraca show that American born children to Mexican parents immigrating to Mexico have a tendency to receive higher remunerations in the labour markets in the short term, due to bicultural advantages that tend to reduce in the medium and long term.

Studies on marginalisation, radicalisation and criminalisation of young immigrants and refugees have mostly examined the experiences in the United States and Europe. They mainly investigate the nexus between immigrant youth and social problems including conflict, crime, and terror (Roy, 2003; Roy, 2008; Gilroy, 2008. Hall and Jefferson, 1993; Kepel, 1997; Andersson, 2003; McKenney, 2006; Eldering and Knorth, 1998; Waters, 1999). As Sirkka Komulainen discusses, the relationship created between migration, terrorism and radicalisation, which caused fear in Europe, directly affect the local and regional debates on solidarity and hospitality relating to immigrant reception as well as integration practices. Some of these issues which were empirically supported in chapters by Massaroni, Horning, Viola and others presented in this volume, confirm the difficulties children face in pursuit of life in safer and better environments.

Consequently, we believe that a youth-based interpretation of the academic-theoretical debates, as well as policies, concerning population movements can help to understand the contemporary global migration better and to provide solutions. To this end, our aim with this volume is to contribute contemporary literature on migration from a perspective discussing young migrants and refugees through four distinctive but interlinked themes. These themes are vulnerability, boundaries, protection, and integration. We believe, young migrants who were taken as children to the Global North, who grew up and socialised in those countries and who are either blocked in host societies or returning to places of origin represent in some way a migration from North to South which is also worth to study further. These young people have been forced to rebuild their lives in social environments to which they mostly have substantial social, cultural, and economic distances. They indeed have an urge to generate conditions of material reproduction once back in their countries of origin. Still, they also need to rebuild their connections with their families, communities, and governments. Therefore, young migrants and refugees as a field of study is an indispensable part of migration studies. These are young people with multiple belongings and composite identities and with significant personal, social, cultural, and human capital.

## Bibliography

Acconcia, G., Chiappero-Martinetti, E., & Graziano, P. R. (2017). The third sector and capability-promoting policies. Capability-promoting Policies: Enhancing Individual and Social Development, 145.

Adams, M. (2009). Stories of fracture and claim for belonging: young migrants' narratives of arrival in Britain. *Children's geographies*, *7*(2), 159-171.

Andersson, M. (2003). "Immigrant youth and the dynamics of marginalisation." *Young* 11.1 74-89.

Bello, B. G. (2011). Empowerment of young migrants in Italy through nonformal education: putting equality into practice. Journal of Modern Italian Studies, 16.3: 348-359.

Berry, J. W., et al. (2006). Immigrant youth in cultural transition: Acculturation, identity, and adaptation across national contexts. Lawrence Erlbaum Associates Publishers.

Bloch, A., N. Sigona, and R. Zetter (2013). "Migration routes and strategies of young undocumented migrants in England: a qualitative perspective." *Irregular Migrants*. Routledge,. 26-42.

Cairns, D. (ed.) (2010). *Youth on the move: European youth and geographical mobility*. Springer Science & Business Media.

Caselli, M. (2017). Immigrants and Local Societies. Why and How to Measure Their Integration. Sociologia Italiana-AIS Journal of Sociology: Aprile 2014, (3), 53.

Eldering, L., & Knorth, E. J. (1998, June). Marginalisation of immigrant youth and risk factors in their everyday lives: The European experience. In *Child and Youth Care Forum* (Vol. 27, No. 3, pp. 153-169). Kluwer Academic Publishers-Human Sciences Press.

Fangen, K., Fossan, K., & Mohn, F. A. (Eds.) (2016). Inclusion and exclusion of young adult migrants in Europe: Barriers and bridges. Routledge.

Fangen, K., Johansson, T., & Hammarén, N. (Eds.) (2011). *Young migrants: Exclusion and belonging in Europe*. Springer.

Gilroy, P., & Lawrence, E. (1988). Two-tone Britain: white and black youth and the politics of anti-racism. In *Multi-racist Britain*(pp. 121-155). Palgrave Macmillan, London.

Gilroy, P. (1993). Between Afro-centrism and Euro centrism: Youth culture and the problem of hybridity. *Young*, *1*(2), 2-12.

Gilroy, P. (2008). "The myth of black criminality." *Ethnicity and crime: A Reader*: 113-127.

Gilroy, Paul. (1981). "You can't fool the youths... race and class formation in the 1980s." *Race & Class* 23.2-3 (1981): 207-222.

Hall, S. and T. Jefferson (eds.) (1993). *Resistance through rituals: Youth subcultures in post-war Britain*. Vol. 7. Psychology Press.

Hirschman, C. (2001). "The educational enrollment of immigrant youth: A test of the segmented-assimilation hypothesis." *Demography* 38.3 317-336.

Holton, G. (2010). Helping young refugees and immigrants succeed: Public policy, aid, and education. Springer.

Kaya, A., and Harmanyeri, E. (2010). 'Tolerance and Cultural Diversity. Discourses in Turkey', Florence: European University Institute.

Kaya, A. (1997). Constructing diasporas: Turkish hip-hop youth in Berlin. Diss. Coventry:

University of Warwick.

Kayaoglu, A. and A. Kaya (2011). "Is National Citizenship Withering Away?: Social Affiliations and Labor Market Integration of Turkish Origin Immigrants in Germany and France." *Discussion papers* 2011033: 25.

Kepel, G. (1997). "Islamic groups in Europe: Between community affirmation and social crisis." *Islam in Europe*. Palgrave Macmillan, London, 48-55.

Limage, L. J. (1984). "Young migrants of the second generation in Europe: Education and labour market insertion prospects." *International Migration*. 22.4 367-387.

McKenney, K. S., et al. (2006). "Peer victimisation and psychosocial adjustment: The experiences of Canadian immigrant youth."

Penninx, R., and B. Garcés-Mascareñas. (2016). "Integration Policies of European Cities in Comparative Perspective: Structural Convergence and Substantial Differentiation." Migracijske i etničke teme 32.2 155-189.

Pfarrwaller, E. and J-C. Suris (2012). "Determinants of health in recently arrived young migrants and refugees: a review of the literature." *Italian Journal of Public Health* 9.3.

Roy, O. (2008). "Al Qaeda in the West as a youth movement: The power of a narrative."

Roy, O. (2003). "EuroIslam: the jihad within?." *The National Interest* 71. 63-73.

Ryan, L. (2011). "Transnational relations: Family migration among recent Polish migrants in London." *International Migration* 49.2. 80-103.

Sandoval, R. and V. Zúñiga (2016). "¿Quiénes están retornando de EstadosUnidos a México?: una revisión crítica de la literatura reciente (2008–2015)." *Mexican Studies/Estudios Mexicanos* 32 (2). 328–356.

Tacoli, C. (1996). "Migrating for the sake of the family'? Gender, life course and infra-household relations among Filipino migrants in Rome." *Philippine Sociological Review* 44.1/4. 12-32.

van Blerk, L. and N. Ansell (2007). "Participatory feedback and dissemination with and for children: reflections from research with young migrants in southern Africa." *Children's geographies* 5.3.313-324.

Waters, T. (1999). *Crime and immigrant youth*. Sage.

White, A. et al. (2011). "Children's roles in transnational migration." *Journal of Ethnic and Migration Studies* 37.8, 1159-1170.

Zúñiga, V. (2018). "The 0.5 Generation: What Children Knowabout International Migration." *Migraciones Internacionales* 9.3: 93-120.

# PART I: PROTECTION AND SUPPORT

# CHAPTER 1

## WHO IS A DREAMER? YOUNG MIGRANT'S CHECKPOINTS, MENTAL MAPS, AND COMMUNITIES OF REFERENCE IN NORTH-AMERICA

Ana Vila Freyer

What meaning do young migrants give to the "Dreamer" concept when they do or don't define themselves as such? The visualisation of young undocumented migrants is reflective of the growing literature on the subject that aims to explain the different ways in which their immigration status has affected their integration in the United States. Throughout the entire 21st century, authors have emphasised the effects of an undocumented immigration situation, its permanent temporality -liminal legality- as a form of legal violence that affects the daily life of children and young people during their transition to adult life (Menjívar, 2006; Gonzales & Chavez, 2012; Gonzales, Ellis, Rendon-Garcia, & Brant, 2018; Anderson, 2014) it also shows how policy decisions impact the transition of young people from childhood, adolescence and the learning process entailed during their transition to illegality (Gonzales & Chavez, 2012). The works stand out for focusing on the way that political decisions affect the subjective experiences, the quality of life of young migrants and their definition, from power, in their capacities as good or bad migrants (Barbero, 2019).

Embracing this trend, this chapter analyses the different ways in which young people identify to or don't identify to the political definition of Dreamer both in Mexico and in the United States. In doing so, three elements are highlighted: the first is that young people do not homogeneously identify as Dreamers, nor grant the same content to it. The second is that this concept contains a sense of belonging to the United States regardless of the place of residence of the youngsters. The third is that having the protection guaranteed by Deferred Action for Childhood Arrivals (DACA) has allowed them to expand their communities of reference and the possibility of becoming visible, either by appropriating or rejecting the identities that arise from the decree's checkpoints.

The work is built on the answers given by the young people to three questions: Do you consider yourself a Dreamer? Can you explain why? What does it mean to you to be a Dreamer? These are part of the 40 closed and open-ended questions of a questionnaire distributed through the *SurveyMonkey* platform between the dates of May 15 and August 31, 2018. In Mexico, its distribution was done with support from the Dream in Mexico, A.C. organisation. From this exercise, 30 responses were obtained, although only 20 surveys were answered in their entirety. In the United States, the survey was distributed among 8 closed Facebook groups identified as groups with Dreamers and DACA Recipients. From this exercise, 75 responses were obtained, of which 40 were completed. Fieldwork in Mexico and the United States also included the conducting of almost 70 personal interviews. The project[1] sought to identify the way young migrants of Mexican origin -citizens, migrants who are documented, undocumented or DACAmented, migrants who returned, voluntarily or not, to Mexico- define their sense of belonging to the two countries.

The answers to the three selected questions were classified using two criteria. The first was to consider whether the adherence to the Dreamer category is determined by internal elements of the individual with which they define their sense of belonging to that country, for example, a Dreamer is an 'American without papers'. With it, the classifications made in relation to the ability of the young people to consider themselves as social actors with the ability to define their sense of belonging to a reference community (Migdal, 2004) were stressed, regardless of the legal-political structures that regulate it territorially. The second classification has to do with the allegiances assumed precisely from these legal-political structures -or checkpoints (Migdal, 2004)- that are external to the individual and that, defined from the state, determine the scope and limits of their membership in the United States, and that Menjívar has defined as liminal legality, to explain the permanent temporality of their legal presence in that country (Menjívar, 2006). In studies conducted in Mexico, the case of young migrants returning to Mexico or established in the United States, have also underlined labour integration (Da Cruz, Back to Tenochtitlán. Migration de retour et nouvelles maquiladoras de la communication. Le cas des jeunes migrants employés dans les centres d'appel bilingues de la Ville du Mexico, 2014), or the transition of fulfilling their dreams of a college degree to the country (Ángel Lara, 2013). The literature focused on young migrants in both countries; however, does not yet explain what meaning do young people give to the Dreamer concept? Does this concept define their sense of belonging to the United States? Do they maintain that sense of belonging once in Mexico? Does the Dreamer concept refer to a strictly American identity?

## Boundaries, virtual checkpoints and mental maps

The argument here is built on Joel Migdal's notions of boundaries, virtual

[1] Field research for this project was funded by the Instituto Estatal de Atención al Migrante Guanajuatense y sus Familias, Government of Guanajuato México.

checkpoints, and mental maps (Migdal, 2004). He defines boundaries as more than the lines dividing spaces on a map, because boundaries, as social constructs, also mark the formal and informal spaces of alterity and belonging. In doing so, Migdal incorporates two elements beyond formal separators: checkpoints and mental maps. As such, Migdal (2004) states "checkpoints refer to the sites and practices that groups use to differentiate members from others and to enforce separation" (p. 6) and mental maps "incorporate (...) the meaning people attach to spatial configurations, the loyalties they hold, the emotions and passions that groupings evoke, and their cognitive ideas about how the world is constructed" (p. 7). All these elements not only establish and maintain the attachment of people to one another but also, they mark the separation between groups.

As such, boundaries can be established by State actions and by communities of reference. State's monitoring devices encases control on the borders: the rules governing people's lives, establish the physical checkpoints, and circumscribe communities of belonging. While social groupings define their own boundaries, virtual checkpoints, and mental maps marking them off from other groupings. The boundaries of social groupings have their own virtual checkpoints and spatial logic (Migdal, 2004). In this sense, state's legal definitions, surveilling checkpoints, and monitoring devices related to immigration – such as DACA- creates not only legal liminality (Menjívar, 2006) but also gives place to new virtual checkpoints on how young migrant groupings include those actions into their mental maps to reestablish their loyalties, sense of belonging and communities of reference.

As the cases discussed here, we find that the liminal conditions created by DACA (Roth, 2018; Abrego & Lakhani, 2015) young migrants protected by the program have crafted mental maps, and as an extension, communities of reference related with the notion of Dreamer. However, their allegiance of belonging to the US include both the undocumented youth migrants settled in the US and those forced to return to Mexico. Even those who have returned voluntarily or were deported back to Mexico have kept their mental maps and sense of belonging to the US and have learnt to include Mexico into their own new mapping. Besides, the notion of Dreamer has not crafted a uniform ascription on the part of the young migrants - enrolled in DACA or not-. They have fought in both countries to fulfil their university studies dream facing not only the abject conditions related to their migratory status but also to their reintegration to their formal community of belonging (Roth, 2018; Ángel Lara, 2013; Gonzales & Chavez, 2012). Finally, being protected by DACA may have created a cleavage between undocumented children and their parents granting a good immigrant status to youth immigrants who are attending a university and working in regular conditions, vis à vis their bad immigrant parents living and working irregularly in the US (Barbero, 2019; Müller-Funk, 2019).

## The social construction of the Dreamer

The appellation of 'Dreamer' comes from the different acts presented in the US Congress to solve the problem of an undocumented population, one taken to the United States as children and that has limited resources to access higher education or good jobs. They grew up, socialised and assimilated in the United States and deem that with their cultural belonging they can accomplish the life they dream of in that country. Since 2001, bipartisan groups of the United States Congress have tried to pass laws that would alter that country's immigration regime that is specifically related to these undocumented youth.

The different versions of the Development, Relief, and Education for Alien Minors (DREAM) Act that have been presented, frozen or rejected in Congress have essentially sought to create conditions that facilitate access to education, permanent residency and, eventually, citizenship to children and youth who have studied and socialised in the United States but who do not have immigration documentation (Barros, 2017; Castañeda, 2017; American Immigration Council, 2017). The youngsters (Rumbaut, 2004) participated in the protest mobilisations against the Sensenbrenner Act in 2006 and against the increase in deportations initiated with the Bush administration but that were intensified by Barack Obama (Gonzales, 2008). It was then that they began to organise their own fight to achieve the promised immigration reform that would guarantee them access to US citizenship. Angel (2013) assures that the concept of Dreamer was shifted to young people because of the support given to the Dream Act of 2009, and because of the political activism developed, above all, to demand that the government of Barack Obama (2008-2016) fulfill its promise of a comprehensive immigration reform.

Scholar research on young undocumented immigrants in the US has evolved according to the political circumstances in that country. As the works show, they have focused on the different forms of assimilation of the so-called 1.5 generation (Rumbaut, 2004) in the United States and in Mexico (Zúñiga, 2019). That is, the migrants who were taken as children to the United States without documents, completed their basic studies (K-12) in that country in order to learn to live an irregular life at the end of adolescence, or wake up to the nightmare of the lack of opportunities associated to their immigration status (Gonzales, 2016; Gonzales & Chavez, 2012; Gonzales, 2018). Starting in 2006, year that the Great Expulsion of migrants began (Hernández-León & Zúñiga, 2016), young people rallied to formalise their situation and pressured the government of President Obama, who had already been named Deporter-in-chief, to issue an executive order on June 5, 2012 to defer deportation actions against young people taken to the US as children (Roth, 2018; Jones, 2018). These studies have also been carried out in Mexico in order to study how, during the same years, the returnee youth sought access to higher education (Sandoval & Hirai, 2016; Ángel Lara, 2013), how they have been integrated into specific Mexican labor market niches (Da Cruz, Back to Tenochtitlán.

Migration de retour et nouvelles maquiladoras de la communication. Le cas des jeunes migrants employés dans les centres d'appel bilingues de la Ville du Mexico, 2014) and how their identities have been impacted after returning to a country that is unknown to them.

President Barack Obama (2009-2017) established DACA to defer deportation and improve labour opportunities to youngsters. DACA guarantees protection against deportation to young people who met a series of requirements, among other things: Having arrived in the United States before the age of 16, and being younger than 31 years old before June 15, 2012; have lived continuously in the US as of June 15, 2007 and be present in the country as of June 5, 2012 and when applying, being currently enrolled in school, have graduated or obtained a high school completion certificate (12 years of school from kindergarten to high school K-12), have a GED - equivalent to high school in Mexico - or have participated in the armed forces for two years, being honourably discharged, and not having a criminal record (Castañeda, 2017; American Immigration Council, 2017).

Ángel (2013) states that the executive order had a "trick" by guaranteeing discretion to the immigration authorities during the verification of the record of the young applicants to the program. Among the requirements that were requested, the final decision was left on the public official that grated the case in order to determine if the person who applied, carries out or carried out activities that could represent a threat to national security or to the public safety of the United States. This guaranteed procedural discretion to the immigration authorities. Likewise, applicants' hand over all their personal information to immigration authorities while recognising their irregular residence in the United States as adults. Lastly, DACA gives new legal consciousness to recipients although it does not guarantee access to citizenship, nor federal resources to carry out further education, nor recognition of residence that would allow for tuition exceptions nor would it guarantee access to certain diplomas in states where immigration status prevents access to them (Roth, 2018; Ángel Lara, 2013; Gonzales, 2016; Abrego, 2018). Of these, 79.4 per cent, 548 thousand people, are Mexican and 8.6 per cent are from the Northern Central American triangle (Zong et al., 2017; Capps, Fix, & Zong, 2017). In September 2017, the Trump administration (2017-2021) granted Congress 6 months to resolve the problem of young immigrants; in light of the failure to approve a new Dream Act in March 2018, federal judges have blocked the cancellation of the program, which stopped receiving new applications in 2018 and has only renewed the existing guarantees. The Supreme Court will deliberate on the issue by the end of 2019 and will issue a resolution in the spring of 2020 (Liptak & Shear, 2019).

### How the Dreamers define themselves?

In this section, we analyse the meaning the Dreamer concept has in the definition given by young migrants in Mexico and the United States. In this exercise, we regroup the 64 valid responses we received. The first division has to do with the spatial separation since while 87.8% per cent of the responses received in the United States considered themselves Dreamers, only 65% considered themselves as such once established in Mexico, after returning voluntarily or involuntarily.

The answers were analysed considering whether or not their allegiances to the Dreamer concept derived from an introjection -meaning the respondents' own mental maps or virtual checkpoints, such as feeling like an 'American without papers'. Within this group, we found a minority group of respondents who define no ascription, instead consider themselves with a capacity of agency assuming control of their life experiences, country of settlement or life expectations. At the other extreme, the ascription or non-ascription to the concept is determined by state regulations or legal checkpoints establishing the boundaries of belonging for the undocumented immigrant youth. These checkpoints grant the state with authority to renew every two years the deferred action to deportation granted by DACA to the young immigrants. Both definitions have outlined the young immigrant's life strategies in their personal life and their strategies of political organisation.

Finally, we present the youth' responses intentionally in the language they answered us, in English or Spanish. These extracts are followed by our free translation to the English language when necessary. For us, it was important to underline the young migrants' multiple belongings, checkpoints and mental mappings expressed naturally in the language they decided to use, well beyond physical borders or the country they are settled in. We also use a code C#USA or C#MX, that means the questionaries' number and the country from which we collected the responses.

### Identifications that respond to the young migrant's internal adherences

Within this group, the allegiances internalised by young migrants have been organised into three categories or virtual checkpoints: those who dream as an 'attribute' of the youth, to the actors 'in control' of their living conditions and, finally, those who build their allegiance to the US from a sense of belonging to a single or multiple reference communities. The first group includes those who call themselves Dreamers, because they are young, and young people dream. The second group considers that they maintain sovereignty in themselves in order to build the life they dream of for themselves, regardless of the circumstances of life. The last group is defined based on a sense of belonging that is unitary or multiple, as "Americans without papers", it includes those who define themselves as a sort of expatriates, as they are considered an 'Americans living in Mexico'. This group includes those who identify themselves as someone who belongs to two cultures and knows how to get ahead in both

(Sandoval & Hirai, 2016)[2].

**Dreamer as an attribute**

Being a Dreamer is a characteristic of the youth. Also including oneself in a community of reference even if the legal checkpoints have not been met. "*[Soy Dreamer] Por que sueño* ([I am a Dreamer] because I dream) (C27USA). "[Being a Dreamer is] to want to achieve your own definition of success regardless of the situation you are in" (C35USA). "*A Dreamer is someone who has goals to pursue and accomplished them no matter how hard it is. Also a Dreamer is someone who does not give up and keeps fighting until is it's accomplished*" (C14USA). "*Una persona que quiera superarse y tener una mejor vida con sus sueños* (a person who wants to improve himself/herself and have a better life with his/her dreams)" (C18USA). *"Un Soñador es una persona que tiene metas de largo y corto plazo, que nunca se da por vencido hasta obtener lo que quiere"* (A Dreamer is a person who has long and short-term goals, who never gives up until he/she gets what he/she wants)" (C24USA). "*Soy un soñador porque quiero salir adelante con mis estudios a pesar de no tener documentos y de todos los obstáculos que me enfrento al no ser residente/ciudadana estaunidense* (I am a dreamer because I want to get ahead with my education despite not having documents and despite of all the obstacles, I face because of not being a resident / citizen of the United States)" (C32USA). *"Un Dreamer es literalmente alguien que sueña. Específicamente es alguien que sueña con poder vivir, estudiar, trabajar, y permanecer siempre en EE.UU. porque se considera ciudadano sin documentación de este país* (A Dreamer is literally someone who dreams. Specifically, it is someone who dreams of being able to live, study, work, and always stay in the United States. because he/she considers himself/herself a citizen of this country that does not have documentation)" (C25USA).

"*Para mí un Dreamer es alguien que quiere seguir sus sueños, aunque le pongan mil obstáculos* (For me a dreamer is someone who wants to follow his/her dreams, even if they put a thousand obstacles in his/her way)" (C23MX). "*[Soy un Dreamer por] El sueño de poder conseguir una superación personal y profesional fuera del país* ([I am a dreamer because of] The dream of being able to obtain personal and professional achievement outside the country)" (C18MX). *"Siempre voy a ser un Dreamer mientras tenga sueños por realizar. Pero no siempre me siento como un Dreamer como tal de los que vivieron allá, ya que ya estoy aquí en México. El tiempo que viví allá me enseñó mucho y agradezco a mis papás por ser los primeros Dreamer para que sus hijos tuvieran una vida mejor que ellos* (I will always be a Dreamer as long as I have dreams to fulfill. But I don't always feel like a Dreamer like the ones that live over there, since I'm already here in Mexico. The time I lived there taught me a lot and I thank my parents for being the first Dreamers so their children could have a better life than them)" (C16MX). *[Soy un Dreamer porque soy alguien] con aspiraciones de mejorar mi situación de educación y laboral para tener mejores oportunidades de tener una*

[2] Sandoval & Hirai (2016) coine the concept 'subjective itinerary' to explain the internal process experienced by returnees recreate their cultural belonging to Mexico and the US.

*mejor calidad de vida* ("[I am a dreamer because I am someone] with hopes of improving my education and employment situations in order to have better opportunities to have a better quality of life)" (C7MX). "I am a Dreamer because just like my parents I have a dream of being in this country for a better life and I want to fulfill the American Dream!" (C9USA).

**Actors in control**

Among those who do not consider themselves Dreamers are those that have a proactive attitude towards the situation they are living. Dream "that's all they do; they dream but don't do anything about it. I take action" (C11MX). Or, those who seek to break the ties that the Dreamer concept represents [I am not a Dreamer, because] "*Un Dreamer está atado al sueño de ser adoptado por un país. Yo me siento libre de vivir dónde quiera y viajar por donde quiera incluso dentro de Estados Unidos con mi B1/B2 visa* (A dreamer is tied to the dream of being adopted by a country. I feel free to live wherever I want and travel anywhere even within the United States with my B1 / B2 visa)" (C12MX). "*[Soy un Dreamer] porque regresé voluntariamente, nunca fui deportado. Regresé para terminar mis estudios en México y un día regresar legal a Estados Unidos* ("[I am a dreamer] because I returned voluntarily, I was never deported. I returned to finish my studies in Mexico and one day return legally to the United States)" (C21MX). "*Ser un Dreamer significa luchar por tus metas, trabajar arduamente y no darse por vencidos ante la adversidad* (Being a dreamer means fighting for your goals, working hard and not giving up in the face of adversity)" (C4MX).

On the other hand, there is someone who claims that "*Me considero un Dreamer porque fuí parte del movimiento político que nos dio DACA, y me benefició de DACA por un tiempo, y estoy activo en organizaciones cívicas con enfoque a derechos del migrante. Para mi eso es un Dreamer, un migrante involucrado* (I consider myself a dreamer because I was part of the political movement that DACA gave us, and I benefited from DACA for a while, and I am active in civic organisations that focus on migrant rights. For me that is a dreamer, a migrant that is involved)" (C11USA). "A Dreamer to me is somebody who has dreams and aspirations of being SOMEBODY in this world, and not only being somebody but also being great and working towards their goals, no matter what." (C34USA).

The concept of Dreamer can also be rejected because "the narrative could be used to create sympathy around my immigration status" (C29USA). Dreamer can also describe someone who denies identification because they reduce their vision to "a person who believes he/she deserves privileges without working for them (...) He/she sees the US as the only country where he/she can survive. He/she wants sympathy of those who have power; however, a "Dreamer" does not have it for others in worse or similar situations than them. An example occurred when Trump's pathetic government announced the end of TPS, the 'Dreamers' did not unite to defend them (…) I personally do not identify as a "Dreamer", although I have lived without documents in the US almost all my life" (C19USA).

## Multiple belongings

This group includes their allegiance to one or two cultures. The claimed belonging to multiple cultures is seen, in some cases, as a comparative advantage for the person who becomes aware of it. "*Un Dreamer es una persona que salió de su país natal y se adapta a una nueva cultura, lenguaje y que lucha constantemente para poder adquirir una educación, a pesar de todos los inconvenientes que se le presentan* (A dreamer is a person who left his/her native country and adapts to a new culture, language and constantly fights to acquire an education, despite all the inconveniences that arise )" (C14MX). "*[Un Dreamer es] Alguien que vive entre dos culturas y utiliza todos sus recursos que aprendió de estas culturas para lograr sus sueños* ([A dreamer is] Someone who lives between two cultures and uses all his/her resources that he/she has learned from these cultures to achieve his/her dreams)" (C1MX). "*[Un Dreamer es una] Persona que emigró a Estados Unidos desde niño y tiene más conocimiento de la cultura estadounidense que la de su país de origen* ([A dreamer is a] Person who emigrated to the United States as a child and has more knowledge of American culture than that of his/her country of origin)" (C16USA). "[Dreamers are] Immigrants that arrived as young children or teenagers and were raised in the USA but have a double identity, Americans/Country of origin" (C40USA).

This group includes those who feel expatriates and maintain their allegiance to the United States from Mexico. "I believe there is one aspect that most of us 'Dreamers' agree we possess. That aspect was that despite the lack of paperwork, we felt American. We pledged allegiance to Ol' Glory in grade school, most likely we feel in love with the state we grew up in" (C19MX). "Deep down I feel like an American since I was raised there" (C20MX). Also, whose virtual checkpoints go beyond a socio-political adscription "Dreamer is a term used and coined for political purpose. I do not identify as a Dreamer because I find it to be a toxic term to use during this fight for protection of everyone. I prefer to identify as an UndocuQueer!" (C2USA)

These definitions include both those that reject the Dreamer label, and those that include it as part of their repertoire of identity or of belongings. One point to note is that sovereignty is their own, and they established their own boundaries independently of physical borders (border lines) or political definitions. They even move across the physical borders with their communities of reference and recreate that sense of belonging even if they are no longer physically in that territory. They are the Dreamers, those who want a better life, those who know that they can achieve a better life regardless of the circumstances and because they have the ability to decide in which country to live. Although some do not seem to recognise it yet, they can choose to be included in one country or another and opt for visas to move across political borders at their will. When assumed as bi-national or bicultural persons, they use this element as an opportunity to carry out their lives by overcoming geopolitical determinations, or they maintain loyalty to belonging to a reference community like the last group. They assume their ability to dream and fulfil their dreams with all the resources that having a mobile life have allowed them.

### Identifications that respond to the young migrant's external adherences

Within this group, young people define their checkpoints and their reference communities by factors external to them. In these cases, their belonging is built or not built by a rationale that determines them, without them having any implication. We have also identified three groups: those who do or don't describe themselves as Dreamers for having socialised in the United States; those who relied on political-legal definitions that create a liminal belonging to the US; and those who define themselves as Dreamers as a result of their status as DACA / Dream Act enrollment. In all three cases, the checkpoints and boundaries are created by the state or their parents, and they only have adapted their lives to the circumstances. The section is thus organised following those constraints of belonging.

#### Socialised in the USA

In this group, we include young people whose checkpoints stand on the socialisation experiences in the US. They define their mental maps on the elements acquired growing up in a country, and it is this element that makes them create a sense of belonging even if it is a marginal belonging. "An undocumented individual that was brought to the US as a minor. I'm basically an American since I grew up in the American culture but lack a piece of paper that grants me the rights of an American citizen" (C30USA). "For me, it means being brought as children and growing up here in the US during the early 1990s/2000s." (C7USA). "A Dreamer is a young individual brought from their birth country to the United States as a child illegally. I consider myself a Dreamer, because I was brought (…) when I was just 7 years old. Texas is the only place I have known as home even though I was not born in Texas" (C31USA).

Those that do define themselves as Dreamers as a result of the decisions of others to whom they sometimes attribute their living conditions. "*Un Dreamer es un estudiante o joven que los padres lo trajeron a Estados Unidos desde bien chiquito y no tiene estatus legal* (A dreamer is a student or young person whose parents brought him/her to the United States from a very young age and that has no legal status)" (C9MX). "Someone who was not born in the states but adapted to the life style of the state and study, works and is working to achieve their dreams and goals" (C20USA). "An undocumented person that was brought here illegally as a child who has attended school here" (C37USA). "A Dreamer is a child that came into the USA with no legal inspection. Living undocumented throughout most of their childhood and adult life but being educated in the USA school system" (C39USA).

## Liminal belonging

The liminal belonging concept refers to a sense of belonging that never seems to become formal or permanent. In these first cases that we will analyse in this section are those that do not consider themselves Dreamers, but that moniker must be given to their parents, their virtual checkpoints to establish their communities of reference makes them heirs of a work culture that does not respond to an individual dream and that also, in addition, fails to formalise "*Mis padres ellos soñaban en una vida mejor. Soñaban en una vida para sus hijos que ellos no tenían* (My parents dreamed of a better life. They dreamed of a life for their children that they didn't have). They want the American dream, I was just a kid moving to a new country. The government dictated that 'Dreamers' are under a certain age group. My parents are the Dreamers because not only did they dream on the American dream but built their dream with hard work and dedication" (C3MX). "A DREAMer is someone (...) who seeks wisdom and strength in her/his ancestors. Someone who values and feels great respect and honour to have such strong parents who gave up a life in their home countries to be able to provide a better life for their children" (C3USA).

Being a Dreamer also means acknowledging your liminal condition, that is, wanting to be part of something that never seems to be yours. As a consequence, it has imposed reference communities, without achieving specific reference points. "A Dreamer is someone who has had their whole life decided by someone else, whether that be your parents or the government" (C12USA). "Dreamers were young kids who were brought over young by their parents to the United States. They want to work legally and be able to take part of society" (C21USA), "A Dreamer is someone who was brought here too young to remember vividly, and that he broke the law while being brought here. I like to compare the Dreamer experience to someone who lives in the shadows, and some day dreams of being allowed to walk into the public without being a symbol of law-breaking" (C22USA).

"After being deported, I realised the true meaning of what a Dreamer is. The people who were taken as children, such as myself, regardless whether they were legally arranged or not to live a normal life in the States (...) It's the media hype that has labeled them as that. So, a Dreamer is the term used to label a person who was either born illegally in the United States or was taken very young and just grew up there. The law owns them and can either grant/remove/cancel or decline their chance to stay (...)" (C18MX). "*Por que vi las oportunidades de estudio que se tiene en Estados Unidos. Me gustaría aprovechar esas oportunidades ya que yo crecí en ese país. Dreamer es soñar con algo que sabes que no es tuyo pero podría serlo* (Because I saw the education opportunities that are available in the United States. I would like to take advantage of those opportunities since I grew up in that country. Dreamer is to dream of something that you know is not yours but it could be)" (C2MX). "*Porque era un estudiante indocumentado*

(Because I was an undocumented student)" (C10MX).

"*Un Dreamer son personas que calificarían bajo el DREAM Act que hasta el día de hoy no pasado. Llegaron a EEUU de niños y quieren seguir estudiando* (A dreamer are people who would qualify for the DREAM Act, which till this day has not yet happened. They came to the US as children and want to continue studying)" (C5MX). "*[Soy] Dreamer porque me identifico con el 'Dream Act' si lo llegasen a pasar. También porque estoy aquí en este país por el sueño americano* ("[I am] Dreamer because I identify with the 'Dream Act 'if it happens. Also because I am here in this country because of the American dream)" (C8USA). "*Un Dreamer solo quiere tener las mismas oportunidades que todos los ciudadanos. Queremos igualdad y equidad sin temer de ser deportados y separados* (A dreamer just wants to have the same opportunities as all citizens. We want equality and equity without fear of being deported and separated)" (C13USA). "I am a Dreamer. I dream that one day I will have equal rights in this country. I dream that one day elected leaders and officials will want me to succeed, not fail. I have a dream that I can make a difference in this world. I have a dream that one day I won't be bounded by boarders. I have many dreams." (C17USA)

**DACAmented**

The third element of belonging is whether or not they have the protection of DACA, which becomes a checkpoint to get out of the shadows and temporarily normalise your life. "I didn't apply for that Act. A student with the papers to be in the country to study" (C6MX). "*Un Dreamer es alguien que aplicó para DACA por los procesos legales. Era un joven inmigrante pero no aplicaba para DACA, entonces no me considero un Dreamer* (A dreamer is someone who applied for DACA through the legal proceedings. I was a young immigrant, but I didn't apply for DACA, so I don't consider myself a dreamer)" (C13MX). "*No soy un Dreamer porque no me encuentro bajo DACA, entonces no soy considerado Dreamer* (I am not a dreamer because I am not under DACA, so I am not considered a dreamer)" (C15MX). "*Yo me metí en problemas con la ley cuando tenía 17 años y no pude obtener DACA* (I got into trouble with the law when I was 17 and I couldn't get DACA)" (C17MX). "*No tengo la edad* (I don't qualify because of my age)" (C38USA).

The existence of DACA is comparable to the possibility of changing their reference communities and their virtual checkpoints. It expands the opportunities for work, for education and, as many studies have found, for life opportunities. "*Soy Dreamer porque gracias al expresidente Obama tengo DACA, un permiso de trabajo que me dio la oportunidad de soñar mas alto y brindarme una carrera y poder ejercerla* (I am a Dreamer because thanks to former President Obama I have DACA, a work permit that gave me the opportunity to dream bigger and to obtain a degree and to be work with my degree)" (C18USA). "I don't believe in that term. I prefer DACA, we'd be Dreamers if they actually had passed it [the Dream Act] (C1USA). "There are different interpretations of Dreamer. Since there is no clear definition of a "Dreamer" I do not identify as one. I simply identify as a Mexican born, current DACA recipient, and immigrant rights activist" (C15USA). "*Haber llegado al pais en un corta edad y no tener estado legal o tener DACA* (Having come to the country at a young age and not having legal status or having DACA)" (C36USA). "A Dreamer is someone who is here to take advantage of the opportunities offered to us. I am a Dreamer because I am going back into my studies wanting to be a better person that I am today and also moving along in the company I work for and proving myself to be a future leader" (C4USA).

The young people included in these three groups are either ascribed or not to the idea of being a Dreamer in relation to the state actions that would facilitate their assimilation to the American society. There are those who recognise the benefit received by being able to come out of the shadows in order to study and work in regular conditions; but also those who prefer not to alter their family loyalties by recognizing themselves as participants of those advantages when their parents were the ones who dreamed of a better life. By creating the concept of Dreamer, the State creates an acknowledgement of an identity, which will never include citizenship status though.

## Discussion and conclusions

This exercise shows the different senses youngsters give to a single concept. The Dreamer concept does not grant a sense of security to young people, and this is reflected in the different contents provided in their responses. The idea of Dreamer creates mental maps that include family and non-family spaces, loyalties, emotions, and passions creating a fluid concept that incorporates different sets of meaning, boundaries and communities of reference. As it has been shown, these series of meanings question family loyalties by excluding - for a matter of legal definition establishing age limits - parents of Dreamers and placing them only as children who changed their country of residence. This point reframes the emotional limits that derive from the dominant discourse in the identity of the United States as a country of migrants, in terms of what (Barbero, 2019) has established as good or bad migrants. It also forces youngsters to include themselves in one group while condemning their families to the other. This is why, in terms of otherness, some young people choose their primary loyalties by emphasizing that the fight for citizenship should not be established only in terms of the dominant political discourse. Accepting the unilateral definition given by DACA and the connection that this decree has with the Dream Act creates a perception of themselves where, if they assume it, they will betray their family roots.

The second point that we want to highlight is about the communities of reference mapped by young people - especially those established in Mexico – to which they kept belonging independently of the place of settlement. This creates a notion of simultaneous belonging that is different from the one created in the notion of transnationalism. Young people, established in Mexico, include virtual checkpoints in their mental maps that do not exclude the undocumented experience that they lived in the United States. But are they Dreamers in Mexico for the same reasons they would be in the United States? This question - as this work shows, does not have uniform answers if we include young people who remain established in the United States through the endless temporality guaranteed by DACA. However, this prevents them from being into permanent contact with their families, with their communities of origin, their national origins, among other things. These elements affect the security that would give them the ability to alternate their daily lives in the two countries, reinforcing a sense of one national belonging over another.

The third point is that as Dreamers - in the political sense of the term - young immigrants wishing to change the boundaries from uncertainty to permanent status - to reevaluate their sense of belonging both to the US and to Mexico; a fact that the political circumstances have blocked for them until now. In the case they reach citizenship, how will they establish their mental maps and virtual checkpoints? How would they integrate their communities of reference in a broader mental map? Would it mean establishing new boundaries in relation to ethnicity, religion or some other characteristic that made them different in the mainstream societies they belong to? Until now, not having papers and having achieved some kind of recognition through DACA has focused their efforts to achieve permanent settlement in the United States, but shouldn't that struggle for recognition also be extended in defence of their right to inclusion both in Mexico and the United States?

Finally, this work aimed to highlight the importance of focusing research efforts on young migrants. The risk of labelling any young person with migratory experience on both sides of the border as Dreamer is that it generates a false idea of homogeneity - young people with university education and/or working in white-collar jobs in the United States that would become an important human capital once established in Mexico - that does not necessarily correspond to reality. In this exercise, we seek to highlight the multiplicity of identifications and symbolic dimensions incorporated by the young people themselves to a simple concept. Making a distinction of their particularity and distinguishing them from those who migrated as adults, as Gonzales and Burciaga (2018) point out, is an effort that allows us to highlight the different opportunities to which young people and parents have access to simply because of their life stories. In the same way, presenting young people with a monolithic vision - be it in identity terms or in the analysis of the positive and negative effects of politics in their daily lives - makes it difficult to see who they really are.

## References

Ángel Lara, H. (2013). ¿Un Sueño Posible? Retos y Dificultades que Enfrentan los Estudiantes Mexicanos Indocumentados por Ingresar a la Universidad en Estados Unidos y en México a

Principios del Siglo XXI. (C. Occidente, Ed.) Tesis de Doctorado en Ciencias Sociales.

Albright, L., Brannon, I., & McGee, K. (2018). *A New Estimate of the Cost of Reversing Daca.* Cato Working Paper No. 49, Cato Institute, Washington.

Abrego, L. J. (2018). Renewed optimism and spatial mobility: Legal consciousness of Latino Deferred Action for Childhood Arrivals recipients and their families in Los Angeles. *Ethnicities, 18*(2), 192-207 DOI: 10.1177/1468796817752563.

Abrego, L., & Lakhani, S. (2015). Incomplete Inclusion: Legal Violence and Immigrants in Liminal Legal Statuses. *Law & Policy, 37*(4), 265-293. DOI: 10.1111/lapo.12039.

American Immigration Council. (2017). *The Dream Act, DACA, and the Other Policies Designed to Protect Dreamers.* Retrieved 2018 febrero, from https://www.american immigrationcouncil.org/research/dream-act-daca-and-other-policies-designed-protect-dreamers

Anderson, B. (2014). *Exclusion, Failure, and the Politics of Citizenship RCIS Working Paper No. 2014/1.* Retrieved from Ryerson Center for Immigration and Settlement: https://www.ryerson.ca/content/dam/rcis/documents/RCIS_WP_Anderson_No_2014_1.pdf

Anderson, J., & Solis, N. (2014). *Los Otros Dreamers.* Ciudad de México.

Barbero, M. V. (2019). Semi-legality and belonging in the Obama era: the Deferred Action for Childhood Arrivals memorandum as an instrument of governance. *Citizenship Studies 23 (1) https://doi.org/10.1080/13621025.2018.1543387*, 1-18.

Barros, M. (2017). Los efectos de DACA en la carrera profesional y las emociones de jóvenes migrantes. *Estudios Fronterizos, 18*(37), 131-148. doi:10.21670/ref.2017.37. a07.

Capps, R., Fix, M., & Zong, J. (2017). *The Education and Work Profiles of the DACA Population.* MPI Issue Brief, Migration Policy Institute, Washington, DC.

Castañeda, A. (2017, septiembre 9). *DACA, el Dream Act y Dreamers.* Retrieved 23 de febrero 2018, from cronica.com.mx: http://www.cronica.com.mx/notas/2017/1042458.html

Da Cruz, M. (2014). Back to Tenochtitlán. Migration de retour et nouvelles maquiladoras de la communication. Le cas des jeunes migrants employés dans les centres d'appel bilingues de la Ville du Mexico. (É. d. Université Aix-Marseille, Ed.) Thèse de Doctorat en Sociologie;.

Da Cruz, M. (2018). Offshore Migrant Workers: Return Migrants in Mexico's English-Speaking Call Centers. *RSF: The Russell Sage Foundation Journal of the Social Sciences, 4*(1), 39–57. DOI: 10.7758/RSF.2018.4.1.03.

Ellis, B., Gonzales, R., & Rendon Garcia, S. (2018). The Power of Inclusion: Theorizing "Abjectivity and Agency under DACA. *Cultural Studies ↔ Critical Methodologies* , 1-12. https://doi.org/10.1177/1532708618817880.

Ellis, B., Gonzales, R., & Rendon Garcia, S. (2018). The Power of Inclusion: Theorizing "Abjectivity" and Agency Under DACA. *Cultural Studies Critical Methodologies*, 1-12. DOI:10.1177/1532708618817880.

Escobar Latapi, A., Lowell, L., & Martin, S. (2013). *Binational Dialogue on Mexican Migrants in the U.S. and Mexico: Final Report.* Washington, DC: CIESAS, Georgetown University.

Gelatt, J. (2017, September). *All Eyes Turn to Congress, Following Trump Decision to Terminate DACA Program.* Retrieved from MPI Commentary: https://www.migrationpolicy.org/news/all-eyes-turn-congress-following-trump-decision-terminate-daca-program

Golash-Boza, T. M. (Ed.). (2018). *Forced Out and Fenced In Immigration Tales From the Field.* Oxford University Press.

González Barrera, A., & Kogstad, J. (2019, junio 28). *What we know about illegal immigration from mexico.* Retrieved junio 2019, from Pew Research Center: http://www.pewresearch.org/fact-tank/2018/12/03/what-we-know-about-illegal-immigration-from-mexico/

Gonzales, R. (2008). Left Out But Not Shut Down: Political Activism and the Undocumented Student Movement. *Northwesern Journal of Law & Social Policy*, 219-239.

Gonzales, R. G. (2016). *Lives in Limbo: Undocumented and Coming of Age in America.* Oakland: University of California Press.

Gonzales, R. G. (2018). Segmented pathways of Ilegality: Reconciling the coexistence of master and auxiliary statuses in the experiences of 1.5 generation undocumented young adults. *Ethnicities, 18*(2), 178-191. DOI: 10.1177/1468796818767176.

Gonzales, R., & Chavez, L. (2012). "Awakening to a Nightmare" Abjectivity and Illegality in the Lives of Undocumented 1.5-Generation Latino Immigrants in the United States. *Current Anthropology, 53*(3), 255-281.

Gonzales, R., & Sigona, N. (2017). Mapping the soft borders of citizenship. An Introduction. In R. Gonzales, & N. Sigona, *Within and beyond Citizenship: borders, membership and belonging* (pp. 1-16). New York: Routledge.

Gonzales, R., Ellis, B., Rendon-Garcia, S., & Brant, K. (2018). (Un)authorized Transitions: Illegality, DACA, and the Life Course. *Research in Human Development, 15*(3-4), 345-359. https://doi.org/10.1080/15427609.2018.1502543.

Gordon, C. (1991). Governmental Rationality: An Introduction. In G. Burchell, C. Gordon, & P. Miller, *The Foucault Effect: Studies in governmentality: with two lectures by and an Interview with Michel Foucault* (pp. 1-52). Chicago, Ill: The University of Chicago Press.

Hernández-León, R., & Zúñiga, V. (2016). Contemporary Return Migration from the United States to Mexico – Focus on Children, Youth, Schools and Families. *Mexican Studies/Estudios Mexicanos, 32*(2), 171-198.

Jones, R. C. (2018). Policy Implications of Deferred Acion for Childhood Arrivals (DACA) on the Educational and Occupational Fortunes of Young Mexican-Born Adults. *Papers in Applied Geography , 4*(3), 229-242. https://doi.org/10.1080/23754931.2017.1396554.

Liptak, A., & Shear, M. (2019, junio 28). El futuro de los 'dreamers' queda en manos de la Corte Suprema de Estados Unidos . *The New York Times*, pp. Retrieved on Sept. 1, 2019 from https://www.nytimes.com/es/2019/06/28/daca-dreamers-corte/.

Müller-Funk, L. (2019). Fluid identities, diaspora youth activists and the (Post-)Arab Spring: how narratives of belonging can change over time. *Journal of Ethnic and Migration Studies*, 1-17. https://doi.org/10.108071369183X.2018.1554300.

Menjivar, C. (2002). Living in Two Worlds? Guatemalan-origin children in The United States and emerging transnationalism. *Journal of Ethnic and Migration Studies , 28*(3), 531-552. (DOI:10.1080/1369183022014659 0).

Menjívar, C. (2006). Liminal Legality: Salvadoran and Guatemala Immigrants' Lives in the United States. *American Journal of Sociology, 111*(4), 999–1037. DOI: 10.1086/499509.

Migdal, J. S. (2004). Mental Maps and Virtual Checkpoints. Struggles to construct and mantain state and social boundaries. In J. S. (Ed.), *Boundaries and Belonging. States and Societies in the Struggle to Shape Identities and Local Practices.* (pp. 3-26). Cambridge: Cambridge University Press.

Roth, B. (2018). The double bind of DACA: Exploring the Legal Violence of Liminal Status for Undocumented Youth, *Ethnic and Racial Studies*, DOI: 10.1080/01419870.2018.1540790.

Rumbaut, R. (1994). The Crucible within: Ethnic Identity, Self-Esteem, and Segmented Assimilation Among Children of Immigrants. *International Migration Review, 28*(4), 748-794.

Rumbaut, R. G. (2004). Ages, Life Stages, and Generational Cohorts: Decomposing the Immigrant First and Second Generations in the United States. *International Migration Review, 38*(3), 1160-1205.

Sandoval, R., & Hirai, S. (2016). El Itinerario Subjetivo como Herramienta de Análisis: Las Experiencias de los Jóvenes de la Generación 1.5 que retornan a México. *Mexican Studies / Estudios Mexicanos, 32*(2), 276–301. DOI:10.1525/msem.2016.32.2.276.

Van Hear, N. a. (2017). Diasporas and Conflict: Distance, Contiguity and Spheres of Engagement. *Oxford Development Studes, 45*(2), 171-184.

Zúñiga, V. (2019, Marzo). Niñas y Niños Migrantes en Escena. *Sinéctica. Revista Electrónica de Educación*, Tomado de https://sinectica.iteso.mx/index.php/SINECTICA/article/view/700.

Zong, J., Ruiz Soto, A., Batalova, J., Gelatt, J., & Capps, R. (2017). *A profile of Current DACA Recipients by Education, Industry, and Occupation.* MPI Fact Sheets.

# CHAPTER 2

# DREAMS OF TRANSNATIONAL SOCIAL PROTECTION: YOUTH RETURNEES IN MEXICO

Victoria Tse

This chapter seeks to broaden existing discussions on social protection and migration with the inclusion of return migration, looking at youth returnees in Mexico in particular. The research asks what formal social protections are provided to youth returnees in the case of Mexico by the Mexican federal government. If no such provisions are made, how do these youth returnees create and piece together their own forms of social protections, and what do their social protection environments look like as they seek to realize their futures back in Mexico? With over 258 million migrants worldwide (United Nations, 2017), many of whom fall outside the purview of formal social protection institutions, there has been an increased interest in how migration impacts social protection and vulnerabilities.

Migrants, who may have migrant-specific vulnerabilities related to their status or socio-cultural particularities, also face specific political and economic related vulnerabilities, such as open access to dirty, dangerous, and difficult jobs (Piore, 1979) but have limited access to the wider labour market and often limited recourse in the legal system. As such, scholarship has focused on how these migrant-specific vulnerabilities necessitate the provision of specific social protections, distinct from those provided to non-migrants (Sabates-Wheeler & Feldman, 2011a).

Little research, however, has been done on social protection as it relates to return migration. This is perhaps due to the belief that returnees return because they have accomplished some goal, and therefore are 'successful returnees.'[1] But this overlooks other reasons for return, such as an inability to adapt, loss of job or income, health-related issues, deportation, etc., and is further compounded by the idea that returnees will be absorbed into the domestic social protection framework when they return, reverting to being 'ordinary' citizens and non-migrants. As such, this chapter seeks to not only expand the

[1] For more on the 'successful' vs. 'failed' return typologies, see de Haas, Fokkema, and Fihri (2015).

discussion of social protection to include the sending state,[2] but also to include returnees.

This chapter focuses on youth returnees in particular for a variety of reasons. Youth migrants have distinct vulnerabilities as compared to their adult counterparts. In their paper on youth vulnerabilities, Hardgrove, Pells, Boyden, and Dornan (2014) outline some of the reasons for this. According to the authors, the transition from dependent childhood to responsible adulthood can be a difficult emotional shift—one that can have not only emotional, but economic, social, and political consequences. The authors also point to the fact that difficulties during youth can negatively impact future capabilities, such as labour market participation and educational abilities. While Hardgrove et al. (2014) focus their paper on youth in general, and not youth migrants in particular, they stress that other risks, such as social exclusion and poverty, can intensify youth vulnerabilities. The Committee on the Rights of the Child (CRC) within the 1990 U.N. Convention on the Rights of the Child acknowledges the particular vulnerabilities of children migrants as well (United Nations Committee on the Rights of the Child, 2012), and emphasizes that migration can, and does, increase the vulnerability of youth.

Youth have largely been excluded from the scholarship surrounding migration, which often focuses on children and young adults as dependents of their parents or grandparents. This chapter finds its foundations in the research of scholars who have stressed the importance of incorporating children and youth voices into migration discussions (Zúñiga, 2018; Bhabha, 2014), and those who have discussed the role of youth voices and youth vulnerabilities in the realm of return migration in the Mexico case (Zúñiga & Hammon, 2015; Espindola & Jacobo-Suárez, 2018). While there exist some studies on youth returnees' realities and vulnerabilities in Mexico, this chapter will expand on these youth returnees' social protections in particular.

The chapter proceeds as follows: Section 2 briefly outlines social protection and transnational social protection, looking at the ways in which social protection and migration are commonly understood. Section 3 follows with a description of the methodology and data collection employed. Section 4 introduces the case study of Mexico and its history of migrant social protection. Section 5 analyzes the different forms of social protection available to youth returnees in Mexico. Section 6 concludes the chapter with some comments on future research.

## Social protection

Social protection has been defined in a variety of ways. In a narrow

[2] This chapter utilizes the term 'sending state' or 'home country' to refer to states from which migrants leave, and 'receiving state' or 'host country' to refer to states to which migrants arrive for consistency with extant literature, understanding that the implications of the use of these terms can, as Délano (2009) and others note, perpetuate asymmetries of power.

economic sense, it refers to social security related provisions. Devereux and Sabates-Wheeler (2004) use an expanded definition, which includes 'all public and private initiatives that provide income or consumption transfers to the poor, protect the vulnerable against livelihood risks, and enhance the social status and rights of the marginalised' in order to reduce their economic and social vulnerabilities (p. iii). In their analysis of social protection and migration, Locke, Seeley, and Nitya (2013) note that a more comprehensive definition of social protection is needed to fully understand the social reality which migrants inhabit. For the purposes of this chapter, transnational social protection will be defined as 'the policies, programmes, people, organizations, and institutions which provide for and protect individuals...in a transnational manner' including pensions, health care, labor market policies, unemployment compensation, housing assistance, education programs, etc. (Levitt, Viterna, Mueller, & Lloyd, 2016, p. 6). This definition acknowledges that social protections can be constructed across borders, which is critical in the study of migration, as migrants are increasingly involved in transnational processes.

As provision can be provided transnationally, migrants may draw on various sources of protection, including both formal and informal sources. In terms of formal social protection, migrants can draw on national protection policies and programs, as well as subnational programs from both the country of origin and the country of destination (see Dobbs & Levitt, 2017; Dobbs, Levitt, Parella, & Petroff, 2018 for an analysis of sub-national provision). While these sources all make up the potential 'social protection resource environments' for migrants (Levitt et al., 2016), this chapter focuses on the formal protections afforded by the sending-state government and on informal social protections, which are often key forms of social protection for migrants (Avato, Koettl, & Sabates-Wheeler, 2010). Avato et al. (2010) define these informal social protection strategies as those 'that migrants themselves pursue in the absence of public provisions. These could include migrant networks existing through established migration routes or local communities and churches providing help for their members' (p. 463).[3]

Within the discussion of transnational social protection and social protection for migrants, four categories of vulnerabilities are usually mentioned: temporal, spatial, socio-cultural, and socio-political, which in turn require specific social protection components. Sabates-Wheeler & Feldman (2011a) describe these categories as follows: access to formal social protection, portability of protections across borders, labour market conditions for migrants, and access to informal networks (p. 21). At the same time, the policies to address these social protection concerns vary from protective measures, preventative measures, promotive measures, and transformative measures to

[3] Migrants have also provided social protection for those left behind, with migration seen as a 'livelihood strategy' to diversify risks and protect against vulnerability (de Haas, 2007; Levitt et al., 2016).

reduce vulnerabilities (see Devereux and Sabates-Wheeler (2004) for an in-depth discussion of the typology for social protection policy intervention).

### Research methods and data collection

To analyze different forms of social protection afforded to youth returnees in Mexico, this research made use of qualitative methods. It consisted of archival work on policy-related documents and semi-structured interviews with key officials from relevant government institutes, civil society organizations, and return youth migrants in order to understand not only the policy framework but also the reality for those who might avail of those policies.

Interviews with government officials (n=9) were conducted in a semi-structured format in Mexico City, Mexico and Austin, Texas, between October 2018 and January 2019. Interviews with several members of civil society groups (n=3) were conducted in San Miguel de Allende, Mexico in November 2019, with ongoing correspondence via phone and email between October 2018 and February 2019. Lastly, interviews with returned youth were conducted (n=12). All interviewees were minors at the time of their entry into the United States—from less than a year, up to 16 years old—and almost all returned when they were young adults (between 16 and 26) with the exception of one who returned at 32 to pursue further studies. Sampling of returnees was conducted through a process of non-random, snowball sampling. Most interviews (n=10) were conducted predominantly in English, as the interviewees felt most comfortable using English. Interviews were conducted over the phone or in person. Due to the undocumented nature of many of the migrants and their family members—some of whom still reside in the United States—any names used in this chapter have been changed.

As a result of the sampling methods and the small sample size, the findings from these interviews are neither representative of all youth returnees in Mexico nor are they representative of all youth returnees. However, the aim of this chapter is to expand the scholarship on social protection and migration through the inclusion of the voices of youth returnees. By bringing light to the challenges that these returnees have faced and how they have been overcome through a process of piecing together informal forms of social protection, this chapter hopes to show the validity and importance of both incorporating youth voices into larger scholarship on migration and of return migration to the study of social protections.

### Mexico: from a 'policy of no policy' to a model for protection

Governments are increasingly involved in the provision of social protection services for their citizens abroad. Some scholars attribute this change in policy to the unravelling and reimagining of nation-states and borders in contemporary politics. Within this, the idea of 'emigrant citizenship' has emerged, suggesting that even while abroad, migrants are still citizens of their home countries, and therefore these home countries are still in part responsible for their well-being (Barry, 2006).

Mexico provides a rich case study for a variety of reasons. The Mexican government has made deliberate efforts to increase protections for its citizens abroad, approximately 98% of whom reside in the United States (Instituto de los Mexicanos en el Exterior, 2017). Additionally, return migration in Mexico has outnumbered outward migration in recent years (Pew Research Center, 2015), and, in 2010, about 1 in 4 of those returnees were minors (Giorguli & Gutiérrez, 2011). Mexico was also chosen due to the nature of its returning youth population. While all youth returnees may suffer from distinct vulnerabilities related to their a) migration history and b) age, returnees to Mexico may also face unique risks related to the length of time they have been abroad. These range from socio-cultural vulnerabilities such as culture shock or inability to reintegrate upon return, language-related vulnerabilities, as well as the potential economic vulnerabilities associated with these socio-cultural distinctions.

Mexico has a highly institutionalized framework of social protection for its migrants, but before the late 1980s, the state took a 'policy of no policy' towards its population abroad (Iskander, 2010). It was only in 1986 with the passage of the United States' Immigration Reform and Control Act (IRCA), which allowed a change in status for 2.7 million undocumented immigrants (Alba, 2013, p. 6), including some two million Mexicans living and working illegally in the United States (Papademetriou, 2004), that the Mexican government began to recognize its migrants. Prior to the IRCA, the government had effectively ignored and 'invisiblized' its population to the north. With the IRCA, their eligibility for status change not only allowed migrants to stay and work in the US legally - it also afforded them new rights and power. Amnesty allowed for a shift in government discourse around Mexican migrants as 'traitors,' especially with increased remittances after the IRCA (Délano, 2009, p. 774).

In addition to post-IRCA border restrictions which ramped up after 1986, fears in the migrant community increased as a result of the passage of Proposition 187 in California in 1994. While later overturned, Prop. 187, which was also known as the Save Our State (SOS) initiative, had the goal of prohibiting undocumented immigrants from accessing basic services from the state, such as non-emergency health care and education (González Gutiérrez, 2006, p. 198). In response, the Mexican government increased the provision of protection for migrants beyond the existing mandates of legal assistance for migrants in distress and documentation services to include social aspects such as health and education, and cultural programming. In this regard, the Mexican state essentially filled the perceived gap in the social protection framework for migrants that Prop. 187 created when it denied access to this population.

In 1990, the then President Salinas created the *Programa para Comunidades Mexicanas en el Extranjero* [Program for Mexican Communities Abroad] (PCME) and the *Dirección General para las Comunidades Mexicanas en el Extranjero* [Directorate General for Mexican Communities Abroad] (DGCME) in order to manage the PCME. The main goal of this new agency was to provide services to Mexicans abroad. Another major policy change occurred in 1996 when the then President Ernesto Zedillo extended political rights for Mexican migrants abroad, creating a law allowing dual nationality and extending the vote abroad.

## Social Protections for Mexican Youth Returnees

Despite renewed interest in migrant social protection by Mexican policymakers and the proliferation of programs and policies towards protecting migrants abroad that came with this acknowledgement, there have been few policies for those who return. In the case of Mexico, García Zamora and Gaspar Olvera (2018) found that youth returnees are at a higher risk for non-attendance in schools and have a lower rate of health service access. Additionally, due to the incompatibility of school systems between the United States and Mexico, they found that access to education and the labour market for youth returnees was particularly difficult. Espindola and Jacobo-Suárez (2018) point to the lack of Spanish language courses as a potential vulnerability for youth migrants, who are often not fully bilingual. Studies have also found that youth returnees face distinct identity difficulties upon return and struggle with feelings of belonging - which can in turn negatively affect their educational attainment (Espindola & Jacobo-Suárez, 2018; Jacobo-Suárez & Jensen, 2018).

The current return migration between the United States and Mexico has been characterized by the increasing involuntariness of return, return for the purposes of family reunification, and as a result of rising anti-immigrant discourse in the United States (Jacobo-Suárez & Cárdenas Alaminos, 2018). When a family member is deported, for example, youth often find themselves returning as well - either voluntarily or because their parent is leaving, giving them no other viable choice. With the rise in anti-immigrant rhetoric and fears surrounding possible deportation increases in the United States, many migrants have self-deported. Despite increased scholarship on gaps in social protections for migrant youth and increased youth vulnerabilities in the current migration system, few social protections have tackled these issues for youth.

## From here to there, and back? Formal social protections for Mexican migrants

Formal social protection, as mentioned, has been limited for youth returnees. Their social protection environments while abroad are made up of the general social protections for migrants (see Imaz, 2011 for a comprehensive overview, abbreviated in Table 2.1) and certain programs that are directly tailored to youth. Consular programs, such as *Ventanillas de Salud* [Health Windows] which provide vaccinations and other medical services, are accessible to youth migrants, although are not youth-specific. Additionally, consulates provide financial-literacy programs, cultural events such as festivals during

Mexican holidays, and documentation related services to help migrants obtain identification for legal purposes in the US when undocumented (*matrícula consular* [consular I.D. card]), which youth can avail of.

Formal social protections specifically for youth migrants also exist, although they are less comprehensive. Mexico has taken key steps to include a "youth focus" in its policymaking, with the 2014 *Ley General de Los Derechos de Niñas, Niños y Adolescentes* [General Law of the Rights of Girls, Boys, and Adolescents]. The law guarantees the protection of children and adolescents and the maximization of their wellbeing by all entities of the state, including economic, social, cultural, and psychological formation. Article 13 stipulates their specific rights, including the rights of children and adolescent migrants in particular, while Article 89 defines special protection for guaranteeing their rights, with an emphasis on repatriated migrants.

The youth migrant specific programs for migrants abroad include *IME Becas* [IME Scholarships], which gives grants to Mexican youth for their studies, while some consulates provide special programs for migrant youth - such as G.E.D. training and college fairs (Interview with Consulate, 2019). A strong focus of social provisions by the Mexican government to youth abroad has centered on the creation of bi-national education schemes. The *Programa Binacional de Educación Migrante* [Binational Migrant Education Program] (PROBEM) was created so that Mexican students living in the United States could access more bilingual teachers, and to help US teachers familiarize themselves with the Mexican educational and cultural context, through exchanges and capacity building.

Currently, there are only two major federal level programs or policies targeting returnees specifically - these are *Somos Mexicanos* [We Are Mexicans], the federal program for return, and the *Fondo de Apoyo al Migrante* [Migrant Support Fund]. For youth returnees, the only youth-specific programs are education policies which seek to facilitate the return of US educated migrants in their access to education and jobs in Mexico, and the existence of special officers deployed within *Somos Mexicanos* to deal with children and youth returnees.

*Somos Mexicanos*, which began in 2014, is the main strategy of the Mexican government to help returning Mexicans via the *Instituto Nacional de Migración* [National Institute of Migration] (INM). The program facilitates the social and economic reintegration of Mexican returnees through coordination with other government institutions, information dissemination, and personalized attention to each returnee, tailored to their own return process (Interview with INM, 2018). They also provide immediate assistance for migrants upon arrival, including basic food and health services, documentation, and emergency housing. Once returnees have settled, *Somos Mexicanos* helps in finding jobs, health services, and options to continue studies (Interview with INM, 2018).

INM also has officers that specifically deal with youth migrants, called *Oficiales de Protección a la Infancia* [Child Protection Officers] (OPI), in accordance with the *Ley General de Los Derechos de Niñas, Niños y Adolescentes*. These officers are trained to help migrant youth in Mexico - both returning Mexicans as well as non-Mexican youth. In practice, however, OPI officers are more likely to interact with non-Mexican youth in an extended manner (Interview with INM, 2018).

**Table 2.1.** Formal Social Protections for Mexican Migrants

| *Government Institution Responsible* | *Program/Policy* |
|---|---|
| *Instituto Nacional de Migración* [National Migration Institute] | Program of Humane Repatriation<br>*Programa Paisano*<br>Program of Migrant Regularization<br>*Grupos Beta*<br>*Mujer Migrante*<br>*Oficiales de Protección a la Infancia*<br>*Somos Mexicanos* |
| *Secretaría de Relaciones Exteriores* [Ministry of Foreign Affairs, SRE] | Consular Assistance and Protection<br>*Instituto de Mexicanos en el Exterior (IME)*<br>*PROBEM*<br>*Programa Plazas Comunitarias*<br>*Ventanillas de Salud*<br>*IME Becas*<br>*Red Consular*<br>*Tu Vivienda en México*<br>*Guía del Viajero*<br>Bi-National Health Week<br>Program of Financial Education |
| *Secretaría de Educación Pública* [Ministry of Education, SEP] | Program of Mexico-USA Teacher Exchange<br>Program of Mexican Teachers Recruitment<br>Secondary Education Accreditation<br>Program of Book Donation for Mexican Children in the USA |
| *Secretaría de Bienestar* [Ministry of Wellbeing] | *Programa 3x1* |
| *Secretaría de Salud* [Ministry of Health] | Program for Migrant Health<br>Repatriation of Sick Migrants |

Source: Adapted by Author from Imaz, 2011, p. 461-462 with Supporting Information from Instituto Nacional de Migración (2019); Secretaría de Relaciones Exteriores (2019); Secretaría de Educación Pública (2019); Secretaría de Bienestar (2019); Secretaría de Salud (2019); Secretaría de Gobernación (2019)

The *Fondo de Apoyo a Migrantes*, while not a program, is a federal fund for returnees. These funds are dispersed to each state in Mexico, based in part on the level of return migration they face, for distribution to help with self-employment activities, for the operation of homes which attend to returnees, to pay for the return of migrants to their location of origin, to help families, and for training in productive capabilities for the purposes of labour market reintegration (Secretaría de Gobernación, 2018). While the distribution of these funds is expected to continue in the future, it relies heavily on the will of the government to allocate the funds, and the way in which the fund is allocated to each state government raises some questions about measurement of return.

**Table 2.2:** Federal Social Protections for Youth Returnees in Mexico

| Program/Policy | Youth Specific? | Migrant Specific? | Returnee Specific? |
|---|---|---|---|
| Somos Mexicanos [We Are Mexicans] | Yes, OPI Officers | Yes | Yes |
| Fondo de Apoyo a Migrantes [Migrant Support Fund] | Not explicitly | Yes | Yes |
| Instituto Nacional de Educación de Los Adultos [National Institute for Adult Education] | Yes, insofar as it helps youth re-enter education system | Yes | Yes |
| Programa Becas Para el Bienestar Benito Juárez [Benito Juárez Welfare Scholarships Program] | Yes | No | No |
| Jóvenes Construyendo el Futuro [Youth Building the Future] | Yes | No | No |

Source: Instituto Nacional de Migración (2019); Secretaría de Educación Pública (2019); Secretaría del Trabajo y Previsión Social (2019)

In addition to these programs and policies, the *Instituto Nacional de Educación de los Adultos* [National Institute for Adult Education] (INEA) has a program to certify migrants' English proficiency, and, as provided through the *Ley General de Educación* [General Law on Education], the government has lowered barriers to entry to returning migrants through the instruction of schools to 'enroll students who lack academic transcripts or who hold transcripts issued in the United States that have not been certified or translated to Spanish' (Ruiz Soto, Dominguez-Villegas, Argueta, & Capps, 2019, p. 15).

Aside from the migrant specific policies for youth, this study also looked into the available social protections for youth in Mexico, regardless of migratory status, as a way to address the notion that returnees are subsumed under domestic protections. There are two key policies for youth in Mexico. *Jóvenes Construyendo el Futuro* [Youth Building the Future] run out of the Ministry of Labor and Social Welfare (*Secretaría del Trabajo y Previsión Social*) is an apprenticeship program which seeks to address youth under- and unemployment. It pairs youth who are neither studying nor employed with a 1-year apprenticeship in the business sector, with the goal of giving youth the skillset and training to be better equipped in the labour market and to increase their chances at formal sector employment. It includes a stipend from the government and covers youths aged 18 to 29 years old (Secretaría del Trabajo y Previsión Social, 2019). The program makes no specific provisions for youth returnees.

In addition to this program, there is the *Programa Becas Para el Bienestar Benito Juárez* [Benito Juárez Welfare Scholarship Program] from the *Secretaría de Educación Pública* [Ministry of Education]. This program provides eligible youth enrolled in public schools with scholarships. The program is split for students enrolled aged 18 and under, and those enrolled in higher levels of education from 18 to 21 years of age (Secretaría de Educación Pública, 2019). Much like the program under STPS, the *Becas Benito Juárez* is focused on youth in general in Mexico, rather than migrant youth in particular.

### Filling the gaps: Informal social protection and return

As the above-mentioned programs and policies show, the social protection environment for Mexican migrants abroad is extensive. But for youth returnees, this framework shrinks significantly. Given this formal social protection environment, how are youth returnees able to re-integrate and adapt to Mexican life? This section looks to tackle this question by analyzing interview data with migrants about their own vulnerabilities and the mechanisms through which they protect themselves against these—often in a transnational way. The adaptation processes of migrant returnees are integral for their reintegration into Mexican society, and function as needed social protections. These adaptation processes often lead to mitigation of risks and vulnerabilities, through allowing migrant returnees to access the job market or enter into the educational system, sometimes addressing their vulnerabilities in a more effective way than through government initiatives.

### Where to turn to? Social protection realities

Throughout the interviews for this research, several key points stood out about the ways in which migrant youth understand their social protection environments upon return. All of the returnees interviewed saw the process of return as the time period in which they needed to protect against future vulnerabilities and regain their livelihoods in Mexico. For some, protections were less about *re*-integration into Mexico, but about *integration* into a country, they were completely unfamiliar with. All of the youth returnees also understood return as a process in which the protections provided by formal institutions included emergency shelter, basic food, and transport offered at the border—they are 'just day one' protections, as one returnee, José, noted—when the real question for returnees is 'what happens for day two or day three or year one.' In those subsequent days after return, the youth turned to other sources to piece together social protections.

In the case of transnational informal social protections from migrant associations in the US, there was the belief that the migrant associations lacked the institutional capacity to facilitate protections for returned members, especially youth. Miguel had been a part of a migrant activist group in the US before he returned, but he did not expect his student migrant advocacy group to help him upon return, because of its focus on protecting those who still reside in the US. For him, organizations in the US were helping to advocate for better rights abroad, but upon return, other organizations or government programs would need to fill this gap.

There has been a proliferation of non-governmental organizations (NGOs) and civil society groups within Mexico whose objective is to provide this informal protection to returning youth. One organization, Dream in Mexico, seeks to create protections to aid returnees in the process of overcoming social vulnerabilities associated with return - such as mental health issues like anxiety and depression, language and cultural barriers, and feelings of belonging and identity - through providing a support network for returnees. Boccagni (2011) stresses that 'in the face of the isolation and severances migration may induce, is a need for psycho-social and emotional support' (p. 225), which is reiterated in this practice by NGOs working on the ground. For Dream in Mexico, these young returnees require services that national government programs cannot necessarily facilitate - such as in the creation of support networks.

In discussions of return, only two returnees were aware of specific government protections and programs for returnees. One, Jesús, emphasized that information is not adequately disseminated by the government about programs in place. When he returned, he tried working with a senator to create better policies for youth returnees but found a lack of willingness to fully commit to the implementation and circulation of information. While most of the returnees interviewed in this study were unaware of government programs, when asked about whether or not government protections for migrants should continue upon return, there were mixed responses. Some returnees doubted the ability and willingness of the government to undertake such programs. One migrant, Alejandro, acknowledged that he was resigned to focus on 'how to come up with the money I need to survive…instead of hoping or thinking the government will do something.'

Most returnees saw communities and support groups for returning youth as the most important way to overcome vulnerabilities upon return. Miguel stressed the need for a resource centre, to establish a network of returnees to create a platform to share lived experiences, based in part on his experience with his migrant advocacy group in the US. 'When we end up sharing stories it becomes about the same thing...you gotta keep your head up' and 'see things at the end of the tunnel…it's not an easy process…you have to live the everyday experience.' There was an acknowledgement that domestic programs for youth, such as the scholarship and apprenticeship programs, could not cover the migrant specific vulnerabilities in the same way as a separate program could.

**Assessing the gaps: Youth returnee vulnerabilities**

In the interviews conducted with returnees, several specific vulnerabilities were mentioned. These vulnerabilities, in turn, were considered key target areas for any potential social protections. Table 2.3 outlines these in an attempt at understanding and making sense of the way in which these risks can manifest themselves in the everyday lives of returnees.

As a starting point, all youth returnees brought up mental health or identity formation as a key risk they faced. For one youth returnee, José, generalized anxiety, as a result of years of living as an undocumented migrant in the US, and the culture shock of returning to Mexico but feeling like he no longer belonged, significantly impacted his ability to continue his education in Mexico. He had returned to Mexico to pursue a career in medicine - which was not possible for him in the US as a result of his migratory status. In addition to mental health, José also brought up the idea of identity formation. 'I didn't know how to have an identity…to be a citizen…to get an ID' because he had lived abroad since he was less than a year old. For José, identity formation was both about learning how to integrate into a society he was unfamiliar with, while at the same time struggling to obtain basic identity documents. Other migrants expressed similar experiences as taking a toll on their adaptation process. Lupe recalled arriving in Mexico, after having spent her entire life in the US, to realize she 'didn't remember anything about Mexico.'

While Lupe had returned to Mexico to continue her education, giving up her right to live and work in the United States under the policy of Deferred Action for Childhood Arrivals (DACA), Lupe felt overwhelmed - unable to easily communicate with her peers. Many of the returnees brought up similar issues arising from inadequate Spanish language abilities as a severe vulnerability they faced upon return. Alejandro simply stated, 'I thought I knew Spanish, I thought I knew Mexico', but in his first year he found his only job prospect was to work at a call centre utilizing his English, speaking to peers in English. For Alejandro, and other returnees, despite their levels of education, call centres are often their first place of employment as they find themselves unable to access other jobs because of this language barrier.

About half of the interviewees returned to Mexico for educational purposes. Their reasons for doing so varied, but most noted that they could not access the formal job market after graduation in the US due to their status, and therefore returned in part to pursue greater post-degree opportunities. Despite the framework in place for the continuation of education in Mexico for returnees with US educational experience, documentation problems caused significant delays in access to education. This had to do, in part, with the nature of return - such as deportation, hasty self-deportation, and general lack of return planning. Additionally, language barriers proved a particularly large obstacle in daily life and within educational settings - such as in classes and exams.

Returnees traced some of these vulnerabilities to the amount of time they had spent in the United States - some of whom had spent nearly their entire lives abroad, had family still living abroad, and considered themselves as American as they did Mexican. Some returnees noted that even though they migrated at an older age - from 13 to 16 - they spent their formative years as a young adult in the United States, and often returned to a completely unfamiliar environment. Additionally, some returned first to their hometowns, only to find that Mexico City was the only place they could find gainful employment or educational opportunities, meaning they effectively 'returned' to somewhere completely new.

When asked about interaction with governments - especially as calls for government involvement supporting migrants or NGOs (Sabates-Wheeler, Koettl, & Avato, 2011) had increased - Miguel noted that when he first returned, 'I never really felt depressed, I felt angry' but felt like he could not complain in Mexico. For Miguel, he did not have the same voice as he did in the United States vis-à-vis the government - to complain, to ask for changes, to advocate. Another returnee, Fernando, noted in passing that he had never experienced police harassment until he returned to Mexico. While a lack of trust in government was not a common thread throughout the interviews, this, paired with a lack of familiarity with the institutional systems in Mexico may have significant effects on the ability of migrant returnees to access certain services.

Lastly, the stigma around return arose in a significant number of interviews. Returnees and NGO groups noted that discrimination against migrant returnees is common, especially those with tattoos, who are believed to be deported gang members. Juana noted that when she and her husband returned to Mexico, people would ask them, 'why did you guys come? What did you guys do? Why are you guys over here?' treating them like criminals. For Juana and her young family, discrimination by community members was a significant obstacle in her return process. Miguel noted that in his research lab, his peers often looked down on migrant returnees, thinking they were lazy and complainers, who 'had it easy' in comparison, making his daily work life difficult. For many of these returnees, discrimination in the US was common, but it was discrimination upon return that was particularly jarring - affecting their sense of identity and belonging.

**Table 2.3.** Categories of Youth Returnee Vulnerabilities[4]

| Determinant of Vulnerability | Examples of Manifestation (Migrant-specific) | Intensified for These Returnees Due To |
|---|---|---|
| Spatial/Environmental | Unfamiliarity with surroundings | Lack of knowledge about area, government programs, jobs, school, community resources, healthcare, etc. (because of length of time abroad, age at which migrated, etc.) |
| Socio-political | Lack of documentation; lack of familiarity with government | Uncertainty interacting with government (trauma from undocumented status in past, unfamiliarity with governance system, language barriers, lack of documentation due to nature of return) |
| Socio-cultural | Linguistic differences, discrimination | Social discrimination based on language, returned status ('failed' returnee stigma), physical appearance (tattoos, etc.) |

Source: Adapted from MacAuslan (2011, p. 185) and Sabates-Wheeler and Waite (2003, p. 14) based on Author's Interviews with Returnees

In order to mitigate these vulnerabilities and risks, all of the returnees relied on either personal networks or civil society organizations to provide them with the social protections they needed upon return - from financial-related needs, such as short-term loans in their first months back in Mexico, language-related support, identity/belonging and mental health support, and documentation issues. They relied not only on family and friends in Mexico, but several of the interviewees pointed to the transnational support of relatives in the US in order to access finances and to deal with documentation issues related to educational access.

Perhaps the most important take away from conversations with youth returnees is the extent to which they share similar self-identified risks and vulnerabilities, and the way that they are able to utilize their own resiliency to create social protections upon return. Conway and Norton (2002) have called on policymakers to 'recognise the costs to households of informal social protection pursued in the absence of the state. In this light, recognition of the ingenuity and resilience of social protection arrangements which have evolved outside the state does not imply … that governments either could or should

[4] In Sabates-Wheeler and Waite (2003) they look at the determinant of vulnerabilities (spatial/environmental, socio-political, and socio-cultural) for each 'stage' of migration. Because this study looks at return, it does not create a separate categorization for each 'temporal' stage of the migration process (transit, in destination, return), but acknowledges temporal aspects such as length of time abroad in other categories. MacAuslan (2011) follows suit.

abrogate responsibility for the provision of social protection, passing the burden on to households, communities, NGOs, and the private sector' (p. 537).

While many returnees were wary of the ability of the government to provide the protections they felt were necessary, there seem to be key areas in which the government can facilitate and extend its own social protection mechanisms to better provide for its migrant youth in their return - especially given the protections for migrants in general awarded already.

In Mexico, there is a need for a more comprehensive policy framework for youth returnees. While the government meets basic protection needs, youth returnees require a more extensive set of long-term protections. This includes issues of mental health and identity formation, but also a strengthening of the existing programs on education and language attainment which could provide relief for those migrants seeking to insert themselves in the local labour market and enroll in further schooling. Additionally, the government could promote a transformative social protection mechanism by creating an anti-discrimination campaign with regard to returnees, to de-stigmatize return, and to emphasize and make visible this growing population in Mexico. This might also entail the inclusion of youth migrant specific provisions within the new administration's youth development initiatives.

With regards to mental health and identity formation specifically, Hardgrove et al. (2014) note that these issues can have spillover effects into other areas of youths' lives, and can negatively affect migrants' adult lives, as their ability to work and access education may be hindered. As such, it seems critical that these issues are addressed, as return migration seems to enhance these vulnerabilities. The Mexican government, for example, currently provides virtual mental health services through an online platform for Mexicans in Ireland, the United Kingdom, and Germany. Through the facilitation of social protections for health and identity, the state would also be mitigating risks that could affect prospects of employment and access to education. In this way, this framework not only protects returnees in the present but also promotes protection in the future as well.

## Conclusion

The path towards realizing the dream of protection for migrants throughout the entire migration cycle is not singular, but instead, there are many potential avenues through which the government - or civil society - can direct its resources and attention to better provide for its youth migrant population, especially upon return. While this study recognizes the limitations in the generalizability of these youth returnees' accounts, it has the goal of beginning a needed discussion about not only the importance of taking into consideration youth experiences in migration, but also the need to expand social protection studies to include return.

All of the youth returnees in this study voiced their desire to remain in Mexico for the foreseeable future - to start and continue their adult lives in their country of birth. Some emphasized that their return to Mexico allowed them to dream of a future in which they could work, receive education, and travel in a way that was impossible in the US. Others pointed to a feeling of permanence and a regaining of control over their lives upon return. But, perhaps most importantly, all of the youth returnees in this study emphasized their desire for future youth returnees to have access to some of the protections they found were missing in their own processes of return. The hope is that future returnees, when faced with the same risks and vulnerabilities as their predecessors, will be able to draw on a wider array of protections and support in order to realize their own dreams in Mexico.

## References


Alba, F. (2013). Mexico: The New Migration Narrative. *The Online Journal of the Migration Policy Institute*, 1–16.

Avato, J., Koettl, J., & Sabates-Wheeler, R. (2010). The Status of Social Protection for International Migrants. *World Development*, *38*(4), 455–466.

Barry, K. (2006). Home and Away: The Construction of Citizenship in an Emigration Context. *New York University Law Review*, *81*(11), 10–59.

Bhabha, J. (2014). Moving Children: Lacunae in Contemporary Human Rights Protections for Migrant Children and Adolescents. *Revue Européenne Des Migrations Internationales [European Review of International Migration]*, *30*(1), 35–57.

Boccagni, P. (2011). Social Protection as a Multi-Actor Process in Ecuadorian Migration: Towards a Transnationalism of Social Rights? In R. Sabates-Wheeler & R. Feldman (Eds.), *Migration and Social Protection: Claiming Social Rights Beyond Borders* (pp. 210–231). Palgrave Macmillan.

Conway, T., & Norton, A. (2002). Nets, Ropes, Ladders and Trampolines: The Place of Social Protection within Current Debates on Poverty Reduction. *Development Policy Review*, *20*(5), 533–540.

de Haas, H. (2007). *Remittances, Migration and Social Development, A Conceptual Review of the Literature* (No. Paper Number 34; pp. i–40). United Nations Research Institute for Social Development.

de Haas, H., Fokkema, T., & Fihri, M. F. (2015). Return Migration as Failure or Success? The Determinants of Return Migration Intentions Among Moroccan Migrants in Europe. *International Migration and Integration*, *16*, 415–429.

Délano, A. (2009). From Limited to Active Engagement: Mexico's Emigration Policies from a Foreign Policy Perspective (2000–2006). *International Migration Review*, *43*(4), 764–814.

Devereux, S., & Sabates-Wheeler, R. (2004). *Transformative social protection* (Working Paper No. 232; pp. 1–30). Sussex, United Kingdom: Institute of Development Studies.

Dobbs, E., & Levitt, P. (2017). The missing link? The role of sub-national governance in transnational social protections. *Oxford Development Studies*, 1–17.

Dobbs, E., Levitt, P., Parella, S., & Petroff, A. (2018). Social welfare grey zones: How and why subnational actors provide when nations do not? *Journal of Ethnic and Migration Studies*, 1–18.

Espindola, J., & Jacobo-Suárez, M. (2018). The ethics of return migration and education: Transnational duties in migratory processes. *Journal of Global Ethics*, *14*(1), 54–70.

García Zamora, R., & Gaspar Olvera, S. (2018). Integración desigual y limitadas oportunidades. Retorno e ingreso a México de niños y jóvenes migrantes mexicanos y de origen mexicano [Unequal integration and limited opportunities. Return and arrival in Mexico of Mexican migrant children and youth]. *Ser-Migrante [To Be-Migrant]*, *5*, 78–94.

Giorguli, S. E., & Gutiérrez, E. Y. (2011). Niños y jóvenes en el contexto de la migración internacional entre México y Estados Unidos [Children and youth in the context of international migration between Mexico and the United States]. *Coyuntura Demográfica [Demographic Moment]*, *1*, 21–25.

González Gutiérrez, C. (2006). Del Acercamiento a la inclusión institucional: La experiencia del Instituto de los Mexicanos en el Exterior [Of Rapprochement to Institutional Incusion: the Experience of the Institute of Mexicans Abroad]. In C. González Gutiérrez (Ed.), *Relaciones Estado diáspora: Aproximaciones desde cuatro continentes [State Diaspora Relations: Approaches from Four Continents]* (pp. 181–220). Mexico City, Mexico: Miguel Ángel Porrúa.

Hardgrove, A., Pells, K., Boyden, J., & Dornan, P. (2014). *Youth Vulnerabilities in Life Course Transitions* (pp. 1–51) [Occasional Paper]. New York, New York: UNDP Human Development Report Office.

Imaz, C. (2011). Public Policies Regarding Migration and Civil Society in Mexico. In *Public Policies on Migration and Civil Society in Latin America: The Cases of Argentina, Brazil, Colombia and Mexico* (pp. 411–478). Mexico City, Mexico: Scalabrini International Migration Network Inc.

Instituto de los Mexicanos en el Exterior. (2016). *Programa Binacional de Educación Migrante [Bi-National Migrant Education Program] (PROBEM).* Retrieved from https://www.gob.mx/ime/acciones-y-programas/programa-binacional-de-educacion-migrante-probem-61464

Instituto de los Mexicanos en el Exterior. (2017). *Población mexicana en el mundo [Mexican population in the World].* Retrieved from http://www.ime.gob.mx/estadisticas/mundo/estadistica_poblacion_pruebas.html

Instituto Nacional de Migración. (2018). *Somos Mexicanos [We are Mexicans].* Retrieved from https://www.gob.mx/inm/acciones-y-programas/estrategia-somos-mexicanos

Iskander, N. (2010). The Creative State: Forty Years of Migration and Development Policy in Morocco and Mexico. Ithaca, United States: Cornell University Press.

Jacobo-Suárez, M., & Cárdenas Alaminos, N. (2018). Los retornados: ¿Cómo responder a la diversidad de migrantes mexicanos que regresan de Estados Unidos?[The Returned: How to Respond to the Diversity of Mexican Migrants Who Return from the United States] (CIDE Report No. DPM 01; pp. 1–19). Mexico City, Mexico: Centro de Investigación y Docencia Económica.

Jacobo-Suárez, M., & Jensen, B. (2018, June 19). *Schooling for US-Citizen Students in Mexico.* 1–13. Los Angeles, California.

Levitt, P., Viterna, J., Mueller, A., & Lloyd, C. (2016). Transnational social protection: Setting the agenda. *Oxford Development Studies*, *45*(1), 2–19.

Ley General de Los Derechos de Niñas, Niños y Adolescentes [General Law on Children and Adolescents]. (2014).

Locke, C., Seeley, J., & Nitya, R. (2013). Migration and Social Reproduction at Critical Junctures in Family Life Course. *Third World Quarterly*, *34*(10), 1881–1895.

MacAuslan, I. (2011). Crossing Internal Boundaries: Political and Physical Access to the Public Distribution System in India. In R. Sabates-Wheeler & R. Feldman (Eds.), *Migration and Social Protection: Claiming Social Rights Beyond Borders* (pp. 183–209). Palgrave Macmillan.

Mexican Embassy of Ireland. (2019). *Ventanilla de Salud Mental [Mental Health Window].* Mexican Embassy of Ireland.

Papademetriou, D. G. (2004). The Mexico Factor in U.S. Immigration Reform. *The Online Journal of the Migration Policy Institute.*

Pew Research Center. (2015). More Mexicans Leaving than Coming to the U.S.: Net Loss of 14,000 from 2009 to 2014; Family Reunification Top Reason for Return. Washington, D.C.: Pew Research Center.

Piore, M. J. (1979). *Birds of passage: Migrant labor and industrial societies.* Cambridge, United Kingdom: Cambridge University Press.

Rosenblum, M. R. (2004). Moving Beyond the Policy of No Policy: Emigration from Mexico and Central America. *Latin American Politics and Society*, *46*(4), 91–125.

Ruiz Soto, A. G., Dominguez-Villegas, R., Argueta, L., & Capps, R. (2019). *Sustainable Reintegration: Strategies to Support Migrants Returning to Mexico and Central America* (pp. 1–38) [Migration Policy Institute Report]. Washington, D.C.: Migration Policy Institute.

Sabates-Wheeler, R., & Feldman, R. (2011a). Introduction: Mapping Migrant Welfare onto Social Provisioning. In R. Sabates-Wheeler & R. Feldman (Eds.), *Migration and Social Protection: Claiming Social Rights Beyond Borders* (pp. 3–35). Palgrave Macmillan.

Sabates-Wheeler, R., & Feldman, R. (Eds.). (2011b). *Migration and Social Protection: Claiming Social Rights Beyond Borders*. Palgrave Macmillan.

Sabates-Wheeler, R., Koettl, J., & Avato, J. (2011). Introduction: Mapping Migrant Welfare onto Social Provisioning. In R. Sabates-Wheeler & R. Feldman (Eds.), *Social Security for Migrants: A Global Overview of Portability Agreements* (pp. 91–116). Palgrave Macmillan.

Secretaría de Bienestar. (2019). Retrieved from www.gob.mx/bienestar

Secretaría de Educación Pública. (2019). Retrieved from www.gob.mx/sep

Secretaría de Gobernación. (2018). *Lineamientos de Operación del Fondo de Apoyo a Migrantes [Operation Guidelines for the Migrant Support Fund]*. Retrieved from http://www.dof.gob.mx/nota_detalle.php?codigo=5516826&fecha=21/03/2018

Secretaría de Relaciones Exteriores. (2019). Retrieved from www.gob.mx/sre

Secretaría de Salud. (2019). Retrieved from www.gob.mx/salud

Secretaría del Trabajo y Previsión Social. (2019). Retrieved from www.gob.mx/stps

UN Committee on the Rights of the Child. (2012). Committee on the Rights of the Child, Report of the 2012 Day of General Discussion on the Rights of All Children in the Context of International Migration [Report]. United Nations.

United Nations. (2017). The world counted 258 million international migrants in 2017, representing 3.4 per cent of global population. *Population Facts, 2017*(5).

Zúñiga, V. (2018). The 0.5 Generation: What Children Know about International Migration. *Migraciones Internacionales, 9*(3), 93–120.

Zúñiga, V., & Hamann, E. T. (2015). Going to a home you have never been to: The return migration of Mexican and American-Mexican children. *Children's Geographies, 13*(6), 643–655.

# CHAPTER 3

# YOUNG MIGRANTS' EXPERIENCES WITH VOLUNTARY LEGAL GUARDIANS IN PALERMO, SICILY

Francesca Viola

According to the Italian Ministry of Labour and Social Policies, as of June 2018, in Italy there were 13,151[1] Unaccompanied and Separated Children (UASC) outside their country of origin[2]; 92.5% of which were males and 99.2% between the ages of 14-17 (Ministero del Lavoro e delle Politiche Sociali, 2018). At the time, the highest concentration of UASC (more than 40%) resided in Sicily (ibid.); research about UASC in this region is, therefore, particularly relevant.

Given the increasing number of UASC arriving in recent years, Italy has established a dedicated protection system aimed at specifically addressing their needs and ensuring their rights are protected (regulated by the DDL Zampa, 47/2017[3]). Among other things, the new law proposes to introduce regional lists of voluntary guardians who are willing, following a screening and certification process, to support UASC in their adaptation process in the host country. It is intended that voluntary guardians will progressively replace institutional and professional guardians, including municipalities' mayors or lawyers, that were previously nominated in the absence of other adult guardians (Defence for Children, 2018). Voluntary guardians will fulfil the role of a

[1] These numbers only reflect official statistics of UASC that are within the system, and do not consider those who flew and continued their journeys on their own. The Italian Ministry of Labour and Social Policies identifies 4,677 UASC (the majority from Eritrea, Somalia and Afghanistan) still minors as of June 2018 and who moved out of the reception system. The figure is a stock figure of all the departures' warnings received in the past years (Ministero del Lavoro e delle Politiche Sociali, 2018).

[2] According to General Comment n.6 of the United Nations Committee on the Rights of the Child "Unaccompanied children" (also called unaccompanied minors) are children [...] who have been separated from both parents and other relatives and are not being cared for by an adult who, by law or custom, is responsible for doing so. "Separated children" are children [...] who have been separated from both parents, or from their previous legal or customary primary caregiver, but not necessarily from other relatives. These may, therefore, include children accompanied by other adult family members (2005: 6).

[3] Law No. 47 of 7 April 2017 on "Provisions concerning the protection measures of third-country unaccompanied children" (known as the "Zampa Law") is in force since 19 May 2017 and is an organic regulation for the protection and taking into care of UASC in the Italian territory, and includes among others provisions on absolute prohibition on rejecting UASC, reception in first-stage and second-stage reception facilities, residence permits, legal guardianship, rules regulating age determination, etc. (INTERSOS, 2017).

guardian as defined by the European Union (EU) Agency for Fundamental Rights[4] (2014) and emphasise the importance of the relational aspect of guardianship in parallel to their legal and institutional role. It is believed that voluntary guardians will be more engaged and closer to UASC's lives and, thereby provide sympathetic accompaniment to UASC as they navigate through the reception system and integration process.

It is widely acknowledged that UASC have positive first impressions of the host country, but over time they experience stressful reactions due to multiple barriers: foreign languages, complex and unfamiliar bureaucratic systems, cultural disorientation, unknown rules, responsibilities and expectations (Roberts et al., 2017; Luster et al., 2009). Studies have also shown UASC do experience anxiety, depression, loneliness and/or isolation, due to the separation from their families, friends and wider social networks in their countries of origin (Derluyn & Broekaert, 2008). Ensuring sympathetic guardian relationships who can link newly arrived UASC with peers, adults, civil society and formal institutions in the host country reduces the above-mentioned stressors allowing a smoother process of adaptation[5] (Aytar & Brunnberg, 2016; Mels et al., 2008) and facilitates children's access to social resources (Sime & Fox, 2015; Smyth et al., 2015). There is broad consensus that guidance, support and proximity of reliable people alongside access to services in the host community, such as health and education, improve UASC's wellbeing in the host country (Costa, 2015; Carlson et al., 2012). Children's engagement with institutions and individuals who aim to develop the child's social capital and support network, tend to improve social inclusion and mitigate against isolation (Costa, 2015) by creating a sense of acceptance, safety and security (Hanberger et al., 2016). The importance of social support, connectedness and meaningful social relationships has also been recognized by the children themselves in a previous study with UASC from Sub-Saharan Africa (O'Toole Thommessen et al., 2017).

In the context of UASC, legal guardians are protective figures responsible for ensuring their rights and best interests are fulfilled (Defence for Children, 2018). This is a challenging task given the many social, cultural and emotional barriers faced by UASC children who have uncertain legal rights and limited financial resources and social networks (Smyth et al., 2015). The legal guardian can provide social, emotional and practical support, esteem and advice to UASC (Cutrona, 2000 in Smyth et al., 2015). However, Costa argues that this is only effective when children and guardians have a strong understanding of the guardian's role and duties (2015). Research carried out in multiple EU countries

[4] "A guardian is an independent person who safeguards the child's best interests and general well-being, and to this effect complements the limited legal capacity of the child, when necessary, in the same way that parents do" EU Agency for Fundamental Rights (2014)

[5] For what concerns the case of Sicily, it has also been argued that UASC's close relationships with third parties who are not involved in the reception system for minors can serve for the monitoring of the reception itself and lead to report cases in which services are poorly provided (Defence for Children, 2018).

found that in Italy, UASC has a fragmented and confused perception of the roles and duties of a guardian (EU Agency for Fundamental Rights, 2010). At the time of this research, legal guardians were still institutional or professional figures who were assigned multiple UASC at the same time and provided formal guidance and services to children. Since the approval of the Zampa law (DDL Zampa, 47/2017[6]) the typology of guardians is being transformed and, presumably, children's experiences and perceptions are also shifting.

Italian regions are currently selecting and training voluntary guardians following the criteria established by the Ombudsperson for Children's Rights. Several voluntary legal guardians have already started exercising their role. Given the anticipated benefits for UASC as a consequence of this policy change, this study explores the perspectives of UASC within the reception system in Palermo and investigates the effects of voluntary guardians upon their lives.

**Study design, Methodology and Ethics**

Qualitative research was carried out with UASC in Palermo[7] to ascertain their experiences of voluntary guardianship. The sample was solicited using a theoretical sampling strategy, following the Grounded Theory method (Glaser & Strauss 1967). Overall, 22 adolescents aged 14-18 were interviewed[8] through seventeen in-depth one-on-one interviews and two focus group discussions each with 3 and 2 participants. The countries of origin of the interviewees are Bangladesh (4), Egypt (1), Gambia (5), Guinea Conakry (2), Ivory Coast (2), Mali (2), Nigeria (4) and Senegal (2). Twenty interviewees were male and two were female[9]. The participants arrived in Italy between September 2015 and November 2017. In duration, they had spent between thirty-four months and eight months in Italy.[10] At the time of the interviews, all lived in migrant reception facilities. None of them were in foster care nor had experienced foster care at any point in their life in Italy. Most of the interviewees had a voluntary legal guardian assigned (16 out of 22), whereas some were still remained under the guardianship of an institution or professional as per the former policy (6 out of 22).

The one-on-one interviews and focus groups were based on semi-structured interview guidelines developed prior to fieldwork. Interviews were audio-recorded with a consensus of the young people and their guardians, and

[6] For additional information, see footnote 3.

[7] In Palermo the first training for voluntary guardians happened in July 2017. Since then several individuals became qualified to be voluntary guardians for UASC. At the time fieldwork for this article was carried out, Palermo had about 150 active voluntary guardians and a population of UASC of about 7000 youths. This data is only approximative and was gathered in June 2018 from a conference on voluntary guardianship organized by the Palermo's Ombudsperson for Children's Rights.

[8] All young migrants interviewed arrived in Italy as UASC. In the remainder of the chapter, the study participants will be referred as "young migrants" or "adolescents".

[9] This percentage is in line with the prevalence of female UASC over all UASC in Italy.

[10] Most of the interviewees arrived in 2017 (17 out of 22), 4 out of 22 arrived in 2016 and one in 2015.

transcriptions were anonymized and coded for analysis following the open coding method (Corbin & Strauss, 1990) using Atlas.ti software.

Steps were taken to guarantee ethical compliance in research with children (Hopkins, 2008; Alderson & Morrow, 2004). Information and consent forms were signed by participants and their guardians; confidentiality and anonymity were guaranteed at all stages of the research project; a referral pathway was prepared with Standard Operating Procedures to follow if interviewees demonstrated signs of distress or disclosed actual events or perceived risks of abuse11 or were evidently isolated and in need of legal advice[12].

The following sections present the results of the analysis of the interviews and discuss the main themes emerging from the conversations with young migrants in relation to voluntary legal guardianship.

**UASC's understanding of the role and duties of a legal guardian**

Those young people who had been assigned a voluntary legal guardian had a stronger understanding of guardianship than those who remained with a professional or institutional guardian. All young migrants who had a voluntary guardian knew their guardian in person, had a familiar relationship with them and in most cases met them multiple times a week, even after they turned 18. Conversely, those adolescents who were not assigned voluntary guardians, and remained under the care of institutional or professional guardians, rarely met them or knew their names. Some interviewees reflected on the fact that their de facto guardian was the person in charge of the reception centre where they lived. In fact, in Sicily, the institutional or professional guardians often sign the power of attorneys to the person in charge of the reception centre or of the cooperative that manages the reception facilities to take responsibilities of guardianship in their behalf. Therefore, in several cases, young migrants could not distinguish between the role of guardians and staff of the reception centre where they resided:

> In reality, all UASC have a guardian, but the guardian is the mayor or the council member… he has 300 guys, he doesn't even know the guys' names, but why is he a guardian? It's fake. There are no meetings with the guardians. Let's say all the guys have a guardian, but if you ask a boy who doesn't have a voluntary guardian 'do you have a guardian?' he will tell you that he doesn't have a guardian, you understand? But in reality, he has a guardian, but it's only a façade." (boy, 18)

When asked about the role and duties of a legal guardian, all interviewees with a voluntary guardian had clarity around their rights and responsibilities vis-

[11] The referral pathway contained list of services and phone numbers that could be used by the youths in case of psychological distress, abuse or risk of abuse. Luckily, I did not have to deal with any of these situations.

[12] The young migrants were referred to the "Ideas Box" project designed by Libraries Without Borders aimed at proposing leisure and training activities for UASC; the "Associazione Porco Rosso" and "Clinica Legale" which respectively provide different kinds of support for migrants, including free legal advice.

à-vis guardianship contrarily to what was observed in a previous research of the EU Agency for Fundamental Rights (2010). On the other hand, young migrants who were not assigned a voluntary guardian were not familiar with the Italian word to define a guardian, and when aware of their right to have a guardian, they emphasized the legal aspects of guardianship rather than the relational ones. Table 3.1 shows interviewees' answers to questions regarding the role and duties of a guardian.

Some of the young migrants without a voluntary guardian were aware of their right to have a guardian and claimed it explicitly by requesting to meet their guardians or to be assigned a voluntary guardian. However, it emerged that many others, not knowing who their guardian was, were not aware of their right to have one. Overall, guardians were not recognized as supportive figures by those young migrants without a voluntary guardian. Nor were they mentioned when recalling worrying episodes, significant challenges or participation in leisure activities. Conversely, all young migrants with a voluntary guardian knew them in person, had an active relationship with them and valued their support. They recognised that the guardian manages bureaucratic issues linked to their request for asylum and their rights within the reception system. Whenever they had problems or feared that they would be transferred to another city against their will, they could phone their guardian, explain their problems and find a solution together. Indeed, they perceived that having a guardian was a guarantee against perceived injustices faced within the reception system.

Moreover, voluntary guardians played an important role in the interviewees' daily lives. They met every week, often multiple times per week, participated in cultural and leisure activities together ranging from eating outside, recreational walking in Palermo and going to the seaside. Unfortunately, some young migrants had high expectations on their voluntary guardians and, at times, mistook their role as providers of basic services[13]. This needs to be carefully considered when training voluntary guardians and in briefing UASC on the roles and duties of guardians.

### "*I cannot deny this luck*": navigating the reception system's dysfunctionalities with voluntary guardians

One common theme was the important role played by voluntary guardians in supporting young migrants to handle adverse events. Many of the interviewees asserted that voluntary guardians gave them courage to denounce poor living conditions in reception centres, express concerns regarding their legal situation in Italy, resist actions not in their best interest such as potential

[13] One of the boys interviewed did not want to be recorded nor that notes were taken. He complained about his guardian because s/he did not buy him clothes nor shoes like he perceives other voluntary guardians do. However, the provision of the economic sustainment of the children and the fulfilment of their basic needs should be granted by the reception facilities and falls beyond the guardian's mandate.

transfers to other localities (which undermines efforts already taken to integrate in Palermo):

> "I realize that the point is not to change the reception centre, but to have a person, like a voluntary guardian, that can help you and sustain you so that your rights will not be infringed or stolen" (boy, 17)

**Table 3.1**. Quotes from young migrants

| The following are quotes by young migrants with a voluntary guardian | |
|---|---|
| Boy, 18 years old | "Yeah, I know some, like my mother, you know… You know, every mother tell her children good mood, you know, good things, you know, every time, so that's what I know, she talks about, every time she talks about, you know, good things, you know, she talks about my future, every time, you know" |
| Boy, 14 years old | "Yes, it has helped me, they help… (…) yes for the documents, and also – many things" |
| Boy, 18 years old | "Is like mums do, you understand? They try to understand the boy and then, ehm, to look after him every day, you understand? Then, with time, it will be known little by little about the school, to get information about how he is performing at school, where the boy goes, his activities and everything that he does" |
| Boy, 16 years old | "In my opinion, is a person that is close to you, that helps you better yourself, that helps you also to have documents; because if you have the guardian you have few problems even if things don't go fast, but you don't be in a hurry she explains you how you get the things. Two people, you with her, so she explains you how things work: you have to study if you want to have these things; she gives you advices like your mother she explains you 'this and this'." |
| Boy, 18 years old | "In my opinion, when you have a guardian she helps you understand things, (…), she helps you live good. The guardian is like a mother or a father. When you are with your family they tell you what is good and what is bad." |
| **The following are quotes by young migrants without a voluntary guardian** | |
| Boy, 16 years old | "No, I don't know" |
| Boy, 16 years old | "Interviewer: Did they explain you what is its role, the role of the legal guardian in your life?<br>Karim: No" |
| Boy, 18 years old | "I don't know" |
| Boy, 17 years old | "The guardian used to help you. With your document also." |
| Boy, 18 years old | "Interviewer: And did you have a legal guardian?<br>Kwame: No, because… when I arrived the person in charge of the reception centre told us that she took the responsibility for all the boys, she is the guardian for everyone. (…) She tells that she is here to help us for the documents, for the enrolment in school. She takes care of all of us." |

One of the youngest interviewees, 14 years old, was moved from a centre where the living conditions were very harsh and enrolled in a regular school with Italian pupils thanks to the intervention of his voluntary guardian. Such action by voluntary guardians mitigates against risky behaviours such as escaping reception facilities in search for better opportunities elsewhere (a common occurrence in the narrations of interviewees and in previous studies, see for example Sanò, 2017). Indeed, having a guardian can per se be a reason not to be transferred to another locality, as the ward should be living in the same municipality as the guardian to facilitate the work. For example, in a centre that shut down, the staff mentioned to all residents: "*the boys without a voluntary guardian will be transferred to Capaci*" (boy, 16) a town farther away from Palermo. A distinction was made by reception facility's personnel between "those with or without a voluntary guardian" and this criterium was used to decide where would they be transferred to. This is a clear case where having a voluntary legal guardian had an instrumental effect in ensuring the best interests of the child were prioritised.

The help that voluntary guardians provide in dealing with the challenges of the reception system was recognized by all young migrants with a voluntary guardian. Bangladeshi boys who attended focussed group discussions agreed that having a voluntary guardian improved circumstances:

> "is different! Because [when you have a] guardian, when there is a problem, [you can] tell him and he comes immediately. Then he tells the people in charge of the centre 'there is this problem'. If there is no guardian, to whom would I ask?" (boy, 18). "Before, I feared to talk if there is a problem, [I think] 'later I cannot stay in this home, I can't go to another home, where do I live?' these thoughts before make me fear. But when the guardian arrived I understood that I can talk to the guardian" (boy, 18).

Voluntary guardians monitor the treatment of children in the reception centres as well as ensuring that the centres provide services to UASC:

> "[a voluntary guardian] pushes the centres to do things for you, to go and find information, to take care of your documents. Because there are many centres that do not care about your documents. And also, about the vaccination that you have to do, they do not care. Without someone that pushes the centre to do all this, it would be difficult, very difficult." (boy, 18)

Finally, interviewees recognized that the personal relationship they have with their voluntary guardians results in a quality of care above and beyond that provided by reception facilities. This increases their ability to speak out and be empowered in acquiring their rights. Voluntary guardians inevitably become a trusted individual to share fears, doubts and concerns:

> "It's better! here without no guardian you cannot talk about your rights. If you have a guardian, it is better. Because when you have needs and when you have problems he will help you." (boy, 17)

Voluntary guardians can enhance young migrants' agency, by supporting them and taking them seriously in their attempts to denounce injustices and perceived violations of rights. This corresponds with findings from other studies (Herz & Lalander, 2017).

**"I am Palermitano now": legal guardians, young migrants and social networks**

All research participants headed out on long journeys alone, often spending many years in transit countries before reaching Italy. Most of them acknowledged how hard it was to leave behind their families and relocate to a new country. Similarly, they all identified the value of making new friendships as well as accessing social support, encouragement and advice from adults and peers in their host country. To that end, the role of voluntary guardians can be vital in supporting children to participate in diverse activities, thereby extending social networks and providing familial care, which was highly valued by young people.

One interviewee reflected that only after he was assigned a voluntary guardian, did he feel included in the society thanks to his ability to "attend courses, make projects or theatre" (boy, 18). Young migrants agreed that voluntary guardians facilitated access to opportunities and information about activities. Those without a voluntary guardian were not informed about things to do, not enrolled in extra courses or projects and spent a lot of their time indoors; "without a guardian (…) you [are] always at home, sleep always, or eat always, you don't do nothing because you don't have anything to do." (boy, 18)

Some of the Bangladeshi boys discussed courses and projects they were referred to by their voluntary guardians and recalled times they went eating outside and participated in cultural and leisure activities with them. Time spent with guardians and activities undertaken together allowed the young people to discover Palermo and its surroundings increasing their sense of well being; "Ada is good, I always go around with her, walking around. Whenever there are things to do she calls me 'Hey Dani today we have to go here, next week we have to go there" (boy, 18). Moreover, the adolescents extend their social network by meeting friends or family of their guardians: "When I go out with her, she says 'this is a male friend of mine, this is a female friend of mine', you understand? (…) I feel happy" (girl, 17).

That said, not all young migrants with a voluntary guardian had the same opportunity to increase their social network, nor to feel part of the local community. Rather, this depended upon the individual characteristics of the young people and their voluntary guardians. Nonetheless, conditional on the adolescents' willingness to participate and the commitment of the voluntary guardian, there is significant potential to increase social networks, access to services and resources, and participation in the host community. Certainly, for the model to be successful, it is necessary that the matching between guardian and ward is made consciously and not left to a random choice (Defence for children, 2018).

UASC who were not allocated a voluntary guardian had a very different experience. These children experienced greater isolation, were less likely to meet friends and displayed more negative attitudes towards their life in Palermo: "if I go out alone, I will be thinking. I'd like to go out with someone, meet the locals, but it's not easy, so I prefer not to go out" (boy, 18). Similarly, another 16 years old boy, preferred not to walk around the city because he did not "like to do that alone". Another boy mentioned that he tends not to go out because he feels discriminated:

> "We stay indoors, we don't go out, for us it is very difficult to go out, well some people are racist, you understand, because with your colour they are racist. [...] the segregation between white and black I can see only in Italy here because it's something, it makes me... it makes me confused sometimes when I think about, 'Ok, why is it that you prefer your dog more than me?', you understand? you can talk to your dog, but you cannot talk to me because of my colour." (boy, 18)

The boy perceived a social barrier in relating to the host population. He did not feel encouraged nor comfortable to talk to locals, had not many experiences spending time with Italians. A similar feeling was perceived by another boy in the year prior to meeting his voluntary guardian. He had felt ashamed to talk to the "*white men*" in the streets because he feared that they would consider him a "*crazy man*". When he finally met his voluntary guardian, his language skills developed and he began to feel comfortable walking around Palermo: "*since I met Marta [voluntary guardian] I know many many friends, I know many many Italians, I improve Italian also. Before I don't speak nothing Italian, even 'Ciao' I don't know*".

Voluntary guardians may not be the only opportunities for young migrants to create ties with the local community; they may also attend school, work or experience transcultural encounters walking around town. Teachers, colleagues, employees at the reception centres and friends of friends all play a role. However, from the age of 16, young migrants are enrolled in adult education rather than in regular schools as 16 is the final age for mandatory schooling for children. In Palermo, public schools for adult education are primarily attended by migrants, with only a few exceptions. Therefore, schools are rarely a space to meet local peers. Occasionally, they build trusted relationships with teachers, or employees working in the reception centres, but these are not institutional relationships guided by a precise mandate.

> "I can say that she [my teacher] is my guardian, too, but she is not like these others, you understand, because (...) she doesn't have to do anything for me, because I cannot ask her for something that, you know, she can do for me." (boy, 18)

Moreover, relationships with teachers and peers at schools as well as staff at reception centres become tenuous without the stability and advocacy that voluntary guardians can provide.

> "Without a guardian is tough. There are many guys who want to continue studying, grow, improve, but without a guardian is tough because today you start studying here, then tomorrow they transfer you outside Palermo, so many people fear this because if there's no one behind, they don't listen to you. They say, 'tomorrow you will be transferred there' and you are here where you started studying, where you have friends, and you will be transferred again, in a new place, you won't have anything, you won't know anybody… it's hard." (boy, 18)

On top of practical support, access to services and the extension of social networks, voluntary guardians occasionally construct a familial environment for children who live in reception facilities and are institutionalized. UASC often compare the relationship with their voluntary guardian in parental terms building ties with the voluntary guardian's nuclear and extended family. They frequently refer to their guardians as "*mum*", "*dad*" or "*parents in Italy*" and acknowledge similarities in the support provided by voluntary guardians with support previously given to them by their parents. Two boys state:

> "I left my family there [in Mali], and I found my family here" (boy, 18)

> "if my family was here, for any problem I would talk to mum and dad, but I don't have mum and dad here, so for any problem I talk to my guardian, it's like with mum and dad" (boy, 18).

In conclusion, voluntary guardians helped to establish social networks, provided guidance and advice that supported understanding and integration in Palermo, established familial environments that allowed UASC to feel cared for and encouraged their participation and familiarization with Palermo. This has reduced social barriers for those adolescents recently arrived in Italy and been a significant influence in their process of integration. Feeling part of the community and feeling "*Palermitano*" is something valued by the young people.

> "I go to the stadium with my guardian's husband and son. If Palermo plays at the stadium I am surely there! This is what is called integration, that you discover things and maybe you like them. Now I support the Palermo team 100%! Yes, it's something I really like." (boy, 18)

Young migrants themselves agreed that voluntary guardianship boosted social inclusion for young migrants by building relationships that go beyond legal obligations and the age of majority. "*[Your guardian] can give you advice, can help you meet new people, so to say that can help you in your path of social inclusion.*" (boy 17)

## "*Now I feel good*": voluntary guardians and UASC's wellbeing

> "When you stay in a family you don't think a lot about your family. That's why I want to live in a family, so I don't think about my family. So I can be quiet in Italy. Because thinking every day is not good." (boy, 18)

Responses from young migrants revealed how voluntary guardianship improved UASC's wellbeing. As mentioned previously, many young migrants have experienced long and often traumatic journeys, are isolated from their families and social networks, and struggle with the process of integration in a new country. These factors represent significant risks for children's wellbeing (Kalverboer et al., 2017; Derluyn & Vervliet, 2012). Children and young people migrating alone may suffer loneliness and isolation in their present lives and may build negative expectations and attitudes regarding their future.

In the conversations with young people, several factors emerged as worrying and stressful for them: (i) the uncertainty of their legal status and the long waiting period to acquire international protection; (ii) the lack of employment, both due to lack of working opportunities and the absence of legal permission to work, which undermines their capacity to provide support to relatives in the country of origin (many young migrants are pressured by family members at home to send remittances believing there to be greater income potential in Italy); (iii) poor living conditions in some reception centres; and (iv) the current political climate and racism present in segments of Italian society. These factors cause young people to feel stressed and angry, and reduce their motivation to take part in activities and plan for the future. Young migrants expressed a great deal of resilience in the face of these circumstances (most of which are beyond their control), many adopting coping strategies to avoid the stress and move on with their life. Young people described meeting friends, taking walks, listening to music, smoking or sleeping as key coping mechanisms:

> "When I go to sleep it means I leave all my thoughts. Because in my life I encountered many difficulties. You understand? Difficulties in Mali, Algeria, Libia, Burkina, Niger, many difficulties. When there are problems like these ones they don't scare me (…). When there's a problem that is more difficult I directly go to sleep. And I move on. Because life is built small small, it's like the stairs. Small small." (boy, 18)

> "When you are working you don't care nothing, you have all your needs. But in the camp here is not easy. Every day when you wake up you will have some stress, so that is your head is not strong you will go smoke! So you will not think no more. It's not easy." (boy, 17)

In most cases interviewees adopted strategies to distract themselves to avoid thinking about overwhelming stresses and concerns. Such coping strategies are defined in the literature as "*avoidant and constrictive behaviours associated with suppression*" and recognized as being problematic in the long term (Goodman, 2004), since they may lead to a reduction in young people's psychological capacities, to withdrawal and detachment from their everyday realities, and to a suppression of their emotions (Van Der Kolk & McFarlane, 1996 in Goodman, 2004).

Through supporting adolescents to better understand their legal status and how to navigate the reception system, by helping them to access basic services, expand their social networks and by simply listening to them and involving them in leisure activities; voluntary guardians generate a positive behavioural spiral which makes the young migrants more aware and less stressed as well as busier, with less time to think:

> "When I go to the cinema or to take walks with my friends I feel good, then when I go home I sleep well. But when you are always at home, and you don't do anything all day, then you think too much, and you get a headache. It's not good." (boy, 18)

Having a free mind helps the youths concentrate on activities they carry out and in thinking positively about their future:

> "Before I used to be very worried because I always think 'how will I do with the documents?' I had a very strong desire in my head, you understand? But as soon as I had my guardian, my head was free, you understand? So, I had the opportunity to study well and do my things." (boy, 16)

Voluntary guardians also have a role in explaining to their wards the timing of asylum procedures, supporting them to be patient and reducing anxiety about applications for international protection. This is naturally aided by focussing on daily studies and everyday activities. This form of guidance and the trust that UASC develop with their voluntary guardians helped them to feel better while dealing with administrative delays in receipt of documents:

> "This helped me to forget to think. Now it's ok. (…) I enjoy myself, I go dancing, and in the end, I feel good. Now I no longer think about the documents, I think about what makes me integrate in the society." (boy, 16)

> "When [my guardian] start to talk about the documents, she says 'don't worry, one day you'll have a document,' I feel my mind is getting steady." (boy, 18)

Voluntary guardians provided emotional support and gave UASC a sense of protection that those without a voluntary guardian did not enjoy. Adolescents without a voluntary guardian had no one in Palermo to talk to or share their thoughts when they experienced anxiety:

> "maybe with the person in charge [of the centre] I could talk a little

bit. In the previous camp, I did that, but here I haven't done that yet, I don't trust [her]." (boy, 16)

"I don't talk to anybody. But… I don't know, like, I sit down, I think, if I cannot stop thinking I go to sleep (…) or I go out, with my friends, so to avoid thinking." (boy, 16)

"I would like to have a guardian if I could share my pain." (boy, 18)

Some of the boys mentioned that after they met their voluntary guardians, they started going to school, while before they refused to because they were not feeling at ease. One of the girls mentioned that after she met her current voluntary guardian, she started going to a psychologist, which helped her reflect on her pain and concerns related to her life in Italy. UASC with a voluntary guardian tended to be more conscious about their educational path and had realistic plans consistent with opportunities in their context. Inversely, UASC without a voluntary guardian were less aware of what may happen in their life and were less inclined to develop plans. For example, one child did not know whether he would start school in the following year; another had no idea how to look for employment in Palermo. Overall, having a voluntary guardian improved the young people's wellbeing in the present and simultaneously encouraged more positive attitudes towards the future[14]:

"When Marta [my voluntary guardian] arrived, I started to go to school, to improve Italian, to talk to people, to meet many many friends, to improve. (…) Now, you know, everything's alright." (boy, 18)

## Conclusions

Respondents revealed dysfunctionalities in the reception system for migrant youth and UASC in Italy. All study participants expressed varying degrees of frustration, anger, stress and anxiety due to poor living conditions in some reception facilities, multiple transfers to different centres and locations, long waiting periods to establish their legal status and overwhelming complexity in navigating the administrative bureaucracy. However, for those young people matched with voluntary legal guardians, they accessed a positive and, often, transformative relationship which demystified the reception process and became a fundamental bridge to services, friendships, care and support. Voluntary legal guardians were integral to their positive experiences and mitigated against the isolation, racism and severe anxiety experienced by those young people without voluntary legal guardians.

The importance of social relations and social support for the wellbeing of UASC in their adaptation process in the host country has been widely discussed in the literature (O'Toole Thommessen et al., 2015; Herz and Lalander, 2017).

[14] These results are in line with a similar qualitative research carried out in Sicily on voluntary guardianship by Unicef (2018)

This study demonstrated how voluntary legal guardians improved the understanding of UASC about the roles and duties of legal guardians, compared to having institutional or professional guardians. In turns, respondents who better understood a legal guardian's function showed a higher degree of understanding of their rights and aspirations, and this is positively correlated with a successful experience of guardianship (Costa, 2015).

From a child-rights perspective, voluntary guardians supported young people in achieving legal status, accessing education (either by enrolling or ensuring reception centres do so), supported their healthcare and helped them to find employment or internship opportunities. In terms of protection, voluntary guardians often prevented unnecessary transfers of young migrants to different centres in unfamiliar localities, (often in isolated places) which has negative impacts upon their mental health. In some instances, voluntary guardians denounced bad practices and violations of children's rights within reception facilities, thereby playing an active role in ensuring the long-term functionality of the system (Defence for Children, 2018). Following protective support from voluntary guardians, young migrants tended to reduce engagement in risky and anti-social behaviours such as participating in violent demonstrations, shouting and vandalism, escaping from facilities or travelling across borders without documents[15].

This study also suggests that voluntary guardians extend young peoples' social networks, boost their ability to access services and resources, and provide a bridge to the host community. These beneficial factors positively contribute to young migrants' wellbeing in line with results from other studies (Dolan & Mcgrath, 2006). In fact, youth migrants who are assigned a voluntary guardian demonstrated more positive attitudes towards their present and future lives, in addition to a higher sense of confidence and motivation vis-à-vis meeting immediate needs, creating plans, and forming desires and aspirations for their lives. In essence, they expressed a greater sense of hope relative to their peers who were not matched with voluntary legal guardians.

In spite of the positive benefits of voluntary legal guardianship, it is worth reflecting on long-term implications and sustainability of a system based on volunteerism. Volunteers are usually engaged citizens willing to offer their time and energy to support UASC and young migrants. However, they may be less competent than professionals on the technicalities and complexities of the asylum system. An effective system of voluntary guardianship should grant access to appropriate training, resources and support at the municipal level. Moreover, to ensure that all UASC can be assigned a voluntary guardian and have similar treatments, UASC should not be concentrated in few municipalities in a specific region of the country but should, as much as

[15] This confirms previous findings showing that voluntary guardianship can facilitate processes of family reunification and reduce the phenomenon of children escaping from the reception system (Genovese, 2018).

possible, be distributed across municipalities and regions of a country. Otherwise, there may be an insufficient number of voluntary guardians to meet the needs of UASC and young migrants, and there would be inequalities experienced by young people in and across reception centres, and the application of guardianship programmes would remain fragmented. This would, in turn, lead to double standards in the reception of UASC and hinder the realization of the rights of all children.

## References

Alderson, P., & Morrow, V. (2004). *Ethics, social research and consulting with children and young people.* Barkingside: Barnardo's. https://doi.org/10.1080/01411920500349808

Aytar, O., & Brunnberg, E. (2016). Empowering Unaccompanied Children in Everyday Life in a New Country. A Resilience Support Centre in Sweden Evaluated from the Perspective of Program Theory. *Social Work Review / Revista de Asistenta Sociala, 15*(2), 35–56. Retrieved from http://search.ebscohost.com/login.aspx?direct=true&db=sih&AN=116705101&site=ehost-live

Bhabha, J. (2004). *Child Migration and Human Rights in a Global Age.* Princeton University Press. Retrieved from http://www.jstor.org/stable/j.ctt5hhrwz

Carlson, B. E., Cacciatore, J., & Klimek, B. (2012). A risk and resilience perspective on unaccompanied refugee minors. *Social Work (United States), 57*(3), 259–269. https://doi.org/10.1093/sw/sws003

Corbin, J., & Strauss, A. (1990). Grounded Theory Research: Procedures, Canons and Evaluative Criteria. *Qualitative Sociology, 13*(1), 3–21. https://doi.org/10.1007/ BF00988593

Costa, N. (2015). Separated and/or Unaccompanied Children Placed in Care: Perspectives and Experiences of Professionals Working in Sweden. *Czech & Slovak Social Work / Sociální Práce / Sociálna Práca, 15*(3), 15–26. Retrieved from http://search.ebscohost.com/login.aspx?direct=true&db=sih&AN=110344015&site=ehost-live

Defence for Children. (2018). Orientamenti formativi sulla tutela volontaria di persone minorenni straniere non accompagnate. Dall'esperienza siciliana alle traiettorie nazionali.

Derluyn, I., & Broekaert, E. (2008). Unaccompanied refugee children and adolescents: The glaring contrast between a legal and a psychological perspective. *International Journal of Law and Psychiatry, 31*(4), 319–330. https://doi.org/10.1016/j.ijlp.2008.06.006

Dolan, P., & Mcgrath, B. (2006). Enhancing support for youg people in need: Reflections on informal and formal sources of helping. In P. Dolan, J. Pinkerton, & J. Canavan (Eds.), *Family support as reflective practice* (pp. 149–164). London: Jessica Kingsley.

European Agency for Fundamental Rights. (2014). *Guardianship for children deprived of parental care (handbook).* https://doi.org/10.2811/7016

European Union Agency for Fundamental Rights. (2010). Separated, asylum-seeking children in European Union Member States: Comparative report. https://doi.org/10.2811/91597

G. Glaser, B., & Leonard Strauss, A. (1967). The Discovery Of Grounded Theory: Strategies For Qualitative Research. Sociology-the Journal of The British Sociological Association - SOCIOLOGY (Vol. 3). https://doi.org/10.1097/00006199-196807000-00014

Genovese, I. (2018). How voluntary guardianship for unaccompanied minors took root in Sicily - Evidence for Action. https://blogs.unicef.org/ evidence-for-action/duty-to-protect-how-voluntary-guardianship-for-unaccompanied-minors-took-root-in-sicily/ 30/7/2018

Goodman, J. H. (2004). Coping with trauma and hardship among unaccompanied refugee youths from Sudan. *Qualitative Health Research, 14*(9), 1177–1196. https://doi.org/10.1177/1049732304265923

Halvorsen, K. (2002). Separated children seeking asylum: The most vulnerable of all. Forced Migration Review (Vol. 12).

Hanberger, A., Wimelius, M. E., Ghazinour, M., Isaksson, J., & Eriksson, M. (2016). Local Service-Delivery Networks for Unaccompanied Children in Sweden: Evaluating Their Effectiveness. *Journal of Social Service Research*, *42*(5), 675–688. https://doi.org/10.1080/01488376.2016.1147516

Herz, M., & Lalander, P. (2017). Being alone or becoming lonely? The complexity of portraying 'unaccompanied children' as being alone in Sweden. *Journal of Youth Studies*, *20*(8), 1–15. https://doi.org/10.1080/13676261.2017.1306037

Hopkins, P. (2008). Ethical issues in research with unaccompanied asylum-seeking children. *Children's Geographies*, *6*(1), 37–48. https://doi.org/10.1080/14733280701791884

Hunner-kreisel, C., Ben-arieh, A., Aber, J. L., & Bradshaw, J. (2016). *Childhood, Youth and Migration* (Vol. 12). https://doi.org/10.1007/978-3-319-31111-1

INTERSOS (2017). Unaccompained and Separated Children along Italy's northern borders.

Kalverboer, M., Zijlstra, E., van Os, C., Zevulun, D., ten Brummelaar, M., & Beltman, D. (2017). Unaccompanied minors in the Netherlands and the care facility in which they flourish best. *Child and Family Social Work*, *22*(2), 587–596. https://doi.org/ 10.1111/ cfs.12272

Luster, T., Qin, D., Bates, L., Rana, M., & Lee, J. A. (2009). Successful adaptation among sudanese unaccompanied minors: Perspectives of youth and foster parents. *Childhood*, *17*(2), 197–211.

Mels, C., Derluyn, I., & Broekaert, E. (2008). Social support in unaccompanied asylum-seeking boys: A case study. *Child: Care, Health and Development*, *34*(6), 757–762.

Ministero del Lavoro e delle Politiche Sociali, D. G. dell'Immigrazione e delle P. di I. – D. I. (2018). (2018). Report Mensile Minori Stranieri Non Accompagnati ( Msna ) in Italia. Dati al 31 Luglio 2018. Retrieved August 20, 2018, from http://www.lavoro.gov.it /notizie/ Documents/ReportMSNA31-07-2018.pdf

O'Toole Thommessen, S. A., Corcoran, P., & Todd, B. K. (2015). Experiences of arriving to Sweden as an unaccompanied asylum-seeking minor from Afghanistan: An interpretative phenomenological analysis. *Psychology of Violence*, *5*(4), 374–383. https://doi.org/ 10.1037/a0038842

O'Toole Thommessen, S. A., Corcoran, P., & Todd, B. K. (2017). Voices rarely heard: Personal construct assessments of Sub-Saharan unaccompanied asylum-seeking and refugee youth in England. *Children and Youth Services Review*, *81*(August), 293–300. https://doi.org/10.1016/j.childyouth.2017.08.017

Roberts, H. M., Bradby, H., Ingold, A., Manzotti, G., Reeves, D., & Liabo, K. (2017). Moving on : Multiple Transitions of Unaccompanied Child Migrants Leaving Care in England and Sweden. *International Journal of Social Science Studies*, *5*(9), 25–34.

Sanò, G. (2017). Inside and outside the reception system. The case of unaccompanied minors in Eastern Sicily. *Etnografia e ricerca qualitativa, Rivista quadrimestrale*, *1*, 121–142.

Sime, D., & Fox, R. (2015). Migrant Children, Social Capital and Access to Services Post-Migration: Transitions, Negotiations and Complex Agencies. *Children and Society*, *29*(6), 524–534. https://doi.org/10.1111/chso.12092

Smyth, B., Shannon, M., & Dolan, P. (2015). Transcending borders: Social support and resilience, the case of separated children. *Transnational Social Review*, *5*(3), 274–295. https://doi.org/10.1080/21931674.2015.1074430

UN Committee on the Rights of the Child (CRC). General comment No. 6 (2005). Treatment of Unaccompanied and Separated Children Outside their Country of Origin (2005). Retrieved from http://www.refworld.org/docid/42dd174b4.html [accessed 6 September 2018]

Unicef. (2018). Minori Stranieri (non) Accompagnati. I risultati di un'indagine esplorativa sul Sistema dei Tutori Volontari in Italia.

Wernesjö, U. (2012). Unaccompanied asylum-seeking children: Whose perspective? *Childhood*, *19*(4), 495–507. https://doi.org/10.1177/0907568211429625.

# PART II: VULNERABILITIES AND BOUNDARIES

# CHAPTER 4

# RELATIONAL PROXIMITY, BOUNDARY-MAKING AND (IM)MOBILITY: MIGRANT CHILDREN'S NARRATIVES OF THE STREETS IN ASHUA AND RABAT, MOROCCO

Chiara Massaroni

Children spend most of their time in three mainly institutionalised settings: school, home and recreational institutions (Rasmussen, 2004). In the Majority World,[1] they also often spend a substantial amount of time supporting the family through work, often outside these three areas, such as in the fields. In both the Majority and Minority Worlds, the street is a fourth – or fifth – place that children occupy, either on their journey from home to one of these institutionalised settings, or as a play space in itself.

The streets, in comparison to school, home or the workplace, are an open structure where rules are less rigid and social sanctions for deviant behaviour are much more ad hoc. On the streets, relationships and encounters are mostly anonymous, and "sign reading" (van Eijk, 2011), recognition of one's "personal front" (Goffman, 1987, p. 34) and "social identity" traits (Goffman, 1979, p. 12) are the main clues that regulate interactions. When the street is part of the neighbourhood, it can, in contrast, become a place where children can informally, and often unsupervised, socialise with peers, thus turning it into a setting for friendly or closer relations (Blazek, 2011; Den Besten, 2010). Adults' control and power over children are potentially more circumscribed in the street, and children's agency is less limited by the power imbalance existing in adult-child relations (Huber & Spyrou, 2012; Robinson & Kellet, 2004). This is particularly relevant for migrant children, who are exposed to a double vulnerability: as children, they are subject to adults' control and power (Robinson & Kellet, 2004); as migrants, they are victims of exclusion and

[1] "Majority World" is an alternative term to refer to the Global South or the Developing World. Similarly, "Minority World" refers to the Global North. This terminology, which is often used in research on childhood (Benwell, 2009; Punch, 2007; Punch & Tisdall, 2012), better highlights the reality that the majority of the world population lives in these parts of the world generally referred to as "developing", and it counters the derogative connotation of terms such as "developing countries" utilised frequently in everyday discuses.

discrimination (Ní Laoire et al., 2016).

The types of encounters and spaces within which these encounters occur have a major influence on identity practices and on the negotiation and creation of boundaries. Boundaries and identities are "situated accomplishments" (West & Fenstermaker, 1995), arising in and through different spaces and relationships. Equally, boundaries and identities are not just something that an individual can claim: they need to be recognised and accepted by the rest of the community (Valentine & Sporton, 2009, p. 736). There is, therefore, a need to make better sense of how the streets and encounters which happen in this space influence the ways in which individuals negotiate their identities and boundaries. This chapter endeavours to address this need and fill this research gap: while there is extensive research on minority ethnic groups or migrant children's boundary-making within the school system (Colombo, 2003; Connolly, 2002; Devine, 2013; Park, 2011), less attention has been paid to open structures such as the street. If neighbourhoods have been the object of some studies (Blazek, 2011; Den Besten, 2010; Spicer, 2008; van Eijk, 2011), the streets, interpreted as a public area which includes but also goes beyond the neighbourhood, used by children with their parents or alone, have received scant attention.

Also, most research on migration, identity construction and social relations focuses on marginalised ethnic groups in the Minority World (Bushin & White, 2010; Colombo, 2003; Devine & Kelly, 2006; Moskal, 2015; Riggs & Due, 2011; Sime & Fox, 2015; Spicer, 2008), reflecting a Eurocentric "myth of invasion" that sees migration as flowing from South to North (De Haas, 2007). My choice to look at Morocco addresses this myopic interpretation. The historical diversity of migration to and through Morocco has been enhanced by the new innovative but ambiguous policy introduced by King Mohammed VI, which promotes the regularisation of migrants in Moroccan society, but fails to adequately eliminate existing barriers to inclusion. Foreign children have been granted access to the school system, but substantial discrimination and challenges to registration persist.

This study focuses on the experiences of young migrant children mostly coming from sub-Saharan Africa and residing in Ashua (pseudonym) and Rabat, Morocco. Data were collected during fieldwork in Morocco, in 2017, using a qualitative multi-method approach. By presenting children and parents' narratives of their experiences in the street, different types of encounters – from anonymous to familiar ones – and networks, relations and use of the street will be explored, reflecting the influence that these dimensions can have on the construction and negotiation of identities and boundaries. Starting by introducing the theoretical framework on which this article is based, as well as the methodology utilised, the article will then look at the different types of relations that children establish in the public realm and explore how these relations affect interpretation of the self and others and contribute to the diverse construction of symbolic boundaries.

**Relationships, identities and boundaries in everyday interactions**

The street is mainly a setting for anonymous interactions, regulated by processes of mutual identity negotiation based almost exclusively on evident traits of the actors' "social identity": "When a stranger comes into our presence, then, first appearances are likely to anticipate his category and attributes, his 'social identity'" (Goffman, 1979, p. 12). The stranger represents a particularly relevant social type. According to Simmel, the stranger is someone who embodies a unity of nearness and remoteness: being visually present and close to us, he/she is perceived as being part of our group itself, while at the same time "his position as a full-fledged member involves both being outside it and confronting it" (Simmel, 1971, p. 144). The interpretation that Schütz provides of the stranger is similar: "the term 'stranger' shall mean an adult individual of our times and civilization who tries to be permanently accepted or at least tolerated by the group which he approaches" (Schütz, 1944). The stranger is not just someone whom we do not know, but someone who comes to join our community for an indefinite amount of time, and whose unknown strangeness becomes therefore much more challenging and threatening than that of a passer-by, as a wanderer might be. His strangeness exists within the clearly defined boundaries of a certain group, towards which he is at the same time both close and distant. This "strangeness" is only relevant in relationships to other members of a community. It arises only in the moment in which the individual tries to enter a new social group for whom he/she is a stranger: when entering, he/she overthrows the "cultural patterns" that generally regulate interactions flawlessly and without crises, based on a commonly established "relatively natural conception of the world" (Schütz, 1944, p. 502). These forms of ambivalent interactions and encounters (Koefoed & Simonsen, 2011) place the individual, simultaneously, both inside a symbolic boundary and outside it.

At the same time, the streets, especially neighbourhood streets, can be a setting for friendly or intimate relations (Den Besten, 2010), which are influenced not only by the superficial "social identity" traits of the actors present, but by some prior knowledge of biographical information (van Eijk, 2011). Strangers interact mostly based on "categoric knowing", or an awareness of each other's role or social status, while "personal knowing" implies interactions constructed around evident social traits as well as some biographical knowledge (Lofland, 1973, p. 16). Strangers and personally known others are not two discrete and separate entities: "the lines between the two are fluid and social life teems with transformation from one to the other" (Lofland, 1973, p. 18).

These two types of relations contribute in different ways to the process of presentation of one's own identity and the creation of boundaries: "encounters between embodied others [...] involve spatial negotiations around the constitution of spaces of familiarity and strangeness and the boundaries and bridges involved in this constitution" (Koefoed & Simonsen, 2011, p. 346). Identity construction is fluid, relational and positional (Jenkins, 1996), and the Self is an "ongoing and in practice simultaneous synthesis of self-definition and definition of ones offered by others" (Jenkins, 1996, p. 20). Identity and boundaries are strongly interlinked: Symbolic boundaries are conceptual tools utilised by individuals to "separate people into groups and generate feelings of similarity and group membership" (Lamont & Molnár, 2002, p. 168). When symbolic boundaries are widely agreed upon, they then become social boundaries and are institutionalised. Only then can they "translate, for instance, into identifiable patterns of social exclusion or class and racial segregation" (Lamont & Molnár, 2002, p. 169).

## Research methodology and setting

This research focuses on the direct experiences of young children. The data for this study draw on fieldwork conducted in Rabat and Ashua in 2017, collected through an adaptation of the Mosaic Approach, a "framework for listening" to young children's perspectives on their everyday lives (Clark & Moss, 2017, p. 13). The Mosaic Approach is a qualitative multiple-method approach, in which various strategies for data collection are utilised to respect children's uniqueness and provide them with various expressive strategies.

Small groups of children participated in multiple 1–2-hour workshops, involving a total of 33 children aged four to 14 years. The tools utilised in the workshops included draw-and-tell activities (Driessnack, 2006; Elden, 2013); child-lead walking tours with cameras through the neighbourhood of Ashua (Clark, 2010); vignette, in which a plausible scenario was presented to the children through pictures (Barter & Renold, 2000); and group conversations.

Data were also collected through daily participant observation over the course of three months in both a non-formal education class and a pre-school in Rabat, attended by some of the children involved in the workshops. Seven parents, three teachers and one headmaster participated in semi-structured interviews and multiple non-formal encounters. These conversations with the adults were used to further enrich the data gathered directly from the children and add details to the mosaic of their symbolic world.

Eight children were originally from Ivory Coast, 18 from the Democratic Republic of Congo (the DRC), one from Cameroon, one from the Republic of the Congo and two from Guinea. Only one family was from Algeria (three children). All children were "first-generation" migrants, some born in Morocco, while others were either born in the country of origin of the parents or "en route". All the children interviewed spoke French at home and French was a language they felt comfortable speaking in, except for one family from Algeria, who spoke mostly Arabic and for which a cultural insider provided language support during the workshops. Nearly all of the children spoke more than one language fluently. The workshops and participant observations were all in French.[2]

The children involved were selected through multi-site snowball sampling, NGOs and diaspora communities. Thorough ethical procedures were established. All children were involved in ongoing assent to participation and multiple forms of consent, signed or agreed upon by various people close to each child were collected. Also, all children were provided with child-friendly leaflets explaining the research and its purposes (Hopkins, 2008) and the names of all the people involved and recognisable place names have been changed. The pseudonyms utilised were all chosen by the children (Tisdall, Davis, & Gallagher, 2009).

### Research setting: Rabat and Ashua

This research focuses on children's narration of their use of the streets within the neighbourhood of Yacoub el Mansour in Rabat, and Ashua, a small town near Rabat. Morocco plays a central role in migration flows within Africa and towards the Minority World. While the country has been considered mostly an area of emigration and transit (Berriane, de Haas, & Natter, 2015), the 2013 migration policy aims at the socio-economic integration of migrants, trying to reshape the country's profile to an area of immigration. Nonetheless, barriers to the effective inclusion of the foreign community still persist.

Migration flows of children and families are largely concentrated in and around Rabat, because of the presence of NGOs, a network of support for migrants through diaspora communities, and access to basic services (CEFA, 2017). Despite the relatively better living conditions enjoyed by this group compared to migrants looking for shelter in northern forests, and the recent political reforms targeting foreigners which have, as many migrants admitted, improved their safety, most participants portrayed Morocco as a temporary residence. Nonetheless, for families with children, leaving is conditional on finding a safe way of accessing Europe rather than attempting to cross the sea or the fences to the Spanish enclaves on the first possible occasion.

Based on this initial analysis, this research was set in Yacoub el Mansour, Rabat and Ashua (pseudonym).[3] Yacoub el Mansour is a large, popular neighbourhood of Rabat. Ashua is a small "ville nouvelle" a few kilometres outside Rabat. Both places have high levels of foreigners, even though official data are not available. While Yacoub el Mansour is a busy and vibrant neighbourhood, Ashua is little more than a ghost city, with poor transport links to the capital and a scarcity of recreational areas and schools. Created to absorb

---

[2] All extracts have been translated from French into English by the author.

[3] I use a pseudonym only for Ashua, not for Yacoub el Mansour in Rabat, because the large number and high density of foreigners living in the latter renders it extremely unlikely that a reader could identify any of the participants of the study. This neighbourhood is one of the largest in Rabat and nearly 40 per cent of the population of Rabat live there.

the rural exodus and become a residential area for those working in and commuting to Rabat, Ashua was planned for 250.000 inhabitants, but now hosts little more than 30,000 people.

### Managing anonymous relations and negotiating social differences: the categoric known "them"

The streets feature predominantly in children's and parents' narratives of their life in Morocco. In comparison with other social settings, such as school, Moroccan streets are more unambiguously described in negative terms, as places of exclusion both for children living in Rabat and those living in Ashua. In most cases, as we see in the account below, exclusion in the streets is constructed in racialized terms.

> Patrick: I think [...] that Moroccans don't have a good image of us, they don't like me much, that's why [...] every time I walk along the street, if there is a guy who passes me or I pass someone else, they call me, like, "nigger", they start insulting me, but I don't care, I pass, me, I don't have any problems, they can say whatever they want.

Patrick is a 14-year-old refugee boy from Ivory Coast living in Ashua. He clearly emphasises the boundaries between "us", "him" and the Moroccan community, and how these boundaries are based on the colour of one's skin. The construction of "me" and "us" stems from the image that others portray of the self (Jenkins, 1996; Valentine & Sporton, 2009), reproducing an ethnically defined boundary. These excluding experiences are generally negotiated within the sphere of anonymous encounters: "in anonymous relations people act without supplying personal information beyond what is superficial or strictly necessary to facilitate the operation" (van Eijk, 2011). "Strangeness" or "otherness" is recognised even before we recognise the individuality of the subject (Koefoed & Simonsen, 2011): what defines the interaction is explicit and visible identity traits, which in the case above take the form of "stigma" (Goffman, 1979). Rather than someone we do not know, the stranger is someone whom "we have already recognised in the very moment in which they are 'seen' or 'faced' as a stranger" (Ahmed, 2000, p. 21). The stranger who arises through these types of encounters is "an effect of processes of inclusion and exclusion" (Ahmed, 2000, p. 6). This type of anonymous exclusion, described by Patrick and many other children and adults, happens most frequently in the streets or on the buses, and it is characterised by strong verbal and physical violence.

### Exclusion and immobility

The violence, discrimination and racism experienced by children in the streets trigger migrant parents' fears for their safety, limiting their access and mobility to these spaces. Allegre, a registered migrant from the DRC and the mother of Flash, 10, and Green Lantern, 5, mentions:

> Allegre: They're locked in the house, in the morning they go to school, they go home, they're locked in, so they're not free. [...] [Flash has some Moroccan friends], but at school only, at school because, well, Moroccans, to receive you at home, it is difficult [...] the children, they cannot go to their friends' houses. And then, outside, to play outside, for me I don't let my children play outside. I won't let my children play outside. I am at home, locked up.

Children's independent spatial mobility is central to understanding their complex dynamics of agency and powerlessness and to gain an idea of their public life in the city. Children's autonomous mobility in the urban area without their parents reflects their independence, and it is a pivotal step towards adult life (O´Brien, Jones, Sloan, & Rustin, 2000). Such a possibility is sensibly hampered for migrant children in Rabat and Ashua.

One crucial consequence of such spatial immobility is the reduced chances for migrant children to freely play outdoors, which is an essential element to ensure children's wellbeing: "time and space to play outdoors is now recognised both as a need and right of children and central to their well-being and development" (Kernan & Devine, 2010, p. 372).

### The symbolic construction of similarities and intimate relations: the personal known "us"

Discrimination and physical exclusion from the use of the streets contribute to reinforcing collective identities that highlight similarities among people and create boundaries around "us". In this process, two forms of "us" are created, one which is intimate and familiar, and refers to the creation of friendship ties and relations that go beyond superficial categorical knowing (Lofland, 1973). The other type of "us" that is created refers to the "symbolic creation of similarity" among an imagined and anonymous group of people sharing some aspects of the same social identity (Jenkins, 1996, p. 105). Here, I am exploring the first idea, the "us" embodied in intimate relations that animate the street environment, as in the case of Directrice, below.

> Directrice: I don't like it here, there are people who are mean [...] here, there are times when they fight, they fight, there is one who can wield a machete, there is another one who can pull a knife; therefore I don't like going for walks here. Sometimes when I want to go for a walk I go with my mother or my father, or on a day when we want to go out and have a little fun, we can go with our grandmothers, our grandparents, and then we have some fun and come home.

Directrice, an 11-year-old refugee from Ivory Coast, foregrounds her dependence on other members of the family to be able to access the streets. The grandparents she refers to do not necessarily represent blood ties, since Directrice's grandparents are not in Morocco. The frequent ambiguity in children's narratives about their family roles is very hard to explain, but here, Directrice probably refers to the practice existing in certain contexts of including non-kin members in the family unit (Coe, 2011), or the frequent use of family names and roles for non-normatively interpreted family members. Consequently, family roles do not necessarily reflect a Minority World interpretation of the household as an entity based on clear blood ties, but rather encompass a much larger group of kin and non-kin, which are ascribed within relationships of familiarity. Hence, Directrice's reference to grandparents implies that the streets can be accessed only with kin or relatives. Since the children can only access the streets with people they are familiar with, and the streets are a setting for the performance of everyday interactions characterised by a high level of intimacy and happening among people who construct their identity as a community.

The streets and neighbourhoods are also a place for the creation of friendship ties. In this case, most of the children mentioned friendships in the neighbourhood built exclusively with other foreigners. This contrasts strikingly with the narratives of their school life, where diverse friendships, which do not essentialise particular ethnic identity traits, are possible. At the same time, the boundaries that delimitate friendship networks constructed and lived in the public realm do not necessarily follow national demarcations (Blokland, 2003): friends are generally identified as other migrants belonging to various national groups, mostly from sub-Saharan Africa. Certainly, conflicts and distinctions within the migrant community exist, and I do not intend to nullify the relevance that specific linguistic, national or religious identities might have for the creation and performance of stronger or weaker networks. Nonetheless, possibly due to the relatively small number of the migrant community and the hostility of the Moroccan community, these forms of identity were toned down, and what emerged was a set of networks and boundaries built as resistance to an unwelcoming local society (hook, 2015). In the case of neighbourhood friendships, children were marking out their immediate social belonging through their sense of difference from the local community, and therefore their minimal share of symbolic repertoire (Cohen, 1994) was constructed around their "otherness" vis-à-vis the Moroccan community.

At the same time, these ties and the boundaries that create a community of "people in the diaspora" against local residents was not limited to the streets of the neighbourhood, it was constructed and performed across multiple sites: relations of friendship, intimacy or familiarity are built with other migrants also living in different cities or neighbourhoods and they are linked together by the proliferation of various diaspora community networks and NGOs that support the migrant community.

### Familial relations in the streets: Children supporting parents through language-brokering

Access to school equips most migrant children with a good ability to speak

Darija, the Moroccan dialect commonly used in the streets. This provides them with bridging social capital that most parents do not possess: because of the difficulties in obtaining a job, they rarely have sustained and prolonged interactions with the local community, hampering their chances of learning the local language. Many children showed pride in their ability to know and recognise particular places in the street environment and navigate street life better than their parents. Many emphasized their role as language-brokers for their parents, where they assist their parents in the interpretation and translation of the language of the new country (Bauer, 2016). In various informal conversations, the children mentioned their role as language-brokers, especially helping their mothers shop in the local souk.

This task, which children did mainly in the urban public realm, overturns the largely held view of migrant children being victims and in need of care and protection. The parental need to protect their children from an unwelcoming local society was reverted to in circumstances in which parents were in need of support to navigate street life. In the example below, Freddy, a registered migrant and father of two from the DRC, talks about an episode of racism and violence that his wife experienced with her children in the streets of Rabat.

> Freddy: It was my wife who was accompanied by the children, she had given her bag to my son – because I have a girl and a boy – and was walking, there was a Moroccan coming the other way, he took [the bag] and inside there was a credit card and a phone, because they were going to the bank to withdraw some money, and the Moroccan took – they tried to call the number, the Moroccan answered the phone but he spoke in Arabic and at that moment neither me nor my wife or children knew Arabic.

From Freddy's words, the task of children's language-brokering includes unravelling challenging and potentially confrontational situations for their parents, which often happen in the streets. When involving challenging issues, as in the example above, language-brokering can place children in in an ambivalent position towards their parents: from one side, it can expose them to tasks which are too sensitive for them and reverses the "normative" role of children as those to be taken care of. At the same time, children can be empowered by this new role they assume within the family (Bauer, 2013), balancing the powerlessness that they may experience as a consequence of the impossibility of independently using the public realm.

### The symbolic construction of similarities and the creation of a collective identity: The streets "chez nous"

In some cases, the impossibility for children to access Moroccan streets is counterposed to images of "back home", where the streets are places of socialisation and leisure.

> Directrice: In our country [Ivory Coast] people like having lots of fun, they like to party and eat attiéké outdoors.

Brunette, a 14-year-old girl, talking about her memories of Congo, mentions:

> Brunette: We play with a skipping rope [with my friends], sometimes we leave, we go around knocking on people's doors and then we run away <<<chuckles>> and then we hang around to laugh.

The accounts of use and access of the streets in their memories of past "homes" embody two different perspectives. In the case of Directrice, an imagined national community emerges (Benedict, 2006), while Brunette refers to what she recalls as her personal experiences back in the DRC. What is relevant here is how the streets are portrayed: both of these extracts dramatically contrast with the narrations of street life in Morocco. Here, the streets are dangerous, hostile places, there – in the DRC or Ivory Coast – the streets were joyful places of encounters and socialisation. Such counterposition in the narration contributes to the dichotomisation between what the 'here' and the 'there' are and represents and reinforces collective identities. The discrimination that occurs on the streets defines whom the strangers are (Ahmed, 2000) and, in opposition, the inclusivity of the streets "back home" creates symbolic boundaries and imagined communities. Such a construction of the streets as a symbol that contributes to identifying a collective identity is more evident in adults' than in children's discourses, as in the example below, between Aaron Cedrick, from Cameroun, and Sonia, the mother of Directrice, from Ivory Coast.

> Sonia: "It's different in our country [chez nous], it's not like here, like in Europe. Especially Ivorian women, if a foreigner comes, we welcome him as a baby."

> Aaron Cedrick: "Yes, that's how it is there [chez nous], we're all together, we don't stay locked in our houses, if I don't see my neighbour after a day, I call him. If I call my friend, he's not going to say no, don't pass by ... we like being together and we all help each other."

The parents also construct the streets at home as a place where children can more easily walk around alone:

> Allegre: I have to control him, I can let him play with the in the garden where I can see him, control him, but I can't let him do like I would back home [au pays], no no...

"Chez nous" or "au pays" do not simply reflect national or ethnic identification: it is a rather fluid and relational identity, and, while its external boundaries are clearly defined in opposition to the "otherness" of Moroccan and European society, its internal margins are porous. "Chez nous" can encompass the multiple micro- and macroscopic meanings attributed to "home" (Antonsich, 2010), reflecting the "home country" or the region or area of origin, or meaning more strictly "at home" or "at my place".

**Boundary-crossing: From anonymity to friendship**

The streets are places where the lines of separation between the Moroccan community and diaspora communities are strongly demarcated. Nonetheless, sometimes these lines are crossed, highlighting the relational and situational nature of the "Stranger" (Schütz, 1944; Simmel, 1971). This attenuation or modification of symbolic boundaries frequently happens when the social actors involved leave the realm of the "unknown other" and interact within a relation of "personal knowing" (Lofland, 1973, p. 16). One's "personal front", such as ethnicity, gender, age, posture etc., is not the only determinant of interaction: due to mutual knowledge of some biographical information, interaction assumes the characteristics of familiarity (van Eijk, 2011). The creation of these familiarity relations is facilitated through neighboured acquaintances:

> Freddy: As a woman, you cannot walk around with a bag on a bus or in isolated places, sometimes even in public places like this [... ] and Moroccans are not going to do anything, they are not going to do anything. Well, one day I asked a friend of mine, a Moroccan friend, because there, where I live, I have already familiarized myself with some Moroccan friends and so I asked him why Moroccans behave like that.

Here Freddy, in the same discourse, broadens the symbolic boundaries when he is referring to his relationships of friendship with his Moroccan neighbours, but he re-emphasizes boundaries when the topic of his enquiry aims at making sense of these lines of separation that exclude the migrant community from Moroccan society. These types of friendship ties with the Moroccan community are mostly expressed by parents in relation to the neighbourhood. Children seem to have little or no access to these types of ties, because of the mistrust of their parents towards the local community and their fear of racism.

In contrast with what other studies have highlighted (O´Brien et al., 2000), the density of population of the setting of these encounters seemed to have no relevance to facilitating or hampering children's chances for spatial mobility in the streets or to the creation of inter-ethic friendships in the neighbourhood. The fear of accessing the streets was equally present in most of the accounts of children and parents living in both Rabat and Ashua. Ashua is a small and extremely quiet village, with few cars circulating, while Rabat is a much more hectic urban setting, and Yacoub el Mansour is no exception.

Contrarily, gender contributed to children's access to the streets: while all the girls talked about the limitations they faced regarding the possibility of accessing the streets, the boys seemed to have more chances to use these spaces. Patrick, in the extract above, mentions that "[he] doesn't care, [he] just pass[es]" when he is insulted in the street, reflecting the fact that he can and does walk the streets alone.

One of the main opportunities for accessing the streets independently that boys have is football, which is described as an activity reserved exclusively for males. Playing football eases boys' street mobility as it builds bridging social capital: most of the time it is not played in ethnically or nationally discrete teams, but rather migrants and Moroccans play side by side, as MoKingston, 14, from the DRC explains, below:

MoKingston: But [laughs] football is for men.

Chiara: It's for men? Why is it for men.

MoKingston: It's for men, it's- well, in short, it's for men, it's not for women.

Chiara: Ah, not for women, only for men.

MoK: Yes, hey, it's hard!

[…]

Chiara: And otherwise, who is the friend who says, who tells, you ... to come and play f-[cross talking]

MoKongston: Jean-Javier.

Chiara: ...he's Moroccan or...?

MoKingston: No, Ivorian.

Chiara: Ivorian, ok ... and are there a lot of Moroccans in the team?

MoKingston: Yes, there are some Moroccans, there are many.

[…]

Chiara: Who is the strongest person in the team?

MoKingston: There is no one who is stronger, it's all of us, together.

Just like MoKingston, nearly all the boys involved in this research played football in a club, or informally with friends. In their narratives, on the football pitch what mattered most was the sense of togetherness as a team, and national belonging in that space had little relevance. These friendships granted these boys access to the "thinking as usual" shared by the group, thus ceasing to be strangers (Schütz, 1944).

It is evident that, through football, friendships crossing symbolic boundaries around nationalities are also plausible within the public realm. Thanks to football, boys are not only allowed independent mobility on the football pitch, but also in the streets, since they can very often access them together with Moroccan football friends, granting them a window of freedom and safety.

## Conclusion

Experiences of exclusion and anonymous interactions happening in the street shape migrant children's symbolic boundaries: as Sara Ahmed pointed out, the exercise of exclusion contributes to constructing the stranger in the community (Ahmed, 2000), and emphasises the caesura and boundaries between the migrant and Moroccan communities.

The impossibility to move around freely and independently in the public realm is also detrimental for children's sense of independence and autonomy, but, in the case of Morocco, such vulnerability and powerlessness are balanced by their linguistic brokering skills, which empower them with a caring and supporting role towards their parents when it comes to navigating street life.

At the same time, racism and exclusion contribute to the symbolic construction of similarities among the diaspora community. While the "otherness" of Moroccan society towards such community is clear, its internal social cohesion is fluid and positional: within different relationships, it can refer to a specific national, ethnic, religious or linguistic identity, or refer to the whole of the sub-Saharan community.

In contrast to the experiences of their parents, the absence of opportunities for migrant children to access relations of personal acquaintance within the public environment contributes greatly to the portrayal of personal identities which emphasise the "symbolic construction of similarities", negotiated in opposition and resistance to an unwelcoming local community.

## References

Ahmed, S. (2000). *Strange Encounters: Embodied Others in Post-coloniality*. Oxford, UK: Routledge.

Antonsich, M. (2010). Searching for belonging - An analytical framework. *Geography Compass*, *4*(6), 644–659.

Barter, C., & Renold, E. (2000). 'I wanna tell you a story': Exploring the application of vignettes in qualitative research with children and young people. *International Journal of Social Research Methodology*, *3*(4), 307–323.

Bauer, E. (2013). Reconstructing Moral Identities in Memories of Childhood Language Brokering Experiences. *International Migration*, *51*(5), 205–218.

Bauer, E. (2016). Practising kinship care: Children as language brokers in migrant families. *Childhood*, *23*(1), 22–36.

Benedict, A. (2006). Imagined Communities: Reflections on the origin and Spread of Nationalism.

Benwell, M. C. (2009). Challenging minority world privilege: Children's outdoor mobilities in post-apartheid South Africa. *Mobilities*, *4*(1), 77–101.

Berriane, M., de Haas, H., & Natter, K. (2015). Introduction: revisiting Moroccan migrations. *Journal of North African Studies*, *20*(4), 503–521.

Blazek, M. (2011). Place, children's friendships, and the formation of gender identities in a Slovak urban neighbourhood. *Children's Geographies*, *9*(3–4), 285–302.

Blokland, T. (2003). Ethnic complexity: Routes to discriminatory repertoires in an inner-city neighbourhood. *Ethnic and Racial Studies*, *26*(1), 1–24.

Bushin, N., & White, A. (2010). Migration politics in Ireland: Exploring the impacts on young people's geographies. *Area*, *42*(2), 170–180.

CEFA. (2017). Etude sur l'accès aux services de base, à l'emploi, au logement, pour la population migrante au Maroc. Rabat, Morocco.

Clark, A. (2010). Young children as protagonists and the role of participatory, visual methods in engaging multiple perspectives. *American Journal of Community Psychology*, *46*(1), 115–123.

Clark, A., & Moss, P. (2017). Listening to Young Children, Expanded Third Edition: A Guide to Understanding and Using the Mosaic Approach. London, UK: Jessica Kingsley Publishers.

Coe, C. (2011). How Children Feel About their Parents' Migration: A History of the Reciprocity of Care in Ghana. In C. Coe, R. R. Reynolds, D. A. Boehm, J. M. Hess, & H. Rae-Espinoza (Eds.), *Everyday ruptures: children, youth, and migration in global perspective* (pp. 97–114).

Cohen, A. P. (1994). Culture, identity and the concept of boundary. *Revista de Antropoligia Social*, *3*, 49–61.

Colombo, E. (2003). Belonging and Identification Among Adolescent Children of Immigrants in Italy. In G. Tsolidis (Ed.), *Migration, Diaspora and Identity: Cross - National Experiences* (pp. 19–35). Dordrecht, Germany: Springer.

Connolly, P. (2002). Racism, gender identities and young children: Social relations in a multi-ethnic, inner city primary school. London, UK: Routledge.

De Haas, H. (2007). The myth of invasion: Irregular migration from West Africa to the Maghreb and the European Union. Oxford, UK: International Migration Institute, University of Oxford.

Den Besten, O. (2010). Local belonging and 'geographies of emotions': Immigrant children's experience of their neighbourhoods in Paris and Berlin. *Childhood*, *17*(2), 181–195.

Devine, D. (2013). 'Value'ing Children Differently? Migrant Children in Education. *Children and Society*, *27*(4), 282–294.

Devine, D., & Kelly, M. (2006). 'I just don't want to get picked on by anybody': Dynamics of inclusion and exclusion in a newly multi-ethnic irish primary school. *Children and Society*, *20*(2), 128–139.

Driessnack, M. (2006). Draw-and-tell conversations with children about fear. *Qualitative Health Research*, *16*(10), 1414–1435.

Elden, S. (2013). Inviting the messy: Drawing methods and 'children's voices'. *Childhood*, *20*(1), 66–81.

Goffman, E. (1979). *Stigma: notes on the management of spoiled identity*. Middlesex, UK: Simon & Schuster.

Goffman, E. (1987). *The Presentation of Self in Everyday Life*. Middlesex, UK: Penguin.

Hook, B. (2015). *Yearning: Race, Gender, and Cultural Politics*. London, UK: Routledge.

Hopkins, P. (2008). Ethical issues in research with unaccompanied asylum-seeking children. *Children´s Geographies*, *6*(1), 37–48.

Huber, V. P., & Spyrou, S. (2012). Introduction: Children's interethnic relations in everyday life – beyond institutional contexts. *Childhood*, *19*(3), 291–301.

Jenkins, R. (1996). *Social Identity*. London, UK: Routledge.

Kernan, M., & Devine, D. (2010). Being confined within? Constructions of the good childhood and outdoor play in early childhood education and care settings in Ireland. *Children and Society*, *24*(5), 371–385.

Koefoed, L., & Simonsen, K. (2011). The stranger, the city and the nation: on the possibilities of identification and belonging. *European Urban and Regional Studies*, *18*(4), 343–357.

Lamont, M., & Molnár, V. (2002). The Study of Boundaries in the Social Sciences. *Annual Review of Sociology*, *28*(1), 167–195.

Lofland, L. H. (1973). A World of Strangers: Order and Action in Urban Public Space. New York, NY: Basic Books.

Moskal, M. (2015). 'When I think home I think family here and there': Translocal and social ideas of home in narratives of migrant children and young people. *Geoforum*, *58*, 143–152.

Ní Laoire, C., Carpena-Méndez, F., Tyrrell, N., & White, A. (2016). *Childhood and Migration in Europe*. Oxon, UK: Routledge.

O´Brien, M., Jones, D., Sloan, D., & Rustin, M. (2000). Children´s Independent Spatial Mobility in the Urban Public realm. *Childhood*, *7*(3), 257–277.

Park, C. C. (2011). Young children making sense of racial and ethnic differences: A sociocultural approach. *American Educational Research Journal*, *48*(2), 387–420.

Punch, S. (2007). Negotiating Migrant Identities: Young People in Bolivia and Argentina. *Children´s Geographies*, *5*(1), 95–112.

Punch, S., & Tisdall, E. K. M. (2012). Exploring children and young people's relationships across Majority and Minority Worlds. *Children's Geographies*, *10*(3), 241–248.

Rasmussen, K. (2004). Places for Children – Children's Places. *Childhood*, *11*(2), 155–173.

Riggs, D. W., & Due, C. (2011). (Un)Common Ground?: English Language Acquisition and Experiences of Exclusion Amongst New Arrival Students in South Australian Primary Schools. *Identities: Global Studies in Culture and Power*, *18*(3), 273–290.

Robinson, C., & Kellet, M. (2004). Power. In S. Fraser, V. Lewis, S. Ding, M. Kelett, & C. Robinson (Eds.), *Doing Research with Children and Young People* (pp. 81–96). Sage.

Schütz, A. (1944). The Stranger : An Essay in Social Psychology Author. *American Journal of Sociology*, *49*(6), 499–507.

Sime, D., & Fox, R. (2015). Migrant Children, Social Capital and Access to Services Post-Migration: Transitions, Negotiations and Complex Agencies. *Children and Society*, *29*(6), 524–534.

Simmel, G. (1971). The Stranger. In D. Levine (Ed.), *On Individuality and Social Reforms* (pp. 143–145). Chicago, IL: The University of Chicago Press.

Spicer, N. (2008). Places of Exclusion and Inclusion : Asylum-Seeker and Refugee Experiences of Neighbourhoods in the UK. *Journal of Ethnic and Migration Studies, 34*(3), 491-510,.

Tisdall, K., Davis, J. M., & Gallagher, M. (2009). Researching with children and young people: Research design, methods and analysis. London, UK: Sage.

Valentine, G., & Sporton, D. (2009). 'How Other People See You, It's Like Nothing That's Inside': The Impact of Processes of Disidentification and Sadavowal on Young People's Subjectivities. *Sociology*, *43*(4), 735–751.

van Eijk, G. (2011). 'They eat potatoes, I eat rice': Symbolic boundary making and space in neighbour relations. *Sociological Research Online*, *16*(4), 1–12.

West, C., & Fenstermaker, S. (1995). Doing difference. *Gender & Society*, *9*(1), 8–37.

# CHAPTER 5

# UNACCOMPANIED MINOR REFUGEES' VULNERABILITIES IN SWEDEN: TESTIMONIALS FROM A VOLUNTARY SUPPORT NETWORK

Amber Horning, Sara V. Jordenö and Tanja Dejanova

The Vocational and Voluntary Network #VISTÅRINTEUT (Eng. "We Can't Stand It", abbreviated: VSIU) was founded in September 2016 by a teacher, two social workers, and an educator. Using Facebook as a way to connect across Sweden, the VSIU network includes nearly 11,000 professionals and individuals who meet and support UMRs. The VSIU network includes teachers, social workers, physicians, psychologists, guardians, welfare officers, counselors, school nurses, and others who came in contact with UMRs at their places of work or in their communities. The VSIU network works to support UMRs in Sweden by organizing protests in connection to deportations, by helping to appeal asylum cases and providing support in the process, by alerting media and the UN to the injustices in the asylum processes and documenting how Swedish society is denying UMR's their fundamental human rights. Most of all, they voluntarily provide housing and emotional support to UMRs. The VSIU network took on the role of the State that, in many cases, stopped providing support for UMRs when Sweden deemed that they were 18 or denied their asylum cases.

Existing literature has focused on how UMRs were vulnerable during their smuggling experiences (e.g., Horning, Jordenö & Savoie, 2020), how they arrived traumatized (e.g., Vervliet et al., 2015), or how they experienced mental health issues in host countries (Jensen et al. (2014). There are few studies focused on how UMRs become vulnerable in Western European or Scandinavian host countries, except for studies about UMRs' mental health symptoms and diagnosis (e.g., Khan, 2017). The studies about other types of UMR vulnerabilities focused on their exploitation en route to the EU (e.g., Brunovkis & Surtees, 2019) or within Southern European host countries (see Chynoweth, Freccero & Touquet, 2017; Freccero et al., 2017). Sweden's asylum policy has been, in the European context, comparatively non-restrictive and coupled with expeditious and straightforward paths to naturalization. Due to this history, it may be only recently that Sweden and its policies and laws have become dangerous to UMRs, and this may explain the current dearth of research on this topic.

We conducted extensive interviews with members of the VSIU network, and we used the Grounded Theory (GT) approach (Glaser & Strauss, 2016) guided by the sensitizing concept (Blumer, 1954) of UMRs' vulnerabilities in Sweden. Based on interviews with VSIU, we found that they perceived UMRs' vulnerabilities as increasingly cultivated or worsened by Sweden's changes to UMR policies and laws. UMRs became more vulnerable to labour exploitation, sexual exploitation, and other types of coercion and abuse that occurs when someone is trying to survive with little to no support.

**Changes to Swedish policies and laws**

In 2015, Sweden received 162,877 asylum applications compared to Denmark's 7,162 and Finland 32,476 (Finnish Immigration Service, 2016), of which roughly 20% (35,369) were UMRs. Upon their arrival, Sweden placed UMRs in the care of the Swedish Migration Board (Migrationsverket). Sweden often housed UMRs in centers, called HVB-hem ("Homes for Care or Housing") or placed them in compensated foster families called familjehem ("family homes"), and they provided them a legal guardian, assigned an attorney for their asylum case and provided them with Swedish language courses at local high schools (högstadium) and Junior Colleges (gymnasium).

However, on November 24, 2015, Sweden introduced a new temporary law[1] intended to reduce the number of asylum-seekers by only issuing temporary residence permits (Wernesjö, 2019). This coincided with Prime Minister Stefan Löfven announcing that the country needed "breathing room" from accepting refugees[2]. Sweden made the Family Reunification Policy and the category of granting asylum due to "severe hardship" effectually impossible. This date marked a watershed moment in Sweden's new restrictive stance on refugees. In July 2019, the Swedish Government voted to extend this temporary law until 2021.

UMRs who arrived from 2015 onwards often had to wait several years for their asylum interviews and decisions. The Swedish Migration Board implemented new ways of interpreting asylum laws, placing the burden of proof of identity on the refugee and arbitrarily changing the age of UMRs to be older than they claimed to be, thus allowing for simpler rejections of asylum claims. In 2016, the Swedish government began using medical age assessments, even though this procedure was deemed unethical by the medical community and

[1] Lag (2016:752) om tillfälliga begränsningar av möjligheten att få uppehållstillstånd i Sverige https://www.riksdagen.se/sv/dokument-lagar/dokument/svensk-forfattningssamling/lag-2016752-om-tillfalliga-begransningar-av_sfs-2016-752

[2] https://www.regeringen.se/artiklar/2015/11/regeringen-foreslar-atgarder-for-att-skapa-andrum-for-svenskt-flyktingmottagande/

inaccurate by scholars (e.g., (Mostad & Tamsen, 2019). UMRs who reached 18 or those whose legal age was changed by the Migration Board lost their legal guardians and accommodations at their HVB-hem ("Homes for Care or Housing"). Often, UMRs were assigned to move to adult asylum camps. If they refused to leave and instead stayed where they had established social and emotional ties and attended school, then the government denied them support for housing and food. This situation incited the beginning of wide-spread homelessness in this group. UMRs who arrived before November 24, 2015, were allowed temporary study permits through the 2018 "Nya Gymnasielagen" policy[3], if they agreed to give up their asylum case, complete specific programs of study and obtain a job within six months of graduation. UMRs struggled due to a lack of qualifying study programs and affordable housing. Finding a job and housing for a young ethnic Swede is not easy, and with UMRs multiple marginalizations and the rise of discrimination (Dalgren, 2016; Herz, 2018), their odds of finding employment are even slimmer. In effect, "Nya Gymnasielagen" became a trap where UMRs could still face the threat of deportation after spending many years in Sweden.

In October 2016, Sweden made the so-called Återvändaravtalet ("Return Agreement") with Afghanistan, promising a ten-year influx of substantial financial aid and infrastructure support if they accepted "returned," i.e., deported refugees. In December 2016, Sweden started deporting Afghani refugees *en masse*, despite the United Nations High Commissioner for Refugees (UNHCR) stating that deporting asylum seekers to Afghanistan equalled "condemning them to death." In 2019, there were nine waves of deportations from Sweden to Afghanistan, in collaboration with Frontex, the European Border and Coast Guard Agency (Swedish Police, 27 November 2019.) The UMRs and Refugee families, along with their advocates, relentlessly protested these actions by the State, through sit-ins, hunger strikes, and demonstrations.

The government has exacerbated UMRs' existing vulnerabilities through restrictive policies, making them extremely vulnerable within Sweden. Few UMRs from 2015, especially those from Afghanistan, have found refuge in Sweden. These already traumatized youth wait in limbo, with few viable opportunities and many setbacks, while witnessing how Sweden systemically deports their peers.

## The general overview of the significant challenges for UMRs

### *Psychological distress and mental health issues*

Mental health professionals recognize UMRs as uniquely - exceptionally - vulnerable to mental health issues, due to predisposing risk factors and a decrease in crucial protective factors (e.g., El Baba & Colucci, 2018; Hasson III, Berger Cardoso & Crea, 2019; Hodes at el., 2018; Jakobsen, 2018). UMRs suffer

[3] https://www.migrationsverket.se/Andra-aktorer/Kommuner/Om-gymnasielagen.html

higher levels of loneliness (Hertz & Lalander, 2017), and this loneliness can be attributed to family separation and an increased risk of PTSD (Geltman, Grant-Knight & Mehta, 2005). The support of a familial adult is vital yet lacking for these children who often have a long, taxing, and psychologically distressing asylum process (Jakobsen, 2018; Seglem, Oppedal & Raeder, 2011).

Jacobsen et al. (2014) found that 41.9% of UMRs who arrived in Norway met diagnostic criteria for a psychiatric disorder, with one-third having post-traumatic stress disorder (PTSD) (Jakobsen et al., 2014). Shahid Khan (2017) reported that approximately 50% of surveyed UMRs had harmed themselves, as compared to 14% of the general population. A National report in Sweden found a nine-fold risk of suicide for UMRs when compared to the general public (Hagström, Hollander & Mittendorfer-Rutz, 2018 cited in Karolinska Institutet, 2018) and Jensen et al. (2014) found an alarming increase in suicidal ideation in a UMR population in Norway. Prior research has also linked adverse life events, psychological distress, and PTSD with self-harm, which is a predictors of suicidal ideation and suicide (Fegert, Sukale & Brown, 2018; Verroken et al., 2014). The particulars of why high numbers of UMRs are engaging in self-harm and committing suicide or engaging in self-injury should be of critical concern to host countries.

In contrast to all the noted issues, many UMRs do not have mental health issues, and some report satisfaction with their life, thanks to harnessing their resilience and protective factors (e.g., Fegert, Sukale & Brown, 2018; Jakobsen, 2018; Jensen et al., 2014).

### *Sexual exploitation*

Refugees are vulnerable to sexual exploitation and abuse, and human trafficking (Brunovkis and Surties, 2019; Godziak et al., 2006). According to Article 3 of the UN's Protocol to Prevent, Suppress, and Punish Trafficking in Persons, they define *Trafficking Persons* is defined as:

> The recruitment, transportation, transfer, harbouring or receipt of persons, by means of the threat or use of force or other forms of coercion, of abduction, of fraud, of deception, of the abuse of power or of a position of vulnerability or of the giving or receiving of payments or benefits to achieve the consent of a person having control over another person, for the purpose of exploitation.

There are numerous reports of refugees being coerced or forced into sex to improve their smuggling outcomes with smugglers or agents (UNICEF, 2017). Chynoweth, Freccero, and Touquet (2017) interviewed shelter workers in Greece who reported that older males exploited 14-17-year-old UMRs by giving them survival items, including food, in exchange for sex. Under the Palermo Protocol (CITE), these minors were not sex workers, but sex trafficking victims. The bright-line classification based on age was designed by lawmakers to protect the welfare of children (Horning, 2013).

Historically and in the 2015, exodus the majority of UMRs have been boys, and from 2008 to 2015, the majority who came to the EU were from Afghanistan (Pew Research Center, 2016). These UMRs were subject to sexual assault by locals in many transit and destination countries, and governments were aware of this (Freccero, 2017). Still, due to ignorance about male rape and the support needed by male survivors, as well as the general chaos of the period, little was done (Chynoweth et al., 2017; Freccero, 2017). Afghanis may be an exceptionally vulnerable population because of higher social acceptance of sexual exploitation of young boys, in particular, due to the cultural practice of Baacha Baz, or "boy play" which is a custom that involves young boys being forced to dress as women, dance seductively for an audience of older men, and many times they are forced to have sex with these men (UNICEF, 2016). These powerful men are often members of the government or terrorist organisations (Jones, 2015). UMRs with a history of Baacha Baz or other forms of sexual abuse can be more vulnerable to sexual exploitation. Despite these complex vulnerabilities and known instances of exploitation and harm, the sexual abuse of UMRs has not been a central policy discussion (Freccero et al., 2017).

### Exploitation in the labour market

Rights and access to employment are necessary for supporting UMRs' resilience and enabling refugees to build sustainable, dignified lives in host countries (Zetter & Ruaundel, 2018). Research on immigrant integration showed that even "social democratic welfare states [such as Sweden] have failed to promote the integration of long-term unemployed young immigrants" (Malmberg-Heinonen & Julkunen, 2006). Consistent implementation is lacking even in countries formally supporting refugees' working rights, which has helped support the rise of underground economies and associated risks, such as marginalization, exploitation, discrimination, and violence (Nicolescu, 2017; Zetter & Ruaundel, 2018).

As a result of these unique challenges, UMRs are a population at high-risk for labour exploitation (Christodoulou & Abou-Saleh, 2016; Plener et al., 2017; UN, 2017). Family poverty, noted as a potential contributing factor in young immigrants' involvement in illegal work (Rossiter & Rossiter, 2009), is often experienced by UMRs who, by definition, have no family who can assist them.

### Discrimination

Negative attitudes toward refugees in host countries are an added stressor (Fegert, Sukale & Brown, 2018). Eide and Hjern (2013) reported high rates of bullying in more homogenous Swedish schools, often resulting in depressive symptoms among UMRs. A study of the general population's views regarding refugees in Germany found that only 20% of surveyed locals were favourable toward accepting more refugees, with the level of willingness depending on refugees' ethnicity (Plener et al., 2017). Extreme right-wing views were associated with less favourable attitudes toward UMRs (Plener et al., 2017).

Feger, Sukale, and Brown (2018) noted that there is a link between hostile media portrayals of UMRs and a decrease in openness to welcome refugees. The virtual world also provides easy access to like-minded individuals and an anonymous platform for hateful rhetoric (Hirvonen, 2013). Online, attacking UMRs as 'predators', 'gang rapists', and 'diseased animals' became frequent, and accountability remained limited (Hirvonen, 2013). With mainstream media also often focusing on the sensational and negative - the crimes committed by male refugees, the cultural clashes, and reintegration challenges - online aggression finds a voice in the offline realm. The virtual world provided easy access to like-minded individuals and an anonymous platform for hateful rhetoric, attacking UMR as 'predators', 'gang rapists' and 'diseased' animals became frequent, and accountability remained limited (Hirvonen, 2013).

## Methodology

We first explored the contours of UMRs' vulnerabilities during their wait in limbo through interviews with UMRs in 2016 (see Horning et al., 2020). We kept in touch with Aresh, a UMR from Afghanistan, via Whatsapp and Facebook. In 2017, Aresh reached out to us for help, as Sweden denied his asylum case three times, and he had no more options to appeal and was facing deportation. Jordenö, being a Swedish citizen, came in contact with Voluntary Network #VISTÅRINTEUT (VSIU), and with their help, Sweden did not deport Aresh. He eventually received a 13-month residence permit to study via the "Gymnasielagen." This experience initiated Jordenö and Horning into the network where they communicated for years and wrote letters to support the asylum cases of UMRs who were victims of trafficking and other forms of sexual assault who would be in grave danger if they were to return to Afghanistan.

It became apparent that the VSIU network had extensive knowledge of UMRs' histories, experiences in Sweden, their vulnerabilities, and the exploitation they have endured. In 2019, we conducted semi-structured interviews with nineteen members of the VSIU network about their experiences voluntarily assisting UMRs from 2015-2019. We asked them about UMRs' experiences in Sweden. These members often were affiliated with several local and national networks supporting refugees, such as FARR (Flyktinggruppernas Riksråd), Stöttepelaren, and Agape. These humanitarian witnesses, advocates, and activists assisted UMRs by helping them find housing, getting them into schools, providing mobile phones and clothes, assisting them with communicating with the Migration Board and other authorities, feeding them, and sometimes becoming their legal guardians. Their roles varied depending on their expertise. Collectively, they have helped thousands of UMRs in Sweden.

The majority of participants from the VSIU network were female: Female

84.2% (n=16) and Male 15.8% (n=3). All of the participants were Caucasian, and most of them were Swedish, with only one being Finnish. Their mean age was 47.8, with a range of 31-72 years old. They were highly educated, with nearly all holding at least a Bachelor's Degree (89.5%, n=17) and almost half of them having a Graduate Degree (47.8%, n=9). In terms of their regular jobs, 42.1% (n=8) were Social Workers, or Psychologists, 15.8% (n=3) were Educators, 15.8% (n=3) had returned to University, 10.5% (n=2) worked for the Justice System, 10.5% (n=2) were Archivists. One was a retired school teacher working for Amnesty. Many of their jobs involved work with youth. All participants were given pseudonyms in order to anonymize accounts.

We qualitatively explored accounts using the Grounded Theory (GT) approach (Glaser & Strauss, 2016). We did not use a purist GT approach because we used the sensitizing concept (see Blumer, 1954) of UMR vulnerabilities in Sweden to guide our analysis. All three authors discussed each case, and we compared notes on relevant quotes and similarities and differences across the interviews. We selected critical quotes by VSIU participants that represented themes in the data. Each section begins with one of their quotes, followed by an exploration of this UMR vulnerability in Sweden. In the findings section, we use the term UMR to refer to those who arrived in Sweden with a UMR status between 2015-2019.

### Psychological distress

> Frida: When we had many suicides, it could be that one person [a UMR] put the picture up on Facebook or Instagram saying "Farewell, goodbye," and you can see it's a bridge or a railway or you can see something on the picture, and we distribute it through the network and in many cases someone recognizes it. Someone says, "I recognize it; I know this place!" They can take a car, or they call the police, and we have saved lives.

Frida is a librarian who learned that there was no current statistical effort to track suicides among UMRs who were undergoing the Swedish asylum process. Taking it upon herself to record all of the attempted and accomplished suicides of UMRs in Sweden, Frida found that suicides increased at critical times, such as during the implementation of the November 24, 2015 law and during the start of mass deportations in 2016. Social media became a place where UMRs inadvertently or directly found help from members of VSIU. However, UMRs who openly threatened suicide sometimes discussed methods and posted images of accomplished suicides on social media, resulting in a tragic ripple effect of more suicide attempts.

Many of the interviewed VSIU members discussed how suicidal UMRs tried to jump in front of trains, hang themselves, drown or overdose from drugs. Frida told us about a couple who took in a suicidal UMR, and they both had to lie on top of him to keep him from hurling himself out of the window. Pelle, a long-time activist, and teacher has lost several UMRs to suicide, but he also prevented many. He felt there was a direct relationship between the broken asylum process and suicides and self-harm among UMRs. Pelle mentioned one case where a young UMR killed himself because the wait for an asylum interview became unbearable. Another complicated case involved a blind UMR who killed himself so that his younger brother would be able to get asylum – as the blind brother had reached 18, the Migration Board suggested he (despite his handicap) could be the guardian for his brother in Afghanistan. Both Pelle and Frida also mentioned how Sweden provides inadequate care for UMRs with mental health problems and has deported UMRs with physical and mental disabilities. They testify how the Migration Board semantically plays down the severity of the mental health issues of UMRs, including suicide ideation and attempts, referring to the UMRs as "being disappointed." If UMRs experience acute mental health issues due to the unfair and traumatic asylum process, then this does not legally grant them asylum; however, this legal exclusion does not reduce how the process is mentally damaging to UMRs.

The pain and subsequent suicidal contagion among UMRs continue as Sweden proceeds with mass deportations. Pelle and Frida, together with many UMRs, are actively protesting deportations outside of the detention centers. They described these protests as traumatic for everyone involved, but in particular for UMRs. The demonstrations are lengthy and typically end with buses leaving with the deportees to a nearby airport where a charted plane is waiting to fly them to Kabul. On deportation in Märsta on September 10, 2019, the protesters heard screaming from inside the detention center, upsetting the crowd. Frida described how she was standing next to a UMR who, when he saw the bus leave with his long-time friend, experienced a seizure and fell into her arms. A second boy fainted and fell to the pavement. An ambulance took them away. UMRs screamed as authorities took away their peers, friends, and brothers. Protesters shouted "Murderers!", 'There is blood on your hands!" In response, the police tried to control the crowd.

### Homelessness

> Elsa: They are really well dressed. They have their little laptop in a bag from their school, with a school mark on it. It's important for them to look like everyone else. And then I drop them off [at the homeless shelter] in the middle of nowhere in Gothenburg, in a place I haven't been to ever, and wouldn't find if someone hadn't shown me first. Leaving them there, every one of them was afraid.

Elsa is heavily involved in UMRs legal cases, and was working with the network Agape, which opened shelters to homeless UMRs. Seeing how the new asylum policies caused a "shadow society" where UMRs were forced into homelessness, drugs, and exploitation by criminal networks, she decided to quit her job and return to school for Legal Studies, focused on asylum cases.

Ingrid is a Judge for the Swedish government. On a drive home from work, she noticed groups of homeless youth – UMRs who lost their regional housing after aging out - on the streets. Ingrid brought some back to her house and continues nightly drives around her town, looking for UMRs in trouble. To make more space available, she and her husband moved their two biological children into their bedroom. Eventually, Ingrid rented an apartment to help house these abandoned kids. She told us, "I can't stand the light of hope in their eyes being snuffed out when I told them I failed to find them housing."

Matts and Alma, a married couple, learned how UMRs they had befriended were moved away from their town, where they had been studying, to an adult asylum camp far away. The reason was that the local politicians refused to support the UMRs after they aged-out of their HVB-hem ("Homes for Care or Housing"). Matts and Alma learned the UMRs experienced depression and even fear in the adult asylum camp and appeared emaciated. They moved a couple of UMRs into their house, and as more UMRs in a similar situation kept coming, they organized for other families to open up their homes too. Eventually, they were able to rent an abandoned building to house more youth.

Many members of the network live in smaller apartments, typical to Swedish cities. They carve out spaces in their apartments so that kids can survive. Often, the VSIU created sleeping spaces by repurposing closets or other rooms or building make-shift walls. Because the government failed to help these kids with their basics for survival (shelter, food, clothing), members of humanitarian networks who are part of civil society (Swedish) help.

UMRs become homeless for several reasons, but a primary reason is that once they are over 18 or have exhausted appeals on their asylum case, they lose the governmental support they received when they first arrived. Their legal guardians, the staff at the HVB hem, teachers, and other adults who were part of their social network, were no longer available to help them navigate Swedish society. The UMRs who were able to get temporary residency permits due to Nya Gymnasielagen are desperate to hold their places in study programs that may eventually qualify them for permanent residency permits. It is difficult for them to find affordable housing due to financial problems and discriminatory landlords. In our interviews, we learned that many UMRs in this situation would keep going to school While being homeless and struggling to feed themselves. We asked the network to list the places where UMRs sleep (see Table 5.1).

Living on the streets or being unstably housed, these UMRs face health problems and other dangers. Ludwig, a member of the network, knew a UMR who lived by eating eggs and tomatoes, noting: "When your diet is that bad, it is going to influence your mind." According to VSIU members, some homeless UMRs develop drug addictions due to the psychological stress of street-life, but also because of one addictive drug called Tramadol that staves off hunger. Many VSIU participants also discussed how UMRs were targeted by local criminal syndicates who tried to recruit them to sell drugs.

**Table 5.1.** Where do young, homeless refugees sleep in Sweden?

| Public spaces | Hidden spaces | Wild spaces | Private Spaces |
|---|---|---|---|
| Public transportation: Buses, trains or subways | Garages | Tents (even in snow) | Shelters |
| Public restrooms | Abandoned buildings | Forests | In private homes (e.g. in exchange for sex). |
| Parks | Shipping containers | Summer cabins | Hostels (paid by members of VSIU) |
| Monuments | Stairwells | Trailers | Hotels (paid by members of VSIU) |
| Children's playhouses in parks | Elevator shafts | Public beaches | Workplaces such as in the kitchen of a pizza restaurant |
| Covered bus stops | Wardrobes (in apartments owned by members of VSIU) | Community gardens | Churches |
| Under bridges | Garden/ outdoor sheds | | Gyms |
| | Abandoned boats | | |

**Survival sex and human trafficking**

> Pelle: If you don't have a place to stay and it's -20C outside, and some older man comes and says, you can stay with me. I'll have sex with you all night, but you can sleep inside and I'll give you food in the morning [you do it].

Pelle is a long-time activist and teacher. He is heavily involved in protests and in petitioning the United Nations (UN) to help UMRs. He works closely with many UMRs, some of whom Sweden is holding in detention centers and others who are undocumented. Only some members of VSIU had heard of UMRs directly discussing sex for pay in Sweden. They surmised that this is due to the stigma attached, especially in Islamic cultures. All VSIU participants heard rumors about greyer areas of sex work, including 'survival sex'. There were many stories of Swedish citizens offering UMRs shelter in exchange for sex, they say. Considering the uninhabitable outdoors during Swedish winters, this can be seen as coercion, and based on the Palermo Protocol, these teenagers are trafficking victims. We learned that some of the UMRs from Afghanistan had been Baacha Bareesh. These boys are generally Hazera, which is a group discriminated against and targeted by the Taliban. Baacha Bareesh are legally classified as human trafficking victims. They have a higher likelihood of re-victimization based on their exploitation history (Sorenson et al., 1991).

Through interviews with the network, we further heard stories about how Swedish women or men who came in contact with UMRs in the roles of advocates developed sexual relationships with them. The representatives of VSIU generally discourage such relations and the members who do this face removal. UMRs who are in relationships with ethnic Swedes, and even have children with them still face deportation. Marriage is not a path to citizenship for a refugee from Afghanistan, as Sweden does not count their passport as a reliable form of identification. One member of VSIU had a friend from the network who offered a room in her small apartment to a boy who arrived as a UMR. When she invited him to live with her, he was stealing clothing to survive. A member of VSIU told us that he was 18, and her friend was in her late twenties when they fell in love and started a relationship. He was well above the age of consent, but that does not mean that this relationship did not begin as survival sex.

As mentioned, Swedish officials have re-assigned age based on inaccurate age assessment tests (Mostad & Tamsen, 2019). Greta, a member of the network, described arbitrary age re-assignment: "They looked at this fifteen-year-old and said, 'you look eighteen,' and they changed his official date of birth." This arbitrary age change could mean that this minor is taken by authorities to live in adult asylum camps, where VSIU says they are at-risk being abused and exploited.

**Labour exploitation**

> Ludwig: They are doing internships or working for a few days to show skills [common in Sweden]. As a Swedish citizen, I know my right to get paid from day one even if it is just a trial. Even if I decide to work for two days and they say they don't want to hire me, I still get paid for those days. It is becoming more common where boys work for a few weeks for free, hoping to get a position that is paid later on, and that is not even in the underground job market.

Ludwig specializes in supporting LGBTQ UMRs who try to get asylum based on their status. He helps them prepare for the Migration Board interviews. He was not aware of any severe cases, but he knew a lot about the everyday labour exploitation against UMRs. While the internship scam described above does not seem severe, it is prevalent. Ludwig discussed how this activity is illegal in Sweden, and Sweden would enforce it if it happened to a Swedish teenager.

Exploitation within the licit sector is a significant issue for UMRs who are getting temporary stay under Nya Gymnasielagen. The problem with this law is the requirement that within six months of finishing school, the UMR has to secure full-time and permanent employment with a minimum of 2 years contract. This stipulation is not only tricky, but it puts employers in a position to easily exploit as their decisions determine asylum decisions. Employers know that UMR lives depend upon jobs, and they can count on long-term and low-cost labour if they hire them, so labour exploitation is inevitable. Elsa who is active in getting UMRs temporary residence permits commented on this "I know that they are stuck in jobs not earning anything […] So...they [UMRs] think they work to save themselves, to get to stay in Sweden on a work permit, but... they don't [get to stay]."

An amendment to the Family Reunification Policy places the burden of financially supporting the family on the UMRs, who are also often in debt to smugglers. Ana, a social worker who spends most of her free time informally counselling UMRs online or by phone, said that UMRs were approached with: "Can you help me to do something?" She stated: "When you look like you are not Swedish, I think that is also how they choose you and try to get you into something […] with drugs." Without the ability for asylum-seekers to work in the licit marketplace, these offers are alluring.

**Discrimination**

> Ana: One boy, he said: "I was sitting down on a bench, and a woman came to me and asked me: 'Where do you come from?' and when I said: 'I come from Afghanistan,' she said: 'Oh when I become a politician, I will clean the country from everybody like you.'

Ana counselled another boy who was harassed by a group of Swedish boys who shouted "rapist" at him. He confessed to her: "I have never even been with a girl in my life." When UMRs first arrived in Sweden in 2015, they placed UMRs in youth-asylum centres in rural areas. According to Elsa, "In Sweden we don't place asylum camps in the centre of the town - we place it in the woods, on an old camping spot or something, with no busses."

All of the participants from the network recounted discrimination against UMRs in Sweden. Many of them said that the boys avoid discussing these incidents due to shame and self-preservation. Pia is a God Man (Legal Guardian), whose UMR was asked to leave by management when trying to visit a local swimming pool. The manager said he asked him to leave because he did not speak Swedish. As this UMR looked at others in the line, some were speaking French, English, and other languages, but the manager did not ask them to leave.

**Discussion**

Many UMRs are at a pivotal moment in their lives, and their situations become worse as their human rights erode. The period of waiting for asylum or facing deportation makes them most vulnerable to exploitation in Sweden. Many are homeless and in desperate need of housing and even food. Their survival instincts may lead them to engage in survival sex or be exploited within the licit or illicit labour market. Due to the mass deportations, many may choose to live undocumented lives or try to get re-smuggled to countries where they have been implementing more humane policies for UMRs, such as France. This population is at extremely high-risk for exploitation in Sweden and other parts of the EU.

Sweden should reevaluate policies for the future waves of UMRs fleeing war, threats, and natural disasters. The Swedish government should change the current Family Reunification policy, which places the financial burden of supporting the family on the UMRs, making it very difficult to bring their families to Sweden. The numerous changes made to this policy since it's introduction left many UMRs without the needed support from their families. Prior research has shown that UMRs experience great loneliness (Hertz & Lalander, 2017), and they arrive at a vulnerable time in their development. Without parental guardians, UMRs are left to navigate their existing trauma and the current trauma of the asylum process alone.

The medical age-assessments have been deemed inaccurate by scholars (Mostad & Tamsen, 2019). The Swedish government should refrain from using age-assessments based on unreliable methods, and re-open cases where decisions were made based on these tests. Further, it has been noted by VSIU and other similar organizations, that officials changed UMRs' ages based on a visual take. Subjective assessments should be forbidden. There should be third-party oversight of changes to government policies for age-assessment. Officials should have a stringent protocol to follow when changing official documents, especially something so crucial as an age for UMRs.

The Swedish government should make a more considerable effort to keep these young people in the regions where they established stable support networks. Loneliness and lack of support contribute to psychological distress, and changes in asylum policies have made it difficult for many to find or maintain stable support networks. Even for those who face deportation, a supportive guardian or a stable network could protect them from added psychological distress, and even suicide. Further, even if UMRs age-out, they should not be denied housing and assistance as they are young people without guidance, and many lack the social capital to navigate the social welfare system successfully, and without the necessities of survival, they are vulnerable to exploitation.

Sweden should adjust current policies for those who arrived as UMRs in the 2015 exodus. The Nya Gymnasielagen policy should be redrafted with a more transparent and more constructive path to permanent residency and citizenship. As the law is written, there is a short window to obtain employment post-graduation, and employers are indirectly given power over asylum decisions, and this renders young people susceptible to labour exploitation and at the mercy of employers. Instead of putting the onus on this vulnerable and discriminated population, Sweden should increase the length of time to find a job, set up programs to ensure success in finding jobs and monitor how employers treat these young workers. The Swedish government should redraft these requirements to ensure that those who successfully pass their study programs have a fair chance to succeed in the Swedish labour market.

The simplest, most humane solution is to give these few thousand, mostly Afghani UMRs from the 2015 exodus, amnesty. First, there were many errors made in their asylum cases, especially based on inaccurate age-assessment procedures. Many UMRs were denied asylum even though they were entitled based on the UN definition. Second, the Swedish Foreign Department persistently warns its citizens that Afghanistan is not safe, yet conveniently deems it safe for UMRs who fled (Kosravi, 2016). This assessment of danger should extend to all. If bombs are dropping in Kabul every week, and the Taliban, who seek to eradicate the Hazera, are absorbing more territory (Jackson & Weigard, 2019), Afghanistan is not safe. At the least, Sweden should not return refugees until Afghanistan is deemed safe for travel by the Swedish Foreign Department.

Deeming Afghanistan safe is another thread in a web of lies about UMR asylum-seekers and their circumstances. Sweden is, in part, responsible for their persisting psychological distress and compounding vulnerabilities, and this should be exposed. The response of a developed social democracy is to take responsibility and afford these young people the safety and security that they legally and ethically deserve. Sweden was considered a model for asylum-seeker treatment and is culturally known for valuing children and young people. We urge Swedish lawmakers and politicians to repair these wrongs and encourage ordinary citizens to become involved. Being involved does not necessarily mean attending protests. However, as participants from the VSIU network have shown, ordinary citizens can use their strengths and expertise to help these young people, and the next wave, and the next, of vulnerable UMRs who have been largely abandoned by host governments.

**Conclusion**

From the perspective of VSIU, UMRs from the 2015 exodus experience multiple vulnerabilities within Sweden. This study supports previous studies that documented UMRs' high levels of psychological distress, including self-harm and suicide (e.g., Khan, 2017). Existing studies are showing that the asylum process is creating high levels of psychological distress (e.g., Jakobsen, 2018), and interviews with VSIU indicate a similar phenomenon. Many prior studies have documented discrimination of refugees by locals in host countries (e.g., Herz, 2018), and this study indicates a similar climate. Few studies are illustrating UMRs vulnerability to sexual and labour exploitation (a few exceptions (Chynoweth et al., 2017 and Freccero et al., 2017) and little to no literature seem to exist about this happening in Western Europe or Scandinavia.

Another theme of vulnerability found in this study that has not been well-researched in this region is the UMRs' susceptibility to criminal syndicates, drug addiction, and homelessness. These findings are alarming, and Swedish policy-makers and lawmakers should be aware of the UMRs' vulnerabilities. Future studies should explore these vulnerabilities in Scandinavia in greater depth in order to create effective programming to support these young people.

## References

Anagnostopoulos, D. C., Giannakopoulos, G., & Christodoulou, N. G. (2017). The synergy of the refugee crisis and the financial crisis in Greece: Impact on mental health. *International journal of social psychiatry*, 63(4), 352-358.

Behtoui, A. (2013). Incorporation of Children of Immigrants: the Case of Descendants of Immigrants from Turkey in Sweden. *Ethnic and Racial Studies, 36(12),* 2141-2159. doi: 10.1080/01419870.2012.696667

Blumer, H. (1954). What is wrong with social theory? *Am. Sociological Review*, *19*(1), 3-10.

Bounds, D., Julion, W. A., & Delaney, K. R. (2015). Commercial sexual exploitation of children and state child welfare systems. *Policy, Politics, & Nursing Practice*, *16*(1-2), 17-26.

Brunovskis, A., & Surtees, R. (2019). Identifying trafficked migrants and refugees along the Balkan route. Exploring the boundaries of exploitation, vulnerability and risk. *Crime, Law and Social Change*, 1-14.

Çelikaksoy, A., & Wadensjö, E. (2019). Refugee Youth Who Arrived in Sweden as Unaccompanied Minors and Separated Children. In: I. Kulu-Glasgow, M. Smit, I. Sirkeci (eds.) Unaccompanied Children: From Migration to Integration, London: Transnational Press London.

Chynoweth, S. K., Freccero, J., & Touquet, H. (2017). Sexual violence against men and boys in conflict and forced displacement: implications for the health sector. *Reproductive health matters*, *25*(51), 90-94.

Côté, J. E., & Allahar, A. (1996). *Generation on hold: Coming of age in the late twentieth century*. NY: New York University Press.

Dahlgren, P. (2016). Moral Spectatorship and its Discourses: The "Mediapolis" in the Swedish Refugee Crisis. *Javnost-The Public*, 23(4), 382-397.

Derluyn, I., & Broekaert, E. (2008). Unaccompanied refugee children and adolescents: The glaring contrast between a legal and a psychological perspective. *International journal of law and psychiatry*, *31*(4), 319-330.

Eide, K., & Hjern, A. (2013). Unaccompanied refugee children–vulnerability and agency. *Acta paediatrica*, *102*(7), 666-668.

El Baba, R., & Colucci, E. (2018). Post-traumatic stress disorders, depression, and anxiety in unaccompanied refugee minors exposed to war-related trauma: a systematic review. *International journal of culture and mental health*, *11*(2), 194-207.

Fegert, J. M., Sukale, T., & Brown, R. C. (2018). Mental Health Service Provision for Child and Adolescent Refugees: European Perspectives. In *Understanding Uniqueness and Diversity in Child and Adolescent Mental Health* (pp. 195-222). Academic Press.

Fili, A., & Xythali, V. (2017). The Continuum of Neglect: Unaccompanied Minors in Greece. *Social Work & Society*, *15*(2).

Fong, R., & Cardoso, J. B. (2010). Child human trafficking victims: Challenges for the child welfare system. *Evaluation and program planning*, *33*(3), 311-316.

Freccero, J., Biswas, D., Whiting, A., Alrabe, K., & Seelinger, K. T. (2017). Sexual exploitation of unaccompanied migrant and refugee boys in Greece: Approaches to prevention. *PloS medicine*, *14*(11), e1002438.

Geltman, P. L., & Cochran, J. (2005). A private-sector preferred provider network model for public health screening of newly resettled refugees. *American Journal of Public Health*, *95*(2), 196-199.

Gericke, D., Burmeister, A., Löwe, J., Deller, J., & Pundt, L. (2018). How do refugees use their social capital for successful labor market integration? An exploratory analysis in Germany. *Journal of vocational behavior*, *105*, 46-61.

Gnatenko, V. (2016). Integration of Unaccompanied Asylum Seeking and Refugee Minors in Sweden.

Gozdziak, E., Bump, M., Duncan, J., MacDonnell, M. & Loiselle, M.B. (2006). The trafficked child: trauma and resilience." *Forced Migration Review,* 25, 14-15.

Glaser, B. G., & Strauss, A. L. (2017). Discovery of grounded theory: Strategies for qualitative research. Chicago: Routledge.

Greeson, J. K., Briggs, E. C., Kisiel, C. L., Layne, C. M., Ake, G. S., Ko, S. J., & Fairbank, J. A. (2011). Complex trauma and mental health in children and adolescents placed in fostercare: Findings from the National Child Traumatic Stress Network. *Child welfare*, *90*(6), 91-108.

Hasson III, R. G., Cardoso, J. B., & Crea, T. M. (2019). Unaccompanied Refugee Minors and Migrant Youth: Policy and Practices in the United States. In *Encyclopedia of Social Work*.

Healy, C. (2016). Targeting vulnerabilities: The impact of the Syrian war and refugee situation on trafficking in persons. International Centre for Migration Policy Development [Internet]. Available from: https://www.icmpd.org/fileadmin/ICMPD Website/Anti Trafficking/ Targeting_Vulnerabilities_EN__SOFT_.pdf

Herz, M. (2018). 'Becoming' a Possible Threat: Masculinity, Culture and Questioning among Unaccompanied Young Men in Sweden.' *Identities*, 1-19.

Hirvonen, K. (2013). Sweden: when hate becomes the norm. *Race & Class*, *55*(1), 78-86.

Hodes, M., & Vostanis, P. (2019). Practitioner review: Mental health problems of refugee children and adolescents and their management. *Journal of child psychology and psychiatry*, *60*(7), 716-731.

Horning, A., Jordenö, S. & Savoie, N. (2020). Double-Edged risk: Unaccompanied Minor Refugees (UMRs) in Sweden and their search for safety. *Journal of Refugee Studies, DOI:* 10.1093/jrs/feaa034.

International Organization for Migration. (2015). Action to Protect Vulnerable and Mobile Populations [Internet]. International Organization for Migration. Available from: https://publications.iom.int/books/addressing-human-trafficking-andexploitation- times crisis-evidenceand-recommendations-0

Jacobsen, J. (2018). Language Barriers during the Fieldwork of the IAB-BAMF-SOEP Survey of Refugees in Germany. In *GESIS Symposium on" Surveying the Migrant Population: Consideration of Linguistic and Cultural Aspects"* (Vol. 19, pp. 75-84). DEU.

Jackson, A., & Weigand, F. (2019). The Taliban's war for legitimacy in Afghanistan. Current History, 118(807), 143-148.

Jakobsen, M., Demott, M. A., & Heir, T. (2014). Prevalence of psychiatric disorders among unaccompanied asylum-seeking adolescents in Norway. *Clinical practice and epidemiology in mental health: CP & EMH*, *10*, 53.

Jensen, T. K., Skårdalsmo, E. M. B., & Fjermestad, K. W. (2014). Development of mental health problems-a follow-up study of unaccompanied refugee minors. *Child and adolescent psychiatry and mental health*, *8*(1), 29.

Jones, S. V. (2015). Ending bacha bazi: boy sex slavery and the responsibility to protect doctrine. *Ind. Int'l & Comp. L. Rev.*, *25*, 63.

Karolinska Institutet. (2018). Significantly increased suicide risk among unaccompanied refugee *minors*. Retrieved from: https://news.ki.se/significantly-increased-suicide-risk-among unaccompanied-refugee-minors

Khosravi, S. (2016). Deportation as a way of life for young Afghan men. *Detaining the Immigrant. Other: Global and Transnational Issues, 169.*

Kisiel, C. L., Fehrenbach, T., Small, L., & Lyons, J. (2009). Assessment of complex trauma exposure, responses and service needs among children and adolescents in child welfare. *Journal of Child and Adolescent Trauma*, *2*, 143– 160.

Knutson, T. (2016). Ordförandena för landets tre migrationskollegier:"Ny lagstiftning leder till sämre integration. Retrieved from: https://www.advokaten.se/Tidningsnummer/ 2016/ nr-6-2016-argang-82/ny-lagstiftning-leder-till-samre-integration/

Malmberg-Heimonen, I. & Julkunen, I. (2006). Out of unemployment? A comparative analysis of the risks and opportunities longer-term unemployed immigrant youth face when entering the labour market. *Journal of Youth Studies, 9*(5), 575-592. doi: 10.1080/13676260601021054

McAlpine A, Hossain M, & Zimmerman C. (2016). Sex trafficking and sexual exploitation in settings affected by armed conflicts in Africa, Asia and the Middle East: systematic review. BMC Int Health Hum Rights, 16.

Mostad, P., & Tamsen, F. (2019). Error rates for unvalidated medical age assessment procedures. *International journal of legal medicine*, *133*(2), 613-623.

Nicolescu, A. F. (2017). The Integration of Refugees into Host Country Labor Markets: Barriers and Best Practices in the EU. *Journal of Identity & Migration Studies, 11*(1).

Omland, G. B., & Andenas, A. (2018). Negotiating developmental projects: Unaccompanied Afghan refugee boys in Norway. *Childhood, 25*(1), 78-92.

Pew Research Center (2016). Number of refugees to Europe surges to record 1.3 million in 2015. Retrieved from: https://www.pewresearch.org/global/2016/08/02/4-asylum-seeker demography-young-and-male/

Plener, P. L., Groschwitz, R. C., Brähler, E., Sukale, T., & Fegert, J. M. (2017). Unaccompanied refugee minors in Germany: attitudes of the general population towards a vulnerable group. *European child & adolescent psychiatry, 26*(6), 733-742.

Ramel, B., Täljemark, J., Lindgren, A., & Johansson, B. A. (2015). Overrepresentation of unaccompanied refugee minors in inpatient psychiatric care. *SpringerPlus, 4*(1), 131.

Sarkadi, A., Ådahl, K., Stenvall, E., Ssegonja, R., Batti, H., Gavra, P., ... & Salari, R. (2018). Teaching Recovery Techniques: evaluation of a group intervention for unaccompanied refugee minors with symptoms of PTSD in Sweden. *European child & adolescent psychiatry, 27*(4), 467-479.

Seglem, K. B., Oppedal, B., & Raeder, S. (2011). Predictors of depressive symptoms among resettled unaccompanied refugee minors. *Scandinavian journal of psychology, 52*(5), 457-464.

Shahid Khan, S. (2017). Are unaccompanied refugee minors in Sweden being pushed towards the risk zone for criminality? Determining the risk and protective factors of unaccompanied refugee minors. *Degree Project in Criminology, Criminology, Master's Programme, Malmo University.* Retrieved from: http://muep.mau.se/bitstream/handle/ 2043/22728/Sadia%20 Shahid%20Khan.pdf?sequence=2&isAllowed=y

Sinha S., Uppal S., & Pryce A. (2008). `I had to cry': exploring sexual health with young separated asylum seekers in East London. Diversity in Health and Social Care, 5:106, 108.

Sivakumaran, S. (2007). Sexual violence against men in armed conflict. *European Journal of International Law, 18* (2), 253-276.

Sorenson, S. B., Siegel, J. M., Golding, J. M., & Stein, J. A. (1991). Repeated sexual victimization. *Violence and Victims, 6*(4), 299.

UNICEF (2017 Feb) A deadly journey for children: the Central Mediterranean Migration Route. UNICEF- Child Alert. 2017Feb:2: 4±6. Available from: https://www.unicef. org/publications/files/EN_UNICEF_Central_Mediterranean_Migration.pdf

UNICEF (2016 Jun). Neither safe nor sound: Unaccompanied children on the coastline of the English Channel and the North Sea. UNICEF [Internet]. 2016 Jun: 11,23,31,44,81; Available from: https://www.unicef.org/media/files/UnicefNeitherSafeNorSound (003).pdf

UNODC. (2019). Retrieved from: http://www.unodc.org/unodc/en/human-trafficking/what-is-human-trafficking.html?ref=menuside

van Reisen, M. E. H. (2016). The Involvement of Unaccompanied Minors from Eritrea in Human Trafficking. [s.n.]

Verroken, S., Schotte, C., Derluyn, I., & Baetens, I. (2018). Starting from scratch: prevalence, methods, and functions of non-suicidal self-injury among refugee minors in Belgium. *Child and adolescent psychiatry and mental health, 12*(1), 51.

Wehrle, K., Kira, M., & Klehe, U. C. (2019). Putting career construction into context: Career adaptability among refugees. *Journal of Vocational Behavior, 111*, 107-124.

Wernesjö, U. (2019). Across the threshold: negotiations of deservingness among unaccompanied young refugees in Sweden. *Journal of Ethnic and Migration Studies*, 1-16.

Zetter, R. & Ruaudel, H. (2018). Refugees' right to work and access to labour markets: constraints, challenges and ways forward. *Forced Migration Review, 58,* 4-7. Retrieved from: https://doaj.org/article/fc0925603c1240a8801ea7749c84601d# ?

# CHAPTER 6

# "I'M IN A GREY ZONE": A NARRATIVE ANALYSIS OF RETURN MIGRATION AND ETHNIC IDENTITY IN MEXICO

Irasema Mora-Pablo

The complex socio-political relationship between Mexico and the United States has created for years the constant migration of Mexicans looking for the "American dream". The present study initially started as an exploration of the lives of university students who were studying a BA in English language teaching (TESOL) and were trying to adapt to the Mexican educational system after living in the United States for many years. The theme of identity construction was at the core of the study, however, as more was revealed from their stories, other issues emerged from the data, such as ethnic identity, their experiences as transnationals, moving back and forth between Mexico and the United States, and how these experiences encouraged them to pursue a career in English language teaching. The data used for this chapter is part of a larger study of return migration and their incorporation into the Mexican educational system at the university level. This research seeks to explore the process of identity construction of students of a BA in TESOL in central Mexico who have had part of their schooling in the United States and have returned to Mexico. In order to do this, it is important to know more about the transnational experience of these students, how they interpret their past and current experiences and how they construct their future professional identity. Concepts such as transnationalism, return migration and ethnic identity will be defined. Then, the methodology that guided this study will be presented, followed by the discussion of results. Finally, conclusions will be provided, as well as comments and implications of this research.

## Understanding return migration from two perspectives

Return migrant refers to the person who comes back to the country of origin with the objective to settle down there, after spending a considerable amount of time in another country (Izquierdo, 2011). This return can be voluntary or forced. The return can be definite, mainly caused by the nostalgia that most immigrants feel for their country of origin. Their permanent stay in the host country can be blurred by the incomplete integration to the new community and due to the strong links they still have with their country of origin (Espinosa, 1998). Mestries (2013) defines how difficult it could be for the immigrant to think about a potential return to the country of origin. This can be due to different factors, such as finding a steady job in the host country, when the immigrant takes his/her family to the host country and the children start their education and socialization process there (Water & Gerstein Pineau, 2015). This makes more difficult the idea of returning to a country they barely know. This is when the returning to the host country goes from being "the Mexican dream" to "the myth of the return", always postponed, and no longer desired (Mestries, 2013, p. 178). Petrón (2009) suggests, these returnees are "immediately classified as native speakers of English because of their fluency and native or native-like pronunciation" (p. 118). This is when they start to be questioned as not being Mexican enough.

**Transnationalism**

To provide a single and comprehensive definition of "transnationalism" is difficult. Authors in different fields have used it to signify different phenomena (Levitt & Waters, 2002). However, for the purposes of this study, the term has been used to characterize the dense social networks that go beyond the national borders, created by the physical, emotional and economic movement of individuals and families, between countries and cultures (Binford, 2000). This perspective seems to offer a fluid interpretation of return migration. Under this perspective, return migration does not necessarily mean the end of the migration cycle. This might represent only a stage, where the person may choose to re-emigrate, or move back and forth between the two countries (Hazan, 2014). The emergent approaches in migration theory describe transnational communities as:

> ...dense networks across political borders created by immigrants in their quest for economic advancement and social recognition. Through these networks, and increasing number of people are able to live dual lives. Participants are often bilingual, move easily between different cultures, frequently maintain homes in two countries, and pursue economic, political and cultural interests that require their presence in both. (Portes, 1997, p. 812)

However, this mobility between the two countries is not always possible for young migrants, as they usually depend on their parents' decision and migratory status. For those who experience this constant back and forth between the two countries, they may start experiencing a sense of inferiority, based on the disadvantageous position in relation to the American citizens. Williams, Alvarez and Hauck (2002) mention that "These disadvantages, coupled with a troubled history of relations between the US and Mexico, fuel antagonism toward Mexican immigration and encourage anti-Mexican stereotypes" (p. 564, citing

Gutiérrez, 1996). This can give us a better idea of how these former immigrant children start developing a sense of identity and this includes feeling part of the community or feeling rejected (Hernández-León, Lakhani & Zúñiga, 2017).

Transnationalism is not the same as immigration. Hornberger (2007) states that "...the latter involves a more permanent affiliation with the host country and separation from the home country while the former may imply no long-term intention to stay beyond what is economically necessary" (p. 326). Therefore, transnationalism can lead to a process of 'becoming other' to both home and host national-cultural contexts (Trueba, 2004), implying the development of transnational identities and social relations. This would mean that transnationals need to develop certain abilities that allow them to negotiate at the same time multiple contexts within local positions, which can become a cumulus of community contexts (Zúñiga, 2000) that symbolically end up becoming a decontextualized cultural limbo.

**Cross-border social network theory**

This theory goes beyond transnationalism, and it might help to understand the capacity of the individual to mobilize different resources that go beyond ethnic and kinship networks. This is intended to be a more dynamic approach to understand return migration since it identifies different types of returnees, as they might portray different levels of preparation but also different levels of readiness (Hazan, 2014). An interesting approach in this view is how the individual can prepare for his/her return to the country of origin. In terms of readiness, the individual feels that he/she has accomplished the original goals for emigration or that he/she can have strong opportunities in the country of origin. His/her skills, knowledge and experiences acquired in the host country, give him/her a feeling that this increases his/her human, social and linguistic capital, something that he/she can mobilize to facilitate his/her successful reintegration in the country of origin (Cassarino, 2008).

Over past several years, more Mexicans have left than migrated to the United States, even after living there most of their lives (Christiansen, Trejo Guzman & Mora-Pablo, 2017; Hamann, Zuñiga, & Sánchez García, 2008; Mora Pablo, Lengeling & Basurto Santos, 2015; Tacelosky, 2018). This includes voluntary returns, as well as deportations (Silver, 2018). Some return migrants remain in Mexico to work in transnational companies where English is mostly used (Anderson, 2015), while others enrol in higher education programs taught in English (Christiansen, Trejo Guzman & Mora-Pablo, 2017; Rivas Rivas, 2013), though admission to these programs often presents social and administrative challenges for returnees because often they are not welcomed back into Mexico.

As Hazan (2014) points out, "Because of its intensity and the characteristics of the returnee population, the return migration phenomenon that has arisen in recent years presents serious challenges and opportunities for both Mexico and the US. It is of the utmost importance both countries, formulate and implement policies capable of addressing it" (p. 3). These policies can be translated in opportunities for these return migrants for work, but also in relation to their studies. However, in terms of work, Mexico has followed a policy of *Laissez Partir* ("let them go"), meaning that potential migrants are not discouraged by the government (Hazan, 2014).

Transnational students bring with them varying degrees of bilingualism and biliteracy (Hamman *et al.*, 2006; Hornberger, 2007; de la Piedra, 2011) and biculturality (Petrón, 2003; Petrón & Greybeck, 2014). These collective skills and experiences are accumulated throughout experiences in both Mexico and the US. These are then internalized and appropriated by transnational students to form their own identity. They can help in understanding their complexities of identity formation and sense of attachment or detachment from one culture or the other.

### Ethnic identity

Cross-border social networks are based upon the idea that migrants share a common identity, based upon a place of origin, culture, customs and linguistic traits associated with it. The individual and group identities are negotiated "within social worlds that span more than one place" (Vertovec, 2001, p. 573). Identity is conceptualized as "an inherently social product that is jointly created by interactants, rather than as a pre-determined, psychological construct that is lodged within each individual's mind" (Park, 2007, p. 341).

As Skeggs (2008) states, "Identity is simultaneously a category, a social position, and an effect" (p. 11). Kidd (2002) defines knowing who one is as having a sense of similarity with some people and a sense of difference from others. The location of identities is "in constant negotiation, both by ethnic group members themselves as well as by outside observers" (Nagel, 1994. p 153). The identities of these return migrants are shaped and re-shaped at different moments of their lives as they continue to rely on their cultural values and backgrounds in order to navigate the current educational moment they face.

Conceptual models describe ethnic identity as a multidimensional construct produced by exploration, resolution, and affirmation (Bernal, Knight, Ocampo, Garza, & Cota, 1993; Umaña-Taylor & Fine, 2004; Umaña-Taylor, Yazedjian, & Bámaca-Gómez, 2004). Ethnic identity results when adolescents engage in culturally specific activities, behaviors, and roles (i.e., exploration), understand group membership (i.e., resolution), and perhaps most importantly, develop positive feelings about the self and the group (i.e., affirmation). Conceptual models also suggest that contextual factors in the family, neighbourhood or peer group and individual characteristics (i.e., language) are potential antecedents of ethnic identity.

The data used for this chapter is part of a larger study of return migration and their incorporation into the Mexican educational system at the university level. The main objective of this research was to unveil the intimate interplay between language and identity by exploring the factors that contribute to the identity formation of returnees. In this chapter, issues of feeling more American or Mexican will be addressed. Also, how their transnational experiences have influenced the participants' decisions for becoming English teachers. In the next section, the methodology that was used for conducting this study will be explained.

## Methodology

Participants in this project share one thing in common: they all lived a number of years in the United States and have returned to Mexico. There were a total of fifteen participants. They signed a letter of informed consent and their names have been changed to protect their identities. In order to explore this phenomenon, qualitative research was used, following an autobiographical-narrative approach. Narrative inquiry provides the opportunity to understand the meanings that participants associate with their own lives and experiences (McClimens, 2002).

According to Maycut and Morehouse (1994), qualitative research "examines people's words and actions in narrative or descriptive ways closely representing the situation as experienced by the participants" (p. 2). Therefore, this research was also based upon a narrative inquiry. Nakamura (2002) mentions that "Narrative inquiry is about building public expression of personal understanding of the events, experiences, and people in our professional lives [...]" (p.117). In order to follow a narrative approach, first, participants were asked to write an autobiography where they could describe their first experiences, when they went to the United States for the first time, how they learned English and if they maintained Spanish, their legal situation, among other aspects. Then, autobiographies were analyzed so follow up questions would emerge in order to ask in their individual interviews. These in-depth interviews allowed participants to reveal and expand on experiences that were crucial in their understanding of the selves, and in turn, allowed the interviewer to interpret these experiences as part of the overall context of participants' current life, resulting in present and future perspectives (Rosenthal, 2007). This was a revealing collaboration between researcher and participants, where the stories and their content were at the core of the interviews (Clandinin & Connelly, 2000; Reissman & Speedy, 2007).

## Context/participants

The research site is the Language Department of a large public university in central Mexico, where the participants are studying an in-service TESOL BA program, and the researcher is a full-time professor. During the last ten years, this program has increased in numbers because many return migrants decide to embrace this career, as this is one of the few that exist in this public university where almost 90% of the classes are in English. This, in turn, becomes an attractive program for these students, since this is a place where they can actually use their English language abilities and make use of their linguistic capital. Most of them, because of their native-like proficiency in English, started to teach the language in different educational levels (primary, secondary, high school, university) before they started their university studies in the BA in TESOL. As the program is attractive to them and they need official documents to validate their role as English teachers at their workplaces, they enrol in the program with the goal of becoming English teachers with credentials to prove they are professionals. As this is part of a larger project, there were 15 participants between the ages of 19 to 30. However, for this chapter, only six were considered, since these are the ones who represented the themes presented in the discussion section. These participants lived in the United States an average of 17 years, but always maintained contact with their home country through relatives, cultural and linguistic practices. After a number of years, they returned to Mexico. The reasons were varied: some of them were deported because they had problems with the police, as they were part of gangs; some others decided to return to Mexico because they did not have legal status in the United States and they were aware of their difficulties to begin university degree programs. Below, a brief description of the participants is offered:

- Neil. He is 27 years old. He was born in Guanajuato. He was taken to the US when he was three years old and never came back to Mexico until he was about to start his university studies. He did not plan to be an English teacher, but this is the only job he found due to his linguistic capital. He is currently working as an English teacher in a primary school

- Oswaldo. He is 26 years old. He was taken to the US (Idaho) when he was nine months old. At home, there was a rule of only Spanish. He used to come to Mexico to visit his parents' family in December, at least every two years. He attended Austin Community College for two years until he finally came back to Mexico to reunite with his family. He is currently teaching English at the University of Guanajuato.

- Rodrigo. Rodrigo is 28 years old, and he moved to the US at the age of 13, as an undocumented immigrant. He had a difficult life in the States as he did not know English, and he got involved in gangs. He was deported, and he always looked for a way to get back to the States. As he saw it was difficult, he started to study a BA in TESOL to become an English teacher

- Joseph. He is 25. He was born in Chicago, but his parents are Mexicans. He lived almost 20 years in the States until he decided to go to Mexico to know more about his parents' country after failing his first year at university. He did not plan to be an English teacher, but a relative suggested he should give it a try.

- Bertha. She is 27 years old. She was taken to the US when he was two, and he lived there for 14 years. Her father made the decision to go back to Mexico, and this was a difficult adaptation process for her. She has an MA in Applied Linguistics now and teaches English at the University of Guanajuato.
- Samuel. He is 30 years old, and he was taken to the US when he was three years old. He lived in the States almost 20 years. He could not afford the university in the US, and he came back to Mexico to see what he could do with his life.

## Data analysis and interpretation

The process of analysing the data was on-going, and there were moments where it was necessary to go back and forth between the autobiographies and the interview transcriptions. As part of the narrative analysis, relying on paradigmatic cognition was useful. This entails "classifying a particular instance as belonging to a category or concept" (Polkinghorne, 1995, p. 9). Similarities across interviews and autobiographies were searched in the data and then grouped them in different categories such as: feeling American or Mexican, sense of attachment to one particular culture, reasons for becoming English teachers and identity formation. Barkhuizen (2013) mentions that "Thematic analyses follow the paradigmatic procedures of coding for themes, categorizing these and looking for patterns of association among them" (p. 11). The themes that emerged from this analysis were diverse. For the purposes of this chapter, first, the issue of feeling more American or Mexican will be addressed. Then, how is it that their previous experiences helped them (or not) to embrace the English teaching profession.

## Feeling Mexican and American in the host country

For the participants, their country of origin is Mexico. At an early age, they were taken by their parents to the United States, which became their host country. Joseph comments on how he actually felt Mexican while being raised in the United States, as he was always encouraged to speak Spanish and to be in contact with his Mexican heritage:

> ...I didn't really feel American because I was actually raised like a Mexican I guess, but you know since I had a lot of influence of school, friends and teachers. I mean they were all American, I mean that in a certain way was a part of me. But I mean at home I ate *tortillas* you know, *frijoles* and talked in Spanish so I don't know...I thought I was Mexican but at the same time, I was a bit American because I have an American nationality.

In his case, Joseph also has the American nationality, which gave him a sense of official belonging to the host country, although he never lost his Mexican identity. Similarly, Neil acknowledges how, while being in the United States, his friends made him feel part of the social group:

> I didn't have an identity because you know my friends accepted me in the States, they knew who I was they knew about me and stuff but I was always the Mexican with them, they were mostly white.

In his account, Neil mentions an important element to consider when defining ethnic identity, and this is physical appearance. In his case, his physical appearance portrays him as someone from Mexican descendant, and he was regarded as such:

> …they would call me by my name and everything, but everyone knew I was Mexican, I mean I'm the only brown person there.

However, when he returned to Mexico, his Spanish was very influenced by his English, after spending a considerable amount of time in the United States. Neil remembers how, in his country of origin, he was seen as Mexican but did not sound like one:

> When I got to Mexico, my accent in Spanish was super heavy. It was really heavy, so then everybody noticed that I wasn't … I was from Mexico; my brown skin told them I was from Mexico. I was from Mexican descend. However, inside I wasn't Mexican, I was more American.

This conflict of identity was more marked when he returned to Mexico, since people recognized him neither as Mexican nor American. To their eyes, he looked Mexican but did not fulfil the expectations of their Mexican counterparts in terms of his linguistic ability in Spanish. Furthermore, he did not feel part of the social group as he felt more identified with his American side. This is similar to what happened to Bertha in terms of self-identification, as she explains:

> I feel more American. I'm still faithful to the United States. My memories are from there, my way of thinking. My mom feels bad. She says: "But you are Mexican" and I tell her "But I didn't grow up here".

For Bertha, it was clear that after spending most of her life in the United States, she felt more American, and she was even questioned by her mother. Having grown up in a different country, this is what Mestries (2013) refers to the difficulties of those children of immigrants who are taken at a very early age to the host country. When they return to Mexico, they have no sense of belonging and do not feel part of their country of origin.

Even more, Bertha comments that she feels *ni de aquí ni de allá* (neither from here nor from there):

I feel like in a 'grey zone'. While I'm in the States, I'm not American enough, and when I'm in Mexico, I'm not Mexican enough. So… people mock me because of the way I speak Spanish [in Mexico], but in the States, they question my physical appearance, not my English. All in all, you can't make people happy!"

For Bertha, after spending several years in the United States, her sense of belonging makes her feel more identified with the American culture. However, even when she tries to belong to the Mexican culture, she feels people do not let her. In contrast, Oswaldo was determined not to let his Mexican side be taken over by his American upbringing, as he states:

> I feel really proud of my heritage, being Mexican, that's why I don't want to lose it because I also saw the other kids whose Spanish wasn't that good, […] and I don't know I guess that I just don't want to lose it, something that was part of me and I didn't want to give it up.

His family made an effort to installed in him this sense of pride about the Mexican culture, but also, his linguistic proficiency in Spanish was something he always wanted to keep developing, as he wanted to avoid being classified as those Mexican-American who do not speak Spanish anymore or that have problems with the language. Even, now that he is an English teacher, his students ask him where he is from, as he shows high proficiency and native-like pronunciation in both languages:

> Sometimes my students ask me where I am from. Honestly, I don't know how to answer. They constantly tell me my English is good and I don't sound like their other teachers… but they also tell me that I look Mexican. I feel Mexican, I am Mexican, but there is this other part of me…

Again, to the eyes of his students, he looks Mexican, but when he speaks English, they do not notice a heavy accent as in the case of other teachers. This makes him feel proud of his commands of the languages but also acknowledges that he still has this American identity that he feels to identify with. And it is precisely this command of the language that Petron (2009) acknowledges as an advantage of these return migrants that opens the doors to a new profession: becoming English language teachers, as it will be discussed in the following section.

## Embracing (or not) the English language teaching profession

Having experienced a process of adaptation and re-integration in the country of origin, these return migrants might face discrimination, isolation and even bullying. For Bertha, for example, coming back to Mexico was a difficult experience, since she had been living in the United States most of her life. Her main language was English, and Spanish was mainly used at home. Therefore, when she arrived in Mexico, people questioned her proficiency in Spanish. Her adaptation process took some time and she even changed their behaviour and the way she socialized among Mexicans

> I became more anti-social. There were people telling me "You speak funny", "Your Spanish is *mocho [corrupted]*" and I was like "Aghh, leave me alone!" but then I started to gain confidence again when I started the BA. It was a long process.

This long process of gaining confidence again started when she began her studies in the BA program. As most of the classes are taught in English, Bertha felt more at ease and found a sense of belonging to a new social group, where she could speak in English and Spanish, and people would not question her level at either language. However, not all participants initially wanted to become English teachers. Their linguistic capital, their high proficiency in English, is seen as an advantage over other counterparts, and this usually gives them access to other job opportunities. This was the case of Neil, as he explains in the following extract:

> I was working in a call-center… and I didn't want to spend the rest of my life there. Someone told me about the BA, and I thought "now I will be an English teacher".

As many other return migrants, his first job when being back in Mexico was in a call center. These call centers are still widely popular among returnees (Durand, 2016). However, Neil did not want to spend his life working in such centers. As he was aware of his linguistic capital, he decided to try a new opportunity and study to become an English teacher. But the decision to become English teachers was not as easy as it might seem for all the participants. Samuel, for example, was hesitant about the idea of starting his studies in this field:

> When I found out about the BA… I wasn't sure if it was the right thing to do. My mom convinced me and I had to do something with my life. […] the problem was the entrance exam; I didn't know many things about Mexican history.

Samuel's mother was a pivotal factor to encourage him to study the BA program. However, one of his main difficulties was the lack of knowledge about the history of his country of origin. This was only one more obstacle that he had to overcome in order to feel that his life was taking direction again, as he had spent almost 20 years in the United States and his school years were in this country. For Bertha, Neil and Samuel, studying the BA was a way of finding a place where they felt embraced, as they found other classmates who had similar experiences. This process helped them develop their self-confidence and also they found a profession they could be part of. However, not all participants had such positive experiences when returning to their country of origin. This is the case of Rodrigo, who found it difficult to adapt to his life back in Mexico:

> I came back in 2007 for three days [...] just for I was just missing out, I wanna go back home. When got here, I realized it wasn't no home for me. Exactly on the third day. I came on a Sunday, on Tuesday I got my airplane ticket to Tijuana, on Wednesday I bounced back. Like that! I was out of place, know what [I] mean? Everything was changed for those years [...] I didn't feel comfortable.

This was the first time he came back to Mexico after spending a few years in the United States. He realized that trying to start again in his country of origin was not an easy task, and therefore, he decided to go back to the United States. He decided to study a BA in 2015. At the moment of the interview, he was back in Mexico and trying to make an effort to find a steady job, a reason to stay in his country. Sadly, shortly after he decided to drop out the program and go back to the United States, as it was very hard for him to adapt to Mexico, his educational system and ways of living in general.

All participants had different experiences and reasons to return to Mexico. Their adaptation process even dictated the way they approached their educational future. The majority embraced the English language teaching profession as a way to put into use their linguistic capital and start a new life in their country of origin. Becoming English teachers was not always their first choice, but it gave them a way to see that they could have a future in Mexico. At times, this was the only job they could find, in a country that did not offer them opportunities upon their return. Sadly, economics of labour migration does not explore the return migration at a macro-level. They tend to focus on micro-level decision models. This means that their focus is on the individual, but not on the institutional context and the opportunities that the country of origin can offer.

## Conclusions

Identity is not singular. These transformations are complex and continual, redefining all aspects of self along the lines of race, ethnicity, professional identity, and so on. Although these issues of social identity are not addressed overtly in the classroom, they are present and have an impact on how participants portrayed themselves and how they became English teachers. They constantly negotiated their identity depending on where they were situated. Their identity process is based upon their lived experiences in two countries: the United States and Mexico. They went through issues of discrimination and being questioned by their Mexican peers about their linguistic proficiency in Spanish. At times they did not feel they fitted completely into a specific national identity; however, they also created a hybrid identity of being bilingual and return migrants. They continually negotiate their identities and emotions and showed flexibility as individuals. Through time the participants seemed to resolve some problems of identity, constant movement and insecurity. One way of solving their identity conflicts was to enrol in the BA program to become English language teachers. They found a place where they felt they belonged and were appreciated, but their integration process was not always easy. Implications for schools in Mexico is that programs that help students with re-immersion and Spanish language learning need to be implemented to provide students with the opportunity to learn academic Spanish necessary for a profession or to study a BA in their preferred field, and not because of their linguistic capital in English. Universities can take advantage of these BA TESOL programs to encourage return migrants to become English language teachers. At a macro-level, we need to consider the economic and political conditions in Mexico, in which there is a need to reintegrate this population in the labour market, but still, few opportunities are offered. This is in a time where job creation is slowing down, and issues of social insecurity are rising. This places a very difficult scenario for return migrants to re-adapt to their country of origin; however, they might find new opportunities for their economic reintegration if they make use of their linguistic capital.

Concerning their teacher identity, they bring a number of positive attributes as teachers because of their lived experiences as transnationals. The data in this project has indicated how complicated it can be to define who they are. Shaping and re-shaping ethnic identity seem to be a common activity for these participants, and now they are at a different stage in their lives, where they can rely on their previous experiences as transnationals but also create their future selves while becoming English teachers.

These participants have shown that they had a life established in the United States and that they like the host country. At times, they feel more identified with it than their own country of origin, and they might think this is a reason for them to re-emigrate. This is a picture which many US politicians and policy makers are unlikely to recognize and even less likely to like. As for Mexico, still much has to be done for institutional programs to work in favour of the reintegration of this return migrants, not only in the economic aspect but also social and educational. Much still needs to be done and there is a need to understand their full migratory experiences (emigration, immigration, return and potential re-emigration) to be able to formulate informed policy and to frame the phenomenon in a more dynamic context.

## References

Anderson, J. (2015). "Tagged as a criminal": Narratives of deportation and return migration in a Mexico City call center. Latino Studies, 13(1), 8–27. doi:10.1057/lst.2014.72

Barkhuizen, G. (Ed.). (2013). *Narrative research in applied linguistics.* Cambridge: Cambridge University Press.

Bernal, M. E., Knight, G. P., Ocampo, K. A., Garza, C. A., & Cota, M. K. (1993). Development of Mexican American identity. In M. E. Bernal & G. P. Knight (Eds.), Ethnic identity:

Formation and transmission among Hispanics and other minorities (pp. 31–46). Albany: State University of New York Press

Binford, L. (2002). Remesas y subdesarrollo en México. *Relaciones. Estudios de historia y sociedad, 23*(90).

Cassarino, J.P. (2008) (Ed.). *Return Migrants to the Maghreb Countries.* Florence: Italy, Robert Schuman Centre for Advanced Studies.

Christiansen, M. S., Trejo Guzman, N. P. & Mora-Pablo, I. (2017). You Know English, so Why Don't You Teach?" Language Ideologies and Returnees Becoming English Language Teachers in Mexico. *International Multilingual Research Journal, 12*(2), 1-17. doi: 10.1080/19313152.2017.1401446

Clandinin, D. J. and Connelly, F. M. (2000). Narrative inquiry: Experience and story in qualitative research. San Francisco: Jossey-Bass.

de la Piedra, M. T. (2011). Tanto necesitamos de aquí como necesitamos de allá: Leer juntas among Mexican transnational mothers and daughters. *Language and Education, 25*(1), 65-78. doi: 10.1080/09500782.2010.535905.

Durand, J. (2016, August 21). La Jornada: Oportunidad histórica. *La Jornada.* Mexico D.F. Retrieved from http://www.jornada.unam.mx/2016/08/21/opinion/016a2pol

Espinosa, V. (1998). *El dilema del retorno: migración, género y pertenencia en un contexto transnacional,*Colegio de Michoacán-Colegio de Jalisco, Zamora, México.

Gutiérrez, D. G. (1996). *Between two worlds: Mexican immigrants in the United States.* Rowman & Littlefield.

Hamann, E. T., Zuñiga, V., & Sanchez-Garcia, J. (2006). Pensando en Cynthia y su hermana: Educational implications of United States-Mexico transnationalism for children. *Journal of Latinos and Education, 5*(4), 253-274. doi: 10.1207/s1532771xjle0504

Hazan, M. (2014). Understanding return migration to Mexico: towards a comprehensive policy for the reintegration of returning migrants. *Center for Comparative Immigration Studies.* University of California.

Hernández-León, R., Lakhani, S. M., & Zúñiga, V. (2017). From children of immigrants to migrant children: Diverse experiences in new places of settlement and the 'homeland'. *Retrieved July, 31,* 2017.

Hornberger, N. H. (2007). Biliteracy, transnationalism, multimodality, and identity: trajectories across time and space. *Linguistics and Education, 18,* 325-334.

Izquierdo Escribano, A. (2011). Times of Losses: A False Awareness of the Integration of Immigrants. *Migraciones Internacionales, 6*(1).

Kidd, W. (2002). *Culture and Identity.* Basingstoke and New York: Palgrave.

Levitt, P. & Waters, M. (eds.) (2002). The Changing Face of Home: The Transnational Lives of the Second Generation. Russell Sage Publications: Nueva York.

Maycut, P., & R. Morehouse (1994). *Beginning qualitative research: A philosophic and practical guide.* London: Routledge.

McClimens, A. (2002). All I Can Remember Were Tablets: Pat's Story. *Journal of Learning Disabilities, 6* (1), 73-88.

Mestries, F. (2013). Los migrantes de retorno ante un future incierto. *Sociológica, 28* (78). Enero-abril, pp. 171-212.

Mora Pablo, I., Lengeling, M. M., & Basurto Santos, N. M. (2015). crossing borders: Stories of transnationals becoming English language teachers in Mexico. SIGNUM, 18(2), 326-348. doi: 10.5433/2237-4876.2015v18n2p326

Nagel, J. (1994). Constructing ethnicity: creating and recreating ethnic identity and culture. *Social Problems, 41* (1). *Special Issue on Immigration, Race, and Ethnicity in America,* 152-176.

Nakamura, I. (2002). Narrative studies to enhance teacher development. *JALT 2000 at Shizuoka,* conference proceedings, 111-118.

Park, J. E. (2007). Co-construction of non-native speaker identity in cross-cultural interaction. *Applied Linguistics, 28*(3), 339–360.

Petrón, M. (2009). Transnational teachers of English in Mexico. *The High School Journal* April/May,

115-128.
Petrón, M. A. (2003). I'm bien pocha: Transnational teachers of English in Mexico. Retrieved from Dissertation Abstracts International.
Petrón, M. A., & Greybeck, B. (2014). Borderlands epistemologies and the transnational experience. *Gist Education and Learning Research Journal, 8*(1), 137-155.
Portes A. (1997). Immigration theory for a new century: Some problems and opportunities. *International Migration Review, 31*(4): 799–825.
Polkinghorne, D. E. (1995). Narrative configuration in qualitative analysis. *Qualitative Studies in Education, 8,* 5-23.
Reissman, C. K., & Speedy, J. (2007). Narrative inquiry in the psychotherapy professions: A critical review. In Clandinin, D. J. (ed.) *Handbook of narrative inquiry: Mapping a methodology.* Pp 426-456. Thousand Oaks, CA: Sage Publications.
Rivas Rivas, L. (2013). Returnees' identity construction at a BA TESOL Program in Mexico. *PROFILE*, 15 (2), 185-196
Rosenthal, G. (2007). Biographical research. In Seale, C., Gobo, G., Gubrium, J. F. & Silverman, D. (Eds.). *Qualitative research practice.* (pp. 48-64). London: SAGE Publications.
Skeggs, B. (2008). The problem with identity. In Lin, A. M. Y. (Ed.), *Problematising identity: Everyday struggles in language, culture and education* (pp. 11–35). New York: Lawrence Erlbaum Associates.
Silver, A. M. (2018). Displaced at "home": 1.5-Generation immigrants navigating membership after returning to Mexico. Ethnicities, 18(2), 208 – 224. doi: https://doi.org/10.1177/1468796817752560
Tacelosky, K. (2018). Transnational education, language and identity: a case from Mexico. *Society Register, 2* (2): 63-84.
Trueba, E. (2004). The new Americans: Immigrants and transnationals at work. New York, NY: Rowman & Littlefield Publishers Inc.
Umaña-Taylor, A. J., & Fine, M. A. (2004). Examining ethnic identity among Mexican-origin adolescents living in the United States. *Hispanic Journal of Behavioral Sciences, 26*, 36–59.
Umaña-Taylor, A. J., Yazedjian, A., & Bámaca-Gómez, M. (2004). Developing the ethnic identity scale using Eriksonian and social identity perspectives. *Identity, 4,* 9–38.
Vertovec, S. (2001). Transnationalism and identity. *Journal of Ethnic and Migration Studies, 27* (4), 573–582.
Waters, M. C. & Gerstein Pineau, M. (2015). The integration of immigrants into American Society. Washington, D. C: The National Academies Press.
Williams, S. L.; Alvarez, S. D. & Andrade Hauck, K. S. (2002). My name is not María: Young Latinas seeking home in the heartland. *Social Problems, 49*:563–584.
Zúñiga, V. (2000). Migrantes internacionales de México a Estados Unidos: hacia la creación de políticas educativas binacionales. En Rodolfo Tuirán (coord.), Migración México-Estados Unidos, Opciones de Política, México, Consejo Nacional de Población/Secretaría de Relaciones Exteriores, pp. 299-334.

# PART III: INTEGRATION

# CHAPTER 7

# INTEGRATION OF THE AMERICAN YOUTH INTO THE MEXICAN LABOUR MARKET

Liliana Meza González and Pedro Paulo Orraca Romano

According to data from 2015 Intercensal Survey, carried out by the Mexican National Institute of Statistics and Geography (INEGI), the total number of people born abroad in Mexico is slightly more than 1 million. The most important contingent of foreigners in Mexico is of American origin, which according to INEGI totals 740,000 people. Of the total number of Americans, those between 15 and 29 years old total 154,400, and represent 21% of the total number of Americans. To put this figure into perspective, it is enough to say that Guatemalans with a population of 42,800 in 2015 was the second largest contingent of foreigners in Mexico. This indicates that young Americans represent almost four times the total number of Guatemalans in the country.

On the one hand, many of the young Americans living in Mexico are the children of Mexicans who spent a few years in the neighbouring country to the north and decided to return, bringing along their children who were born in the United States. For example, of the total number of Americans in Mexico, 85% are between 0 and 24 years old. On the other hand, some young Americans in Mexico are the product of the cross-border dynamics in the northern part of the country, where women who live in Mexico (and who normally have high educational levels and come from medium-high or high socioeconomic backgrounds) choose to give birth in the United States, so that their children have the US citizenship with the purpose of improving their long-term educational and economic prospects (Vargas and Coubès, 2017)[1]. This situation gives young American migration a special characteristic: they are not really immigrants; nonetheless, they are foreigners in their own country.

[1] With the INEGI's data it is not possible to measure the phenomenon of cross-border birth. This article is based on the idea that young Americans are mainly the children of Mexicans who returned to their country after residing in the United States. Zúñiga (2018: 96) calls these children and young people "0.5 generation" which refers to those children of migrants who lived the first years of their lives in the United States and are currently living in Mexico. They are called as such because while living in Mexico they are immigrants, but at the same time they can be considered Mexicans, regardless of their country of birth.

It is well known that young people have different characteristics and work-related problems than those of adults. Their transition to adulthood passes through their integration into the labour market after school, and the obstacles that young people face to obtain their first job and to remain in it can lead to situations that affect their working life over time (Meza, 2018). This phenomenon is known as "scarring effect" and is well documented in the literature [see Nilsen and Holm-Reiso (2011), among others].

Several studies have addressed problems of integration into the host society that children and teenage migrants face [see Heckman (2008), Lu and Zhou (2013) and Gutiérrez and Giorguli (2018), among others]. Young Americans must deal not only with the problems of labour integration faced by young people in general but also with those caused by their migrant status; for example, poor command of the local language, their oral expressions, their different customs and accents, among other factors. Nevertheless, their knowledge of the English language, their years in the American school system, and their experience abroad are likely to put them at an advantage over their Mexican peers. It is possible that Mexican employers have a preference for hiring young people of American origin, which would imply favourable treatment for them in the Mexican labour market.

In the case of young Americans in Mexico, although they are not considered immigrants in the traditional sense of the concept, their integration into the host society has to pass through the four stages that Esser (2006) suggests[2].

The purpose of this chapter is to analyse the conditions under which young people born in the United States and living in Mexico are being integrated into the Mexican labour market, in comparison with their same age Mexican peers. For this purpose, young people are classified into three age groups: 15-19, 20-24 and 25-29. The analysed variables are labour income and unemployment probabilities, informality, non-remunerated work, agricultural labour, construction labour, self-employment and caretaking jobs.

The study shows that young Americans have almost always had remunerations that are higher than the ones received by their Mexican peers, although this advantage diminishes over time. Given that young Americans have higher levels of schooling, it is important to ask whether their wage advantage is explained by their observable characteristics or by their

[2] The stages of integration that Esser (2006) proposes are: a) "acculturation", which is the transmission and acquisition of language, cultural standards and skills needed to interact in society; it can be compared to socialization. B) "placement", which means having a position in society, e.g. in the education system, in the professional or work aspect or in the acquisition of citizenship, which confers rights and a sense of belonging by having a social position and the economic, social and cultural capital to allow socialisation. C) "interaction", which includes the formation of relationships and networks in which there is feedback from different individuals, such as friendships, marriages or general memberships that migrants acquire in relation to the host society. Finally, d) "identification", which implies that the individual sees him- or herself as an element of a collective body or social system; this element implies an emotional and cognitive component of the sense of belonging.

unobservable characteristics. For this, Blinder-Oaxaca decomposition exercises are included, and they show that the unobservable characteristics of these young people are the ones that explain, to a greater extent, their income advantage, which suggests that they receive preferential treatment from Mexican employers. The study also finds that young Americans are more likely to work in the informal sector and to be non-remunerated workers, which shows difficulties in their initial integration which is explained, in part, by the destruction of social networks that the migratory experience of their parents may have brought. This outcome also suggests that young people of American origin have a larger support network, which allows them to work without remuneration or informally in order to gain work experience. Another finding is that young Americans are less likely than young Mexicans to work in the agricultural and construction sectors, implying that their labour integration, once achieved, has better conditions than that of their Mexican peers. Finally, the study reports that young Americans are more likely to work as caretakers, at least in 2015. This can be explained by better working conditions in this sector; by its prevalence in rural areas for workers who are not engaged in agricultural labour; and by its employment stability, which makes it appealing to the best labour market candidates [see Butler et al. (2014)].

**Literature review**

Because this study examines the process of labour market integration of young Americans in Mexico, several areas of labour economics and international migration are relevant to our research. For example, studies focusing on the labour market integration of young people, and in particular young immigrants, are of special interest. There are also studies examining the process of economic assimilation of the migrant population and studies investigating issues of temporary migration or remigration. No other study, to our knowledge, focuses on the labour conditions of young American workers in Mexico.

Some of the individual factors that make integration of young people into the labour market difficult include lack of work experience, lack of experience related to job hunting, and restrictions or unwillingness to move geographically, among others (Mocanu and Zamfir, 2016: 402). Likewise, their high unemployment rates are partly explained by the fact that they are in a state of transition, moving from school to the labour market and from living with their parents to living independently, which leads to frequent entries and exits in the labour market (Vela, 2007). Structural factors that prevent them from entering the labour market include the lack of connection between the educational offer and the labour requirements demanded by companies. In addition, in times of economic uncertainty or recession, young people tend to be the least likely to be employed and the most susceptible to losing their jobs because of their limited experience, seniority and low bargaining power (Weller, 2007).

At the microeconomic level, problems in entering the labour market result in postponing young people's emancipation, which may include postponing marriage and buying a house. At the macroeconomic level, it implies less use of national human resources, which cost is exacerbated when experiencing a demographic bonus (Calves and Schoumaker, 2004; Meza, 2018).

One of the prominent studies that focus on the integration of young immigrants into the labour market is Perreira et al. (2007), which examines this process for the case of young immigrants in the United States. The analysis shows that, in relation to their native peers, immigrants have lower labour participation rates during their secondary and high school studies. It is argued that this arises because immigrants and natives have significant differences regarding their families' socioeconomic characteristics, social networks, and job opportunities. According to Behtoui and Olsson (2014: 792), immigrants' parents play an important role in their child's integration process into the labour market, where their education and position in the labour market gives them different levels of access to economic and social capital and therefore provides them different resources to access higher educational levels and better-paid jobs.

Froy and Pyne (2011) examine the ethnic minority groups' and young immigrants' job performance in developed countries. It is observed that young people have higher unemployment rates than the adult population and that, among young people, immigrants are more prone to be unemployed. However, this finding depends on the country of origin and destination, the demographic characteristics of individuals and the time of residence in the destination country. Behtoui and Olsson (2014) analyse the educational and job performance of young migrants from Bosnia-Herzegovina, Chile and Somalia in Sweden. The authors conclude that education investments are less profitable for young immigrants than for natives because they tend to hold subordinate positions, making it difficult for them to gain access to a social and economic status that suits their skill level and merits.

Carrasco and Riesco (2011) analyse the path of labour integration of young immigrants in Spain. The study finds that, regarding immigrants, Spaniards have lower activity rates, lower employment rates and lower unemployment rates. In addition, while 38.0% of immigrants live exclusively on their income, this figure drops to 23.0% among Spaniards, where they in turn receive a personal income 12.0% higher than that of immigrants.

The age at which young immigrants arrive to the country of destination plays an important role, where those who arrived at an early age perform much more similar to natives, as opposed to those who arrived during their teenage or adult years (Allensworth, 1997; Behtoui and Olsson, 2014). Furthermore, numerous studies have shown that there are important differences in the labour integration of immigrants according to how long they have lived in the destination country, their levels of human capital and their demographic characteristics. The usual observation is that the job performance of immigrants tends to improve as they adapt to that market (Chiswick, 1978); however, this does not imply that they achieve a performance comparable to that observed among the native population, where a considerable gap is commonly observed regarding this group (Borjas, 1994).

In the short term, the worst performance of the immigrant population occurs due to incomplete information on the country of destination and local labour dynamics and the flawed transfer of skills when migrating from one country to another. These skills may include the language, certificates of study, occupational licenses, and specific skills of more defined tasks. In the medium term, immigrants make investments that complement the skills they bring with them, thus increasing the transferability of these skills in the destination country, and they invest in acquiring new skills in order to increase their productivity and income (Chiswick et al., 2005: 335). Due to the restrictions that they sometimes face when integrating themselves into a new country, as well as among the young, self-employment is often the last option for certain immigrant groups.

In the case of young Americans in Mexico, it is expected that they will perform well in the national labour market, due to the good level of education they bring with them, their command of the English language and their knowledge of the country, resulting from the fact that a significant number of them are of Mexican ascent. If we add this to the fact that working in Mexico carries the opportunity cost of not working in the United States, this suggests that the wages of young Americans will be higher than those of young Mexicans.

Finally, because of the large wage differences that prevail between Mexico and the United States, it is likely that a significant number of young Americans in Mexico will migrate at some point in their lives to their country of birth. Cuecuecha et al. (2017) analyse this phenomenon by focusing on the international remigration of American children living in Mexico. Their study indicates that, indeed, a high percentage of them return at some point in their lives to the United States. It is observed that among minors, the most common objective for which they remigrate is their incorporation into the American school system; while among the population 18 years of age and older, work represents an important determinant of remigration.

This means that, on several occasions, the presence of young Americans in Mexico will be temporary. Dustmann and Görlach (2016) argue that the behaviour and decisions regarding investments in human capital, labour supply and migrant's consumption in the destination country vary depending on whether their stay in the country is permanent or temporary. If their migration to Mexico is temporary and at some point, they plan to return to the United

States, the high wage differentials motivate them to value leisure more or reduce their labour supply when they are in Mexico (the country with the lowest wage) and to work more when they are in the United States (the country with the highest wage). At the same time, young Americans who are temporary migrants will be less willing to invest in specific human capital for Mexico because it will be of little use to them once they leave the country and seek to enter the American market. In the case of permanent migrants, they will distribute their leisure consumption and labour supply decisions more evenly throughout their life cycle and will be more willing to invest and acquire human capital in the destination country (Dustmann and Gorlach, 2016: 100).

## Data, methodology and descriptive statistics

This section describes the data used in the estimations included in this paper. It also describes the methodology used and shows some socio-demographic and labour descriptive statistics of the analysed populations.

### Data

First, data from the 2015 Intercensal Survey (EIC 2015) is used. The purpose of the survey was to update the socio-demographic data on the population living in Mexico, specifically in the year between the census conducted in 2010 and the one to be conducted in 2020. The sample of this survey comprises 6.1 million dwellings[3].

Second, data from the 2010 and 2000 population and housing censuses are used. In order to analyse the 2010 data, the census sample of about 2.9 million dwellings in the country was taken. A basic survey and an extended one that includes labour information were applied to those surveyed who were included in the 2010 census sample. Unfortunately, it was not possible to use all of the data from the 2010 census because labour information was only captured through the extended survey, and this was only applied to the census sample.

With respect to the 2000 census, the basic questionnaire included questions on the labour market integration of those surveyed; however, in order to exclude those young people who worked in the United States, a census sample was used to obtain information on approximately 2.2 million homes. The expansion factors were used in all the estimates. The three samples used are representative at national, state, municipal and local levels of more than 50,000 inhabitants. Although none is representative of the foreign population, in all cases, there are enough observations to make the estimates (see table 1). The results, however, should be taken with caution.

The samples used in this study are restricted to individuals between 15 and

[3] The study excludes, in all of the years, people who live in Mexico and work in the United States. According to the 2015 Intercensal Survey, the municipalities located along Mexico's northern border house approximately 86,600 people between 18 and 65 years old who work in the United States. Orraca (2019) estimates that this population has an income 121.7% higher than the one received by their peers who live and work in Mexico.

29 years old. Since the estimates make use of data about occupied persons and not only wage earners, the dependent variable in the income equations is labour income. To simplify the nomenclature, we refer to the labour income as a wage. All wages are in real terms, base 2015.

**Methodology**

To understand how the integration into the labour market of young people of American origin living in Mexico has evolved over time, this study carries out cross-sectional analyses for each of the years for which data is available. For cross-sectional analyses, firstly, Mincer equations similar to those proposed by Chiswick (1978) in his work on wage differentials between immigrant and native workers are estimated. The baseline model, estimated by the ordinary least squares (OLS) method, is as follows:

$$\log w_i = X_i \Theta + \delta A_i + \lambda A_i^2 + \gamma_0 I_i + \varepsilon_i \text{ .............. } (1)$$

where $w_i$ is the labour income or wage of worker i; $X_i$ is a vector of socio-demographic characteristics that include educational level, head of household, gender, whether or not he/she had lived in Mexico 5 years before the survey and his/her area of residence[4]; $A_i$ represents the age of the worker and estimates his/her potential labour experience; $I_i$ is a dummy variable that indicates whether the worker is of American origin or not, and $\varepsilon_i$ is a stochastic error. This model includes a second-degree polynomial for the age variable to establish a quadratic relationship with the wage. For 2015, the model is estimated using monthly labour income, because the survey did not include the question about worked hours, but for 2000 and 2010, the dependent variable is the hourly labour income. In our case, the coefficient $\gamma_0$ represents the percentage wage differential between young Mexican workers and young people of American origin.

The previous regressions were estimated both for the entire young working population, as well as for women and men separately. To understand the reasons behind the wage differentials estimated with the Mincer equations, Blinder-Oaxaca wage decomposition exercises were carried out for each of the years of the analysis. This procedure classifies the wage differential between two groups of workers, partly explained by differences in the observable characteristics of the workers, such as education, age or job experience, and partly explained by the coefficients assigned to each of these characteristics (called the "unexplained part"). The unexplained part of the differentials is generally attributed to discrimination (when the differential is positive, i.e. it favours the first analysed group), as it shows the prices that would be paid to

---

[4] The regions of origin are grouped according to their degree of marginalisation, which is calculated by the National Population Council with census and 2015 Intercensal survey data.

the disadvantaged group if their characteristics were paid at the same rate as which the advantaged group is paid. When the unexplained part of the differential is higher than the explained part, and when this differential is negative (when it favours the supposedly disadvantaged group), it is said that there is a favourable treatment for the second population group. Similarly, if the part of the differential attributed to the unobservable characteristics is positive, it means that if the group at a disadvantage were paid the same as the other group for its observable characteristics, the former would receive a higher remuneration, implying that they are being discriminated by employers.

**Table 7.1**. Number of observations (expanded)

| | 2000 | 2010 | 2015 |
|---|---|---|---|
| Young Americans | 47,684 | 118,393 | 138,138 |
| Ages 15 to 19 | 25,438 | 71,454 | 77,956 |
| Ages 20 to 24 | 13,987 | 30,432 | 42,998 |
| Ages 25 to 29 | 8,259 | 16,507 | 17,184 |
| MEN | | | |
| Young Americans | 21,252 | 56,104 | 63,327 |
| Ages 15 to 19 | 11,768 | 34,147 | 37,052 |
| Ages 20 to 24 | 5,834 | 14,760 | 19,038 |
| Ages 25 to 29 | 3,650 | 7,197 | 7,237 |
| WOMEN | | | |
| Young Americans | 26,432 | 62,289 | 74,811 |
| Ages 15 to 19 | 13,670 | 37,307 | 40,904 |
| Ages 20 to 24 | 8,153 | 15,672 | 23,960 |
| Ages 25 to 29 | 4,609 | 9,310 | 9,947 |

Source: 2015 Intercensal Survey (EIC 2015) and 2010 and 2000 Population and Housing Censuses.

For a better understanding of the integration process of young people of American origin into the Mexican labour market, probabilistic equations were also estimated -with cross-sectional data and for each of the years of the analysis- where the dependent variables are the risks of becoming unemployed, informal and non-remunerated worker. Furthermore, probability equations were calculated to determine the probability of young American workers to perform as agricultural, construction, self-employed and caretake workers.

Probit regressions were estimated as follows:

$$prob(y) = \beta_0 + \beta_1 X_{1i} + \beta_2 X_{2i} + \beta_3 X_{3i} + \beta_4 X_{4i} + \beta_5 X_{5i} + \beta_6 X_{6i} + \beta_7 X_{7i} + \beta_8 X_{8i} + \beta_9 X_{9i} + u_i$$

| Independent variable | Description |
|---|---|
| $X_{1i}$ | Age |
| $X_{2i}$ | Age$^2$ |
| $X_{3i}$ | Accumulated years of schooling |
| $X_{4i}$ | Economic sector in which the individual works |
| $X_{5i}$ | Gender |
| $X_{7i}$ | Head of household |
| $X_{8i}$ | Recently arrived in Mexico |
| $X_{9i}$ | Young people of American origin |
| $u_i$ | Random error |

Regressions were estimated for the whole population as well as for women and men separately. Marginal effects were estimated as a way of facilitating the interpretation of the coefficients.

**Descriptive statistics**[5]

Table 7.2 shows, in 2015, the average age for young Americans were 19.5 years, while it was 21.7 years for young Mexicans.

The schooling level is very similar between the two populations, although that of young Americans is higher. The proportion of women is also higher among young Americans in comparison with Mexicans.

According to the figures in table 7.2, just over 15% of young Americans arrived in Mexico between 2010 and 2015, as the variable "recent" accounts for the population who five years before the survey was conducted lived in the United States[6]. Another interesting fact is that Mexican and American girls have slightly higher levels of schooling than boys. Furthermore, men are more likely to be heads of household and women are more likely to be daughters of the head of household. However, it is noteworthy that young Americans of both genders are less likely to be heads of household than Mexicans, suggesting better family networks that allow them to postpone their independence.

Table 7.3 presents key labour force data on young Mexicans and Americans and, for comparative purposes, on the remaining population in Mexico. Figure 7.1 shows the labour incomes of the analysed populations, while figure 7.2 presents the percentages of workers in four sectors: primary, manufacturing industry, services and trade.

[5] The descriptive statistics in this section refer only to the year 2015.

[6] The "recent" variable cannot be not used to measure the phenomenon of cross-border birth, as it is likely that a significant number of young American of the 0.5 generation have arrived in Mexico more than 5 years before the 2015 EIC survey.

**Table 7.2.** Descriptive socio-demographic statistics by age and gender groups

| | Young Mexicans | Young Americans | Remaining population of Mexico |
|---|---|---|---|
| Age | 21.72 | 19.51 | 44.13 |
| Accumulated schooling years | 10.37 | 10.82 | 9.17 |
| Women (%) | 50.91 | 54.15 | 52.83 |
| Head of household (%) | 12.11 | 7.09 | 48.00 |
| Child of the head of household (%) | 12.31 | 9.70 | 32.81 |
| Recent (%) | 0.38 | 15.10 | 0.82 |
| MEN | | | |
| Age | 21.63 | 19.35 | 44.10 |
| Accumulated schooling years | 10.26 | 10.70 | 9.41 |
| Head of household (%) | 19.01 | 10.88 | 73.76 |
| Child of the head of household (%) | 1.70 | 1.16 | 7.03 |
| Recent (%) | 0.51 | 14.03 | 1.13 |
| WOMEN | 21.80 | 19.65 | 44.16 |
| Age | 10.48 | 10.92 | 8.95 |
| Accumulated schooling years | 5.44 | 3.88 | 24.97 |
| Head of household (%) | 22.54 | 16.93 | 55.81 |
| Child of the head of household (%) | 0.25 | 16.01 | 0.54 |
| Recent (%) | 0.25 | 16.01 | 0.54 |

**Table 7.3.** Labour descriptive statistics

| | Young Mexicans | Young Americans | Remaining population of Mexico |
|---|---|---|---|
| Monthly income | 5018.11 | 7126.46 | 6894.83 |
| Primary sector % | 10.73 | 8.25 | 10.27 |
| Manufacturing industry sector % | 28.35 | 20.20 | 24.22 |
| Services sector % | 37.07 | 47.00 | 41.98 |
| Trade sector % | 20.16 | 22.67 | 17.77 |
| MEN | | | |
| Monthly income | 5110.28 | 6900.08 | 7363.47 |
| Primary sector % | 14.99 | 12.24 | 14.85 |
| Manufacturing industry sector % | 33.41 | 24.83 | 29.44 |
| Services sector % | 30.59 | 40.58 | 34.44 |
| Trade sector % | 17.45 | 20.83 | 15.49 |
| WOMEN | | | |
| Monthly income | 4845.24 | 7486.08 | 6063.66 |
| Primary sector % | 2.69 | 1.90 | 2.06 |
| Manufacturing industry sector % | 18.79 | 12.85 | 14.89 |
| Services sector % | 49.32 | 57.21 | 55.48 |
| Trade sector % | 25.28 | 25.60 | 21.86 |

Source: Self-estimates based on the 2015 Intercensal Survey, INEGI.

**Chart 7.1**. Monthly income 2015

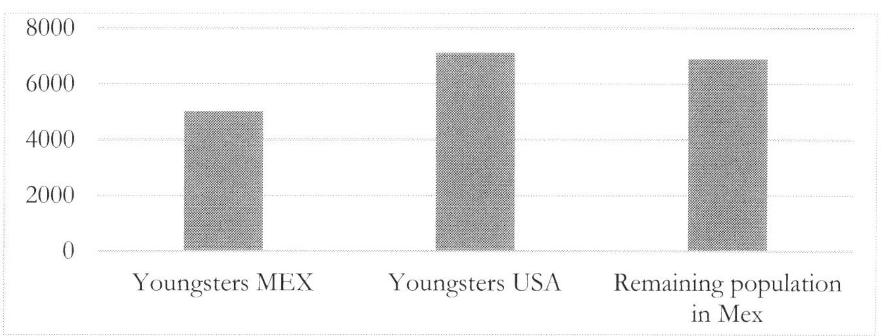


Source: Own estimates based on the 2015 Intercensal Survey, INEGI.

Chart 7.2, on the other hand, shows that young Americans are inserted to a lesser extent than Mexicans in both the agricultural and manufacturing industry sector, while they are inserted to a greater extent in the services and trade sectors.

**Chart 7.2**. Workers by sector and by population group 2015

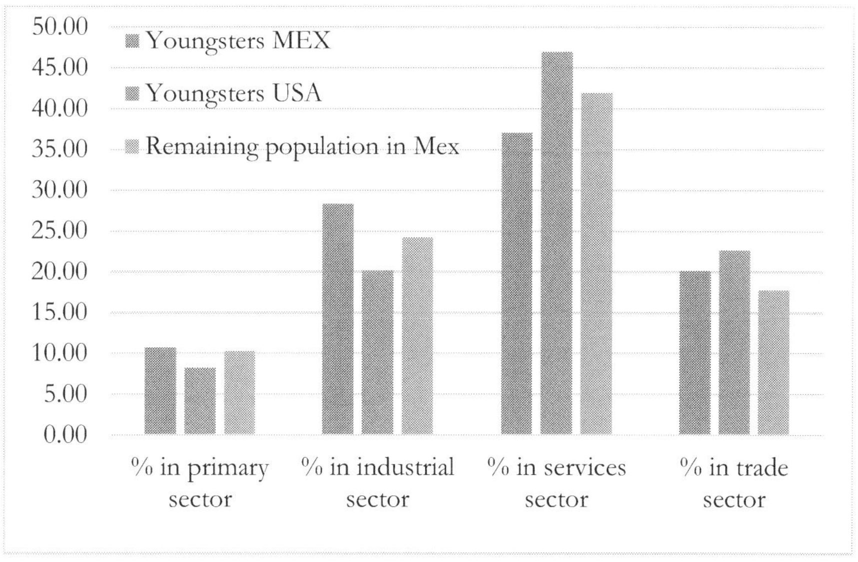


Source: Own estimates based on the 2015 Intercensal Survey, INEGI.

The one question worth asking is, where are the young Americans located throughout Mexico? Chart 7.3 shows the percentages of young Americans in relation to the total population by state. The state with the highest percentage of young people from the United States is Baja California, followed by Chihuahua, Colima, Sonora and Tamaulipas.

**Chart 7.3**. Young Americans compared with the overall population of 2015

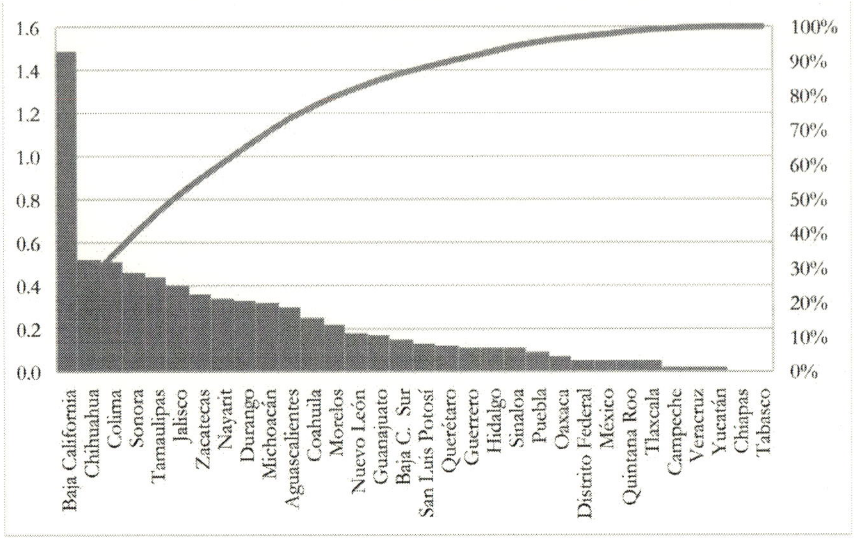

Source: Own estimates based on the 2015 Intercensal Survey, INEGI.

## Results

### Wage differentials

Table 7.4 shows the results of the estimates of the wage equations, and in particular, the coefficients of the dummy variable that indicates that the observation is a person of American origin who falls within a specific age range. In this case, young Americans are those between 15 and 29 years old.

**Table 7.4**. Wage differentials between young Mexicans and Americans by age and gender group

| | 2000 | | 2010 | | 2015 | |
|---|---|---|---|---|---|---|
| Young Americans | 0.3726 | *** | 0.2617 | *** | 0.0719 | *** |
| Ages 15 to 19 | 0.1646 | *** | 0.0686 | *** | -0.0566 | *** |
| Ages 20 to 24 | 0.3683 | *** | 0.2894 | *** | 0.0379 | *** |
| Ages 25 to 29 | 0.6275 | *** | 0.4709 | *** | 0.2637 | *** |
| MEN | | | | | | |
| Young Americans | 0.4002 | *** | 0.3203 | *** | 0.0702 | *** |
| Ages 15 to 19 | 0.1548 | *** | 0.1433 | *** | -0.0846 | *** |
| Ages 20 to 24 | 0.4125 | *** | 0.3166 | *** | 0.0252 | *** |
| Ages 25 to 29 | 0.6616 | *** | 0.5799 | *** | 0.3250 | *** |
| WOMEN | | | | | | |
| Young Americans | 0.3208 | *** | 0.1753 | *** | 0.0722 | *** |
| Ages 15 to 19 | 0.1636 | *** | -0.0698 | *** | 0.0016 | |
| Ages 20 to 24 | 0.3034 | *** | 0.3089 | *** | 0.0514 | *** |
| Ages 25 to 29 | 0.5561 | *** | 0.2934 | *** | 0.1700 | *** |

***/ Significant at 99 % confidence

Age, age squared, schooling, position in the household, region and recent are the control variables
Source: Own estimates based on INEGI's census and intercensal survey data.

It is especially remarkable that almost all the coefficients of interest were positive and significant at 99% confidence, except for young men between 15 and 19 years old in 2015 and women between 15 and 19 years old in 2010 and 2015. This suggests that throughout the first 15 years of the 21st century, young Americans almost always received higher remuneration than those of their Mexican peers, even after controlling for their observable characteristics. This differential becomes higher as the age of the group increases. Generally, the differentials in the male group are higher than the differentials of the female group, although there are some exceptions. Chart 7.4 presents these wage differentials by year, for young people classified by age group of both genders.

**Chart 7.4.** Wage differentials between young Mexicans and Americans, 2000-2010-2015

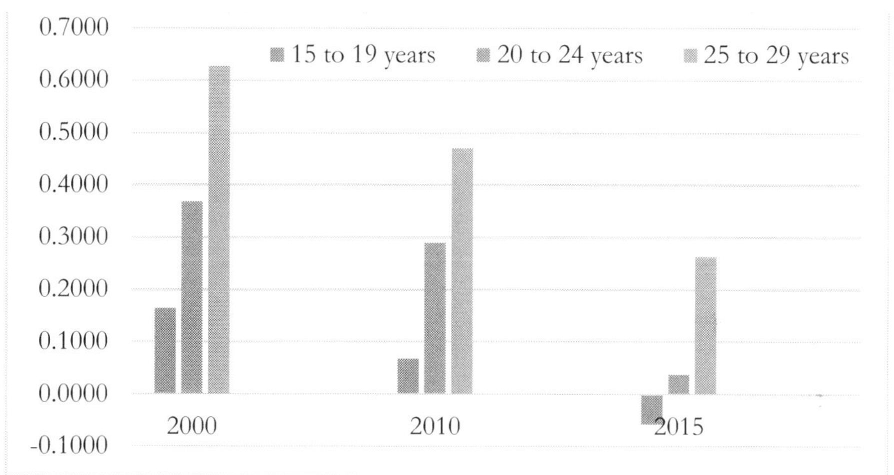


Source: Own estimates based on 2015 intercensal survey and 2010, 2000 censuses, INEGI.

One may notice how the differentials fall over time for the three age groups. Probably, the fact that the difference in formal education between young Mexicans and American has closed over time (due to the longer years in school among the Mexican population), is behind this result[7]. By economic sector, we have that the highest differentials are observed in the services sector and the lowest in the manufacturing industry sector. Also, in this case, wage differentials fall over time. In 2015, there is no longer a differential in favour of young Americans within the primary sector (see Chart 7.5).

[7] Based on data from the censuses and the Intercensal Survey, while in 2000 the difference in formal years of education between young Americans and young Mexicans was 1.47 years, for 2010 this difference was 0.61 years and, for 2015, it was only 0.44 years.

**Chart 7.5**. Wage differentials by sector: young Americans versus Mexicans, 2000-2010-2015

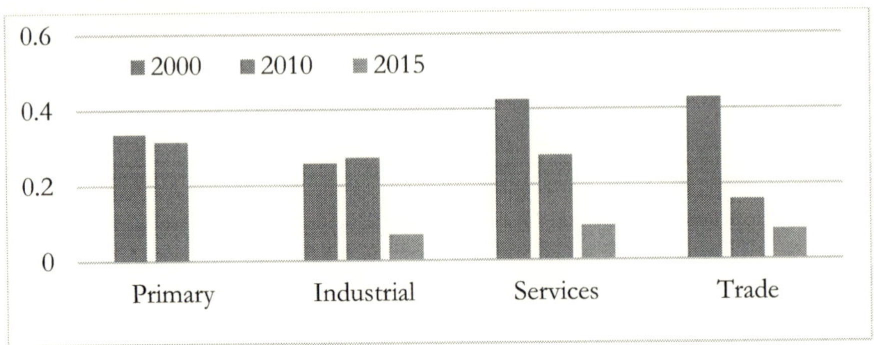


Source: Own estimates based on 2015 intercensal survey and 2010, 2000 censuses, INEGI.

**Blinder-Oaxaca decompositions**

Facing a scenario of wage differentials that favour young people of American origin in Mexico, it is worth asking if these are explained by the higher educational levels of these young people or if they result from the favourable treatment from Mexican employers, due to unobservable characteristics such as their education in the United States, command of English, among others. The decomposition exercises were carried out for the three years of the analysis and for men and women separately. Table 7.5 presents the results of the decomposition exercise for the year 2000; table 7.6 for the year 2010, and table 7.7 for the year 2015.

**Table 7.5**. Blinder-Oaxaca decompositions (Hourly wages logarithm, 2000)

| | Young Americans | Young American men | Young American women |
|---|---|---|---|
| Group 1 Predictions | 3.7162*** | 3.7040*** | 3.7398*** |
| Group 2 Predictions | 4.4865*** | 4.5219*** | 4.4226*** |
| Differential | -0.7702*** | -0.8179*** | -0.6828*** |
| Endowments | -0.1025*** | -0.1097*** | -0.1113*** |
| Coefficients | -0.6487*** | -0.7032*** | -0.5487*** |
| Interaction | -0.0190*** | -0.0049*** | -0.0227*** |
| Explained | -0.1215*** | -0.1146*** | -0.1340*** |
| Unexplained | -0.6487*** | -0.7032*** | -0.5487*** |
| Explained % | 15.7751 | 14.0115 | 19.6251 |
| Unexplained % | 84.2249 | 85.9763 | 80.3603 |

***/ Significant at 99 % confidence
Source: Own estimates based on 2000 Population and Housing census data.

Once again, decomposition exercises show that, during the three years of analysis, young Americans received significantly higher labour incomes compared to those of their Mexican peers. This differential falls over time[8].

[8] It is important to remark that, in 2015, we use log monthly real labor incomes, while in 2000 and 2010, we use log real hourly labor incomes. This explains the differences in values and means that the differentials might not be completely comparable over time.

Notice how in 2000, 84% of this differential was explained by the unobservable characteristics of the young people. This proportion increases to 98% in 2010 and to 108% in 2015. The unexplained portion of remunerations is consistently higher for men than it is for women. Also, notice how the unexplained part of the income differential is negative in all cases, which implies that if young Americans received the same payment for their observable characteristics as young Mexicans, then they would receive lower incomes. This means that during the first fifteen years of this century, young Americans have received preferential treatment when compared to young Mexicans.

**Table 7.6**. Blinder-Oaxaca decompositions (Hourly wages logarithm, 2010)

| | Young Americans | Young American men | Young American women |
|---|---|---|---|
| Group 1 Predictions | 2.9835*** | 2.9709*** | 3.0062*** |
| Group 2 Predictions | 3.3073*** | 3.3409*** | 3.2514*** |
| Differential | -0.3237*** | -0.3700*** | -0.2452*** |
| Endowments | 0.0894*** | 0.0917*** | 0.0698*** |
| Coefficients | -0.3179*** | -0.3728*** | -0.2244*** |
| Interaction | -0.0953*** | -0.0889*** | -0.0905*** |
| Explained | -0.0059*** | 0.0028*** | -0.0207*** |
| Unexplained | -0.3179*** | -0.3728*** | -0.2244*** |
| Explained % | 1.8227 | -0.7568 | 8.4421 |
| Unexplained % | 98.2082 | 100.7568 | 91.5171 |

***/ Significant at 99 % confidence

Source: Own estimates based on the 2000 Population and Housing census data.

**Table 7.7**. Blinder-Oaxaca decompositions (Monthly wages logarithm, 2010)

| | Young Americans | Young American men | Young American women |
|---|---|---|---|
| Group 1 Predictions | 8.3326*** | 8.3702*** | 8.2635*** |
| Group 2 Predictions | 8.4515*** | 8.4799*** | 8.4074*** |
| Differential | -0.1188*** | -0.1096*** | -0.1438*** |
| Endowments | 0.0522*** | 0.0653*** | 0.0245*** |
| Coefficients | -0.1287*** | -0.1267*** | -0.1395*** |
| Interaction | -0.0422*** | -0.0482*** | -0.0288*** |
| Explained | -0.0100*** | 0.0171*** | -0.0043*** |
| Unexplained | -0.1287*** | -0.1267*** | -0.1395*** |
| Explained % | -8.4175 | -15.6022 | 2.9903 |
| Unexplained % | 108.3333 | 115.6022 | 97.0097 |

***/ Significant at 99 % confidence

Source: Own estimates based on the 2000 Population and Housing census data.

### Probability models

To conclude with the analysis of the conditions of labour integration of young workers of American origin living in Mexican territory, seven different types of probabilistic equations were estimated, according to what was discussed above. The results of the probabilistic regressions are shown in table 7.8.

It is worth mentioning that while, in 2000, young Mexicans and Americans were virtually equally prone to be unemployed, by 2010 both men and women of American origin were more likely to be unemployed than their Mexican peers. This is probably the effect of the crisis. In 2015, this probability fell or was reversed.

Indeed, in 2015, underage Americans have lower probabilities of being unemployed than their Mexican peers, but those who are of legal age have higher probabilities of being unemployed, although the probabilities are lower than in 2010. This suggests that the crisis affected the unemployment probabilities of these population groups differently and that young people of legal age suffer more from the loss of their families' social capital, which affects their unemployment rates.

**Table 7.8.** Probabilities of young Americans compared to young Mexicans, by gender. Marginal effects

| | 15-19 years old | | | 20-24 years old | | | 25-29 years old | | |
|---|---|---|---|---|---|---|---|---|---|
| | Men | Women | Both | Men | Women | Both | Men | Women | Both |
| **2000** | | | | | | | | | |
| Unemployed | 0.0000 | 0.0058 | 0.0035 | 0.0095 | 0.0000 | 0.0053 | 0.0000 | 0.0000 | 0.0000 |
| Informal | 0.0446 | 0.0442 | 0.0463 | 0.0398 | 0.0715 | 0.0519 | 0.0774 | 0.1414 | 0.0998 |
| Non-remunerated | 0.0195 | 0.0260 | 0.0224 | 0.0311 | 0.0429 | 0.0347 | -0.0190 | 0.0000 | -0.0086 |
| Agricultural labour | 0.0000 | -0.0318 | 0.0000 | 0.0000 | 0.0158 | 0.0000 | -0.0576 | 0.0180 | -0.0345 |
| Construction labour | -0.0458 | 0.0038 | -0.0276 | 0.0000 | 0.0039 | 0.0076 | -0.0421 | 0.0000 | -0.0274 |
| Self-employment | 0.0000 | 0.0000 | 0.0000 | 0.0501 | 0.0292 | 0.0414 | 0.0662 | 0.0739 | 0.0689 |
| Caretaker job | -0.0046 | 0.0000 | -0.0053 | 0.0000 | -0.4492 | -0.0166 | 0.0000 | 0.0000 | 0.0000 |
| **2010** | | | | | | | | | |
| Unemployed | 0.0330 | 0.0205 | 0.0283 | 0.0513 | 0.0179 | 0.0390 | 0.0409 | -0.0297 | 0.0181 |
| Informal | 0.0547 | 0.1048 | 0.0718 | 0.1940 | 0.1020 | 0.1625 | 0.1797 | 0.1185 | 0.1495 |
| Non-remunerated | 0.0152 | 0.0072 | 0.0123 | 0.0209 | -0.0158 | 0.0113 | -0.0118 | 0.0000 | -0.0058 |
| Agricultural labour | -0.0595 | -0.0280 | -0.0491 | -0.0643 | -0.0220 | -0.0498 | -0.0258 | 0.0000 | -0.0186 |
| Construction labour | -0.0176 | -- | -0.0156 | 0.0277 | -0.0076 | 0.0134 | -0.0367 | 0.0138 | 0.0140 |
| Self-employment | -0.0247 | 0.0000 | -0.0165 | -0.0200 | 0.0478 | 0.0097 | -0.0174 | 0.0322 | 0.0065 |
| Caretaker job | -- | 0.0275 | 0.0085 | -- | 0.0062 | 0.0019 | -- | 0.0268 | 0.0092 |
| **2015** | | | | | | | | | |
| Unemployed | -0.0044 | -0.0065 | -0.0058 | 0.0243 | -0.0026 | 0.0092 | 0.0123 | 0.0027 | 0.0068 |
| Informal | -0.0100 | -0.0202 | -0.0143 | -0.0084 | -0.0203 | -0.0117 | 0.0000 | -0.0389 | -0.0189 |
| Non-remunerated | 0.0156 | 0.0171 | 0.0167 | 0.0053 | 0.0000 | 0.0041 | 0.0000 | 0.0167 | 0.0124 |
| Agricultural labour | -0.0141 | 0.0000 | -0.0102 | -0.0262 | -0.0077 | -0.0200 | -0.0208 | -0.0087 | -0.0169 |
| Construction labour | -0.0054 | 0.0000 | -0.0037 | -0.0148 | -- | -0.0109 | -0.0199 | -- | -0.0147 |
| Self-employment | -0.0214 | 0.0131 | -0.0086 | 0.0000 | 0.0273 | 0.0108 | 0.0368 | 0.0841 | 0.0567 |
| Caretaker job | 0.0358 | 0.0794 | 0.0508 | 0.0373 | 0.0490 | 0.0419 | 0.0098 | 0.0259 | 0.0170 |

Non-zero values in the table are at least significant at 95% confidence. Values that do not appear to imply that the independent variable predicted perfectly a failure.
Among the control variables we have age, age squared, schooling, position in the household and recent.
Source: Own estimates based on INEGI's censuses and intercensal survey data.

As for informality, table 7.8 shows that in 2000 and 2010, Americans had higher rates in comparison with Mexicans. In 2015, this result is reversed, which implies that the labour integration conditions of this population group have improved over time. It is interesting to observe that in the first two years of the analysis, young Americans, both men and women, have a positive and significant probability of entering the informal sector in greater proportions than young Mexicans. In 2015, this probability was reversed, as is the probability of unemployment, suggesting an interesting pattern: as wage differentials in favour of Americans fall, their working conditions improve over time. It is known that the economic crisis brought a significant return of

Mexican migrants coming from the United States. It is possible that this has normalized the presence of young people of American origin and that the productive sector is increasingly matching them with young Mexicans, who are increasingly more educated.

Regarding non-remunerated jobs, Table 8 shows that younger Americans, both men and women, are positively and significantly more likely to perform non-remunerated jobs in the three years of the analysis. This can be related to the lack of their parents' social capital, surely explained by their migratory process and their recent arrival in Mexico: It also suggests stronger family networks that allow young Americans to gain work experience through a non-remunerated job. On the other hand, American men between 25 and 29 years old have a negative and significant probability of doing non-remunerated jobs, especially in 2000 and 2010. Probably, the preferential treatment by the productive sector found in the previous section is primarily focusing on older young people.

The following three categories (agricultural labour, construction labour and self-employment) reflect jobs with precarious characteristics. It is worth mentioning that young Americans are consistently less likely than Mexicans to be inserted in the agricultural and construction sectors, although in some cases, and especially in those of older age, there are higher probabilities of becoming self-employed.

In general, the higher educational levels of American youngsters may be the reason for the above results, although it is possible that their unobservable characteristics, such as their command of the English language, make them more likely to work in the service and trade sectors. The result associated with self-employment contradicts the idea that older young Americans are the ones who benefit the most from the favourable treatment that young Americans receive in Mexico. However, the literature on migration highlights the idea that immigrants are more prone to set up businesses in the destination country (Fairlie and Lofstrom, 2015), so that higher self-employment and better quality work for older young people of American origin are not likely to represent a contradictory finding.

Finally, care work distinguishes itself as quality work, with low rotation and better conditions compared to many other occupations. This work can be done in both the informal and formal sectors. As it was expected, and especially in 2015, young Americans are inserted in a higher proportion than their Mexican counterparts in this type of jobs, which again reflects the national productive sector's favourable treatment.

## Conclusions

This chapter analysed the process of labour market integration of young Americans in Mexico, which was compared with that of young Mexicans. On the one hand, it was shown that Americans generally receive higher incomes than Mexicans, where this advantage is largely explained by their unobservable characteristics, suggesting that they receive preferential treatment in the national labour market. On the other hand, younger Americans tend to work in lower quality jobs, as they are more likely to work in the informal sector or as non-remunerated workers. This result changes over time, and in 2015 there is no longer this lower quality of work for Americans, which suggests improvements in their integration, along with the fall of the wage differential that is in their favour. Likewise, few are employed in the primary sector or in the construction industry, and a greater proportion is dedicated to services and trade. These results show an interesting pattern: as wage differentials in favour of Americans fall, their working conditions improve over time. As we have said, the economic crisis brought a significant return of Mexican migrants coming from the United States. It is possible that this has normalized the presence of young people of American origin and that the productive sector is increasingly matching them with young Mexicans, who are increasingly more educated.

Our work emphasizes that, despite the considerable increase in the number of school years observed in Mexico in recent years, the level of schooling of young Mexicans is lower than that of young Americans. Moreover, the wages of young people in Mexico, regardless of their country of birth, are lower than those of adults. Although this is partly a product of their reduced work experience, it also shows the need to build a stronger link between the knowledge and skills offered by educational institutions and those demanded and well paid in the labour market.

Further research that may complement the findings presented here includes examining in more detail the unobservable factors that explain the higher wages of young Americans, which may be picking up, for example, differences in the quality of education, levels of English language proficiency, or skills, among others. It is also essential to compare the integration process into the labour market of young Mexicans with young people from other countries, particularly those in the developing countries, or whose parents are not Mexicans. This would provide additional information on how differences in language, ethnicity, and social networks are related to integration and job performance of young immigrants. Finally, longitudinal data to analyse who are the immigrants who stay and who are those who return to their country of origin would make it possible to study possible transitions between countries, providing valuable information on the process of economic assimilation of the immigrant population in Mexico.

## References

Allensworth, E. (1997). Earnings mobility of first and "1.5" generation Mexican-origin women and men: A comparison with U.S.-born Mexican-Americans and Non-Hispanic Whites. *International Migration Review,* 31(2): 386-410.

Behtoui, A. and Olsson, E. (2014). The performance of early age migrants in education and the labour market: a comparison of Bosnia Herzegovinians, Chileans and Somalis in Sweden. *Journal of Ethnic and Migration Studies,* 40(5): 778-795.

Borjas, G. (1994). The economics of immigration. *Journal of Economic Literature*, 32(4): 1667-1717.

Butler, S., Brennan-Ing, M. and Wardamasky, S. (2014) Determinants of longer job tenure among home care aides: what makes some stay on the job while others leave? *Journal of Applied Gerontology*, 33(2): 164-188.

Calves, A.E. and Schoumaker, B. (2004). Deteriorating economic context and changing patterns of youth employment in urban Burkina Faso: 1980-2000. *World Development*, 32(8): 1341-1354.

Chiswick B. (1978). The effect of Americanization on the earnings of foreign-born men. *Journal of Political Economy*, 86(5): 897-921.

Carrasco. C. and Riesco, A. (2011). La trayectoria de inserción laboral de los jóvenes inmigrantes. *Papers. Revista de Sociologia*, 96(1): 189-203.

Chiswick, B., Lee, Y. L. and Miller, P. (2005). A longitudinal analysis of immigrant occupational mobility: A test of the immigrant assimilation hypothesis.

Cuecuecha, A., Lara, J. and Vázquez, J. (2017). La reemigración de niños estadounidenses que viven en México. *Papeles de Población*, 23(91): 93-116.

Dustmann, C. and Görlach, J.S. (2016). The economics of temporary migrations. *Journal of Economic Literature*, 54(1): 98-136.

Esser, H. (2006) Migration, language and integration. AKI Research Review 4. Berlin. Germany.

Fairlie, R. W. and Lofstrom, M. (2015). Immigration and entrepreneurship. In B. Chiswick and P. Miller (Eds.), *Handbook of the Economics of International Migration* (pp. 877-911). Amsterdam: Elsevier.

Froy, F. and Pyne, L. (2011). *Ensuring labour market success for ethnic minority and immigrant youth.* OECD Local Economic and Employment Development Working Papers No. 2011/09. Paris: OECD Publishing.

Gutierrez, E. and Giorguli, S. (2018). Children and youth in the context of international mobility patterns in Mexico. *Carta Económica Regional*, (121): 33-58.

Heckman, F. (2008). Education and the integration of migrants: Challenges for European education systems arising from immigration and strategies for the successful integration of migrant children in European schools and societies. NESSE Analytical Report 1.

Lu, Y. and Zhou, H. (2013). Academic achievement and loneliness of migrant children in China: School segregation and segmented assimilation. *Comparative Education Review*, 57(1): 85-116.

Meza, L. (2018). Dinámica de las condiciones laborales de los jóvenes en México: análisis comparativo 2000-2014. In: A. E. Latapí (Compilador), *Factores domésticos en el pronóstico de vida de los adolescentes y jóvenes de hogares de bajos ingresos en México. Enfoque multiregional y diacrónico.* México: CIESAS.

Mocanu, C. and Zamfir, A.-M. (2016). Jobs for youth–Is there a labour market for youth in Romania? *Practical Application of Science*, 4(1): 401-407.

Nilsen O. and K. Holm Reiso (2011). Scarring effects of unemployment. *Mimeo.* Norwegian School of Economics.

Orraca, P. (2019). Cross-border earnings of Mexican workers across the US-Mexico border. *Journal of Borderlands Studies*, 34(3): 451-469.

Perreira, K., Harris, K. M. and Lee, D. (2007). Immigrant youth in the labor market. *Works and Occupations*, 34(1): 5-34.

Vargas, E. and Coubès, M.L. (2017). Working and giving birth in the United States: Changing life strategies of transborder life in the north of Mexico. *Frontera Norte*, 29(57): 57-82.

Vela, F. (2007). Transición demográfica, estructura por edad y el desempleo de los jóvenes en México. *Política y Cultura*, 28: 252-280.

Weller, J. (2007). La inserción laboral de los jóvenes: características, tensiones y desafíos. *Revista de la CEPAL*, 92: 61-82.

Zúñiga, V. (2018). The 0.5 generation: What children know about international migration. *Migraciones Internacionales*, 9(3): 92-120.

# CHAPTER 8

# THE NEXUS BETWEEN THE MIGRATORY AND ACADEMIC EXPERIENCES OF YOUTH: THE CASE OF TRANSNATIONAL STUDENTS IN GUANAJUATO, MEXICO

Omar Serna Gutiérrez

The aim of this qualitative study is to present the academic and migratory experiences of four transnational high school students in the state of Guanajuato, Mexico and to align such findings with a view of transnationalism that takes into consideration deterritorialized knowledge acquired through migratory experiences. From these experiences, all transnationals acquire – to different degrees – transnational funds of knowledge and a different type of imagination which allows them to envision themselves as members of other communities. To understand the transnational experience, one must consider research into the phenomenon and into the biographies of such students as seen in the discussion of the data.

## Transnational students' experiences as knowledge

Empirical studies have brought forth that transnationals acquire from their migratory experiences sets of knowledge which are "accumulated [...] between countries" (Sanchez & Kasun, 2012, p. 75). I utilize concepts which are deeply rooted in Vygotskian sociocultural theory that include: funds of knowledge, funds of identity, funds of linguistic knowledge, and funds of cultural knowledge. I then present these concepts as an interrelated framework for understanding transnational students' knowledge.

### Funds of knowledge

In 1990, Luis Moll along with colleagues and pupils, collaborated on a project in Arizona which brought students' experiences into the classroom. As a result, the concept and approach to the teaching of funds of knowledge (Moll, Velez-Ibañez, Greenberg, & Rivera, 1990) were coined. The concept is attributed to Wolf's (1966) discussion on the household economy. Moll et al. (1990) took the concept from anthropology and adapted it to education, and they defined funds of knowledge as an "essential part of a broader set of activities, social relationships, related to the households' functioning in society" (p. 34) that are "historically accumulated and culturally developed" (Moll, Amanti, Neff, & González, 1992, p. 133). The application of the concept in education sustains that "people are competent and have the knowledge, and their life experiences have given them that knowledge" (González & Moll, 2002, p. 625). This view is a step away from the assumption that biculturalism and bilingualism are obstacles in education which are typical of deficit perspectives.

Following this definition, in the case of transnational families' funds of knowledge are sets of transnational tools which help them navigate through society and are acquired through social interaction. González, Moll, & Amanti (2005) argue that funds of knowledge can "become cultural resources for teachers as they document their [transnational students] existence and bring them to bear on their work" (p. 19). This implies that teachers must become knowledgeable of this background and incorporate it into their lessons. This is done by accessing students' homes and gathering data which in turn becomes an educational resource in the classroom.

Although a funds of knowledge approach to teaching has gained grounds among researchers and has contributed to changes in educational practices which viewed students as deficient, one of the key arguments is that such approach is based on adult household practices and knowledge (Moll, 2005; Rios-Aguilar, Kiyama, Gravitt, & Moll, 2011). Funds of knowledge are then the transnational individual's acquired survival skills and experiences based on his or her family's background. Thus, this approach relies on an adult view of knowledge and tends to leave out those which have been appropriated by individual transnational youth students. An approach which seeks to incorporate such knowledge sets is known as funds of identity.

**Funds of identity**

Funds of identity is a shift from the adult, collective knowledge to personalized sets of knowledge. It is defined as "historically accumulated, culturally developed, and socially distributed resources that are essential for people's self-definition, self-expression, and self-understanding" (Esteban-Guitart, 2014, p. 752). The first part of this definition is in line with the definition of funds of knowledge in which these are accumulated, developed, and distributed resources. Such resources become funds of identity when "people actively internalize family and community resources to make meaning and to describe themselves" (Esteban-Guitart & Moll, 2014a, p. 33). In essence, funds of identity are sets of knowledge which the individual has appropriated from his or her family's funds of knowledge. A funds of identity approach not only takes household knowledge into account but also student' interests which may benefit the classroom.

Researchers in the area have identified different types of funds of identity (see Charteris, Thomas, & Masters, 2018; Esteban-Guitart, & Moll, 2014a; 2014b; Joves, Siques, & Esteban-Guitart, 2015; Poole, 2017a; 2017b) that are classified according to their source and content. To identify funds of identity, researchers have also employed different qualitative methods (see Brito-Rivera, Subero, & Esteban-Guitart, 2018; Saubich & Esteban-Guitart, 2011; Subero, Vujasinovic, & Esteban-Guitart, 2016). From the types of funds of identity and the array of methods to identify them, this project focuses on the accumulated and acquired funds of linguistic and cultural knowledge which were discovered through semi-structured interviews. These are explained in depth in the following two sections.

### Funds of linguistic knowledge

Basing his work on Moll's et al. (1990) funds of knowledge, the concept of funds of linguistic knowledge was first coined by Smith and later applied to his studies (2001a; 2001b; 2006). Smith (2001a) defines funds of linguistic knowledge as those which "encompass what speakers know about their language(s), including how languages are learned and used" (p. 381). The author has used the concept as a tool for teachers and a resource for schools and has encompassed funds of linguistic knowledge as part of the repertoire of transnational bilingualism (Smith, 2001a, p. 433).

Studies have identified skills that transnationals possess which are a result of their transnational bilingualism, these include those such as language brokering (e.g., culture and language mediating practices which include translating and interpreting for parents and other adults) (Mora Pablo et al., 2015). These skills are often utilized to the transnational's advantage. The importance of funds of linguistic knowledge in professional decisions and the demand it has in the current Mexican context has been explored (see Mora Pablo et al., 2015; Mora Pablo et al., 2015). In addition, inquires have discovered that the linguistic needs of transnational students are not being met and, to make matters worse, they have found that English classrooms in Mexico often do not foster any new learning as the level of English of transnationals is well above mainstream students (Tacelosky, 2013).

Furthermore, research has also demonstrated that transnational bilingualism (Smith, 2001a) is often perceived from a deficit perspective which educators often have trouble interpreting. Thus, transnational bilingualism in Mexico is often seen as something negative, as it may represent a non-prestigious variety of both English and Spanish (Smith, 2006). Knowing transnational students' funds of linguistic knowledge would entail much more work in terms of diagnostics, but an awareness of these funds would aid in their academic success. Awareness of their linguistic abilities also entails acknowledging their funds of cultural knowledge.

## Funds of cultural knowledge

A sub-category of these sets of knowledge are funds of cultural knowledge in which cultural capital and social capital are covered. Cultural capital is defined as "knowledge, skills, and other cultural acquisitions, as exemplified by educational or technical qualifications" (Bourdieu, 1991, p. 14). Similarly, Colemans' (1988) concept of social capital which are the resources serving functions utilized to fulfil specific goals.

Studies which have incorporated the notion of funds of knowledge and identity into their theoretical framework have concluded that both teachers and students would benefit from such sets of knowledge (see Charteris, Thomas, & Masters, 2018; de la Piedra, 2011; Esteban-Guitart & Moll, 2014a; 2014b; Frausto Hernández, 2017; Hamann Zuñiga, & Sánchez García, 2006; Hornberger, 2007; Joves, Siques, & Esteban-Guitart, 2015; Kasun, 2014; 2015; Olmedo, 2004; Petrón, 2003; Petrón & Greybeck, 2014; Poole, 2017a; 2014b; Sánchez, 2007). Studies such as the ones previously listed have identified that transnational students bring with them varying degrees of bilingualism and biliteracy (Hamann Zuñiga, & Sánchez García, 2006; Hornberger, 2007; de la Piedra, 2011) and biculturality (Petrón, 2003; Petrón & Greybeck, 2014). For this reason, it is vital to conceptualize transnational students' knowledge sets.

## Conceptualizing transnational knowledge

Thus far, I have outlined the transformation of the concept of funds of knowledge and how it has progressed into a personalized account of transnational knowledge. I have divided funds of identity into two sub-categories which include funds of linguistic knowledge and funds of cultural knowledge. Such a distinction does not mean separation. Instead, it should imply overlap as culture and language go hand in hand.

Funds of transnational knowledge includes funds of knowledge, funds of identity, funds of linguistic knowledge, and funds of cultural knowledge. I argue that these knowledge are a result of the transnational experience. Figure 8.1 describes the interrelatedness of transnationals' knowledge.

Figure 8.1 shows how, in the case of transnational students, funds of knowledge serve as a source for collective skills and experiences. These are accumulated throughout experiences in both Mexico and the US. They are then internalized and appropriated by transnational students to form their own funds of linguistic knowledge and funds of cultural knowledge. It is with these last two that schools can capitalize on with transnational students.

**Figure 8.1.** Transnational Knowledge

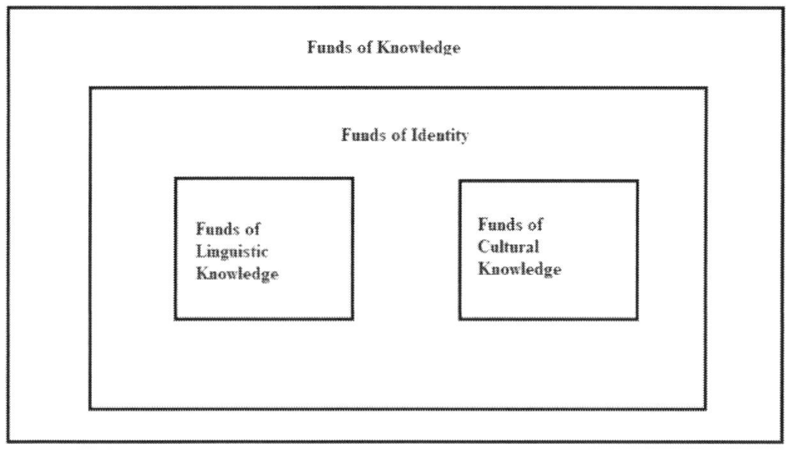


### Imagined Communities: Portrayals of National and Self Identity

Transnationalism inspires in those involved new sets of knowledge which in return, allow them to imagine themselves as members of multiple communities. In his seminal work, which was later revised, Anderson (2006) conceptualized the notion of the nation and nationalism. He theorized that these were imagined communities because "members of even the smallest nation will never know most of their fellow-members, meet them, or even hear of them, yet in the minds of each lives the image of their communion" (2006, p. 6). In his discussion, he argues that the imagination is moulded by ephemeral and temporal cultural artefacts. Imagination is defined by Wenger (1998) as a "process of expanding oneself by transcending our time and space and creating new images of the world and ourselves" (p. 176). This conception of imagined communities and imagination is helpful in understanding the national identity of transnationals as they may portray a sense of in-betweenness, but in their imaginations, they display a sense of belonging to one nation more than to another. This is further discussed in the data as the student participants speak of their futures and where they envision themselves.

### Data collection techniques

For this qualitative study, semi-structured interviews were carried out. This type of interview allows for a "co-construction of meaning regarding a topic [or theme]" (Janesick, as cited in Hernandez Sampieri, Fernandez-Collado, & Baptista Lucio, 2006, p. 597). Moreover, this allows the interviewer to provide "guidance and direction [and] elaborate on certain issues" (Dörnyei, 2007, p. 136). This flexibility allowed me to receive answers to my prepared questions and it also left space for other emergent areas that I did not expect. During the interview, participants were asked about their experiences both in the US and in Mexico regarding their education, family, academic and social aspects of their (re)integration processes.

**Context and participants**

According to Lamy (2013), Guanajuato has a 100-year history of involvement in international migration, in which the first migrants immigrated to Chicago to work on the construction of the railroad. This history has placed the State of Guanajuato within the 'traditional' region, which is comprised of Aguascalientes, Colima, Durango, Guanajuato, Jalisco, Michoacán, Nayarit, San Luis Potosi, and Zacatecas (Durand, 1998). However, contemporary socio-political and economic events have situated Guanajuato among the top five states with the most return migration (CONAPO, 2015).

This research took place at two public high schools affiliated to the University of Guanajuato. The official name of this high school is *Escuela de Nivel Medio Superior* (ENMS). From the ten campuses spread across the state, the two selected are located in the cities of San Luis de la Paz and Silao.

San Luis de la Paz is an agricultural city located in the north-eastern region of the State of Guanajuato. It has a population of 101,370 and is classified in terms of migration to the US as "high" (INEGI, 2010). This classification places the city among those with the highest numbers of immigrants in the State. The high school in San Luis de la Paz was opened in 1974 and in 2008 consisted of approximately 333 students (Programa Educativo, 2010). From this point, the high school in San Luis de la Paz will be referred to as ENMS 1.

Silao is an industrial city located in the central region of the State of Guanajuato. It has a population of 143,024 and is classified in terms of migration to the US as "medium" (INEGI, 2010). The ENMS in Silao was opened in 1975 and in 2008 consisted of approximately 618 students (Programa Educativo, 2010). The high school located in this city will be referred to as ENMS 2.

A total of four students were selected to participate in this study: Juanita, Norma, Carmen, and Janet. As shown below, all of the participants were young women. This is coincidental as initially two males were interviewed but opted out of the study. Table 8.1 describes their demographic information.

**Table 8.1.** Participant's demographic information

| Pseudonym | Location | Age | Hometown | Semester |
|---|---|---|---|---|
| Juanita | ENMS 1 | 16 | San Luis de la Paz | 3rd |
| Norma | ENMS 1 | 19 | Doctor Mora | 5th |
| Carmen | ENMS 2 | 16 | Silao | 3rd |
| Janet | ENMS 2 | 16 | Silao | 3rd |

### Transnational academic and migratory trajectories

As part of their migratory experiences, transnational youth display unique academic trajectories which can be described in terms of their movement between two nations and education systems. Below, the profile of each participant is presented to highlight their particularities. Each profile consists of the participants' migratory and academic experiences.

### Norma

Norma was born in Doctor Mora, Guanajuato. At the time of the interview, she was 19 years old and in the 5th semester of high school at the ENMS 1. Typically, students in the fifth semester are between the ages of 17 and 18; however, she was 19 because she did not attend one school year in the US.

When her family, consisting of her mother, father, brothers and sisters, emigrated to the US, she had not yet been in school in Mexico. She and her family spent a total of seven years in Tucson, Arizona and she studied until third grade in the US. Throughout these seven years, they were deported three times because they did not possess the necessary legal documents to remain in the country. She stated that each time they were deported, they returned and settled once again as a family. For a child, these types of experiences can be traumatic and will undoubtedly shape their beliefs and imagined selves.

When asked about her experience in US schools, Norma mentioned her age as a positive factor in her socialization and language barriers in academics. As already mentioned, Norma had not yet attended school in Mexico, and her first experience in academic settings was in the US. She recalls that because of her age, she did not encounter many problems adapting to a new school. One could say that her experience paralleled with her peers as school was also new for most of them.

Perhaps a major difference in Norma's socialization, when compared to her peers, is that of linguistic differences. In the interview, she recalled how she and her friend resolved issues with communication:

> They would help me, and I would try to make myself understood. We

would help each other. (Norma)

Although not mentioned by Norma, it can be understood that she and her friend employed communication strategies, either linguistic or paralinguistic, and they relied on each other through scaffolding. Despite being successful in communicating with her friends, her status as an emerging bilingual had an impact on academics.

> In my first year at elementary school, I did not understand much. It was then that they changed my teacher to one that spoke both languages. She really helped me a lot. [...] I remember very little of her, but she was very kind to me and always helped me and explained activities to me. (Norma)

Two issues raised in the quote above. First, Norma's linguistic abilities were not fully diagnosed; therefore, she had been placed in a regular classroom with proficient or native English speakers. Second, perhaps an area that the Mexican education system could learn from is that her linguistic abilities were catered for and she was placed with a bilingual teacher. For transnational students enrolled in the public education system, it is common that the only exposure to the English language that they receive is in general English classes. The problem with this is that these classes are often mixed-level and are well below transnational students' linguistic needs.

Norma's stay in the US lasted until she was in third grade of elementary school. After several deportations that she and her family experienced, her family decided to return to Mexico for family reasons. The reasons for return among migrants vary from legal matters to family issues, among others. In Norma's case, an older brother encountered some problems in the US and returned on his own to Mexico. In Mexico, he suffered an accident that caused a great commotion among his family. When asked why she and her family returned, she replied:

> They were family reasons. My brother had returned before because he had some problems there [US], so he returned to Mexico for a year. Then, he had an accident, and my mom became worried, and we all had to return. Because we were all older, it was not easy to adapt to Mexico. (Norma)

As a result of her brother's accident, her family opted to return to Mexico. The decision was made due to her mother's concern. This represents the role of her mother in the family as an active decision-maker. Her mother's role contradicts the role which women typically play in transnational families (Boehm, 2012). Traditionally, this role was portrayed as women being the ones who cared for the home and children while male members were involved in decision making regarding family matters.

Upon her return to Mexico, Norma was confronted with a new school which involves not only a different physical setting, but also different norms, expectations, and language. Among these new norms is that of enrollment. In Mexico, students must enroll months before the first day of class to ensure their place. However, Norma's family knew someone at the school:

> [...] the lady who was in charge of the office was my father's relative, and I believe that had a lot of influence because we arrived one day, and we went to the elementary school, and they talked to her [the relative], and that same day they left me there. I was not even prepared. (Norma)

Having a relative in charge of the admissions facilitated her enrollment. In the interview, she sounded surprised and stated that she "did not have a pencil on her" at that time. Her experience brings forth common practices which may not be fair for others. Although her enrollment process was easier than others, she still faced other challenges. One such challenge involved, once again, was language. When asked what her greatest challenge was when returning to Mexico, Norma replied:

> School, because I was reading and writing in English and it [returning] was something sudden that we had to return and I did not know much – well I knew Spanish, but I could not communicate much, and I did not know how to read and write Spanish. So, I struggled in elementary school. (Norma)

In Norma's transnational profile, it is revealed that she and her family remained together through her transnational experience and even returned permanently because of a family matter. Throughout her profile, family plays a crucial role. She also seems to be following her sister's transnational academic trajectory as well. In the interview, she mentioned that she wishes to remain in Mexico to study at the same university as her older sister. Her mother and sister have reinforced Norma's imagined self as a student in Mexico.

Norma's transnational profile reflects migration trends which exemplify the shift from the head of the family (e.g., male figure, typically the father) only migration to entire families sojourning. Moreover, it demonstrates the changes in roles regarding gender and decision making among transnational families, and it also reflects the importance of family as they all returned to Mexico when a member of the family was in trouble. In summary, her family's reasons for return were both political and familial (King, 2000).

### Juanita

When interviewed, Juanita was sixteen years old and lived and studied in San Luis de la Paz. She was a third semester student at the ENMS 1. She was born in the US and studied and lived in the US during multiple time periods while also keeping contact with Mexico. Although Juanita was born in Arcadia, Florida, she claims her a nationality as the following:

> I am Mexican. I was born in Florida, but I have lived all my life here [Mexico], I am the daughter of Mexican parents. (Juanita).

As stated above, Juanita was born in the US and has lived most of her life in Mexico. For her, nationality is based on two factors; the amount of time lived in Mexico and her parents' nationality. This excerpt highlights her affiliation to a nation and its relationship with family and heritage. Perhaps, this is due to her short stays in the US:

> From the point I was born, I was there at different times. I was there three years, and we returned, and when I was six years old, we returned [to the US]. After that, we returned to Mexico. (Juanita).

The second time she returned, she lived in Palestine, Texas for less than a year. During this stay, she lived with an aunt, her mother and siblings. Her mother's migratory status contrasts with the norm, as it were her mother who possessed legal documents and her father, who remained in Mexico due to his migratory status. However, when asked why she returned, she placed the load of the decision on her father:

> Well, it was only my siblings and I that left [to the US], and my father stayed here [Mexico]. It was he who said, "Go, and study English", and we left. However, I think that he couldn't be without us. Right away, he said, "come back". I did not want to come back because I had been there for half a year and I had adapted. I had liked it there, and I wanted to learn English. I came back forcefully. It was because of my father that we returned; if not, we had only returned on vacations. (Juanita).

The above represents the weight of decisions from adults which may often not coincide with the desires of children (Boehm, 2012). It is clear that Juanita's desire was to remain in the US and continue learning English. Her reaction to her father's resolution was not pleasant:

> I cried; I acted rude with my father. There were times when I did not want to answer [the phone] because I knew he would say "come back". I would tell him "I do not want to go" because I want to learn English and I had liked it there. (Juanita)

The excerpt above shows that Juanita wanted to be a member of two imagined communities, one of English learners and the other of nation state membership in the US. After her father's request, her siblings dropped out of school leaving her still enrolled. Her father suggested that she could stay if her older brother also stayed to look after her.

Although she and her brother are close in age, he did not want to remain in the US. From Juanita's experience, the role of children and specifically women in most traditional Mexican families is portrayed (Boehm, 2012; Lamy, 2013; Romo & Mogollon-Lopez, 2016; van Dijk Kocherthaler, 2013). Her father chose to send them to the US, and it was he who decided that they must return. Within her family, the role of male members is portrayed as that of decision makers and guardians. In addition, Juanita's brother's choice of not to remain in the US reflects what King (2000) and Durand (2004) call voluntary return due to difficulties adapting to the host country.

Interestingly enough, Juanita's transnational profile consists of many contradictions which reflects how we, as people often view the world around us. Juanita's membership of imagined communities seems to be divided and demonstrates an in-betweenness. In the first excerpt, she describes herself as Mexican; however, she also asserts that it "feels horrible to be from there" – referring to the U.S – and not know the language. Not knowing English can be attributed to her constant movement between two educational settings in which she spent most of the time in Mexico and as she claims had little contact with English.

> I really do not dominate the language [English]. I really did not speak Spanish well over there [US] and we returned to Mexico [...] then I did not practice English here. I understand it [...] I also practiced it with my father but not that much and it was not the same [...] and in school, it is as if we did not take the class [English] and it is until now that I am learning in school, but I do not know much. (Juanita)

As in Norma's case, Juanita faced linguistic challenges. With Norma, these seemed to affect her in academics, but with Juanita, these had an impact on her identity.

**Carmen**

Carmen was sixteen years old and at the time of the interview, she was a third semester student at the ENMS 2. Her father had been in the US before her immediate family settled there. She was born in Chicago, Illinois and resided there for ten years before she moved to Mexico for the first time.

For Carmen's family, the year 2010 was a not a memorable year as the foreclosure crisis hit the US. This economic crisis affected not only the country's economic stability but also the lives of homeowners and their families. Carmen attributes her family's return to the crisis:

> One of the motives behind our return was that we had been renting a house in Carpentersville. [...] Rent had gone up way too much, I believe that it was a period of crisis that the United States suffered. So, my parents decided to return here to Mexico because my father had his own house. (Carmen)

Although Carmen's family did not own a house in the US, they had their own house in Mexico. From the previous statement, it is implicit that this house was the product of remittances which had been invested in purchasing or building the house. Above, Carmen states the principal reasons for their return. The 2010 foreclosure crisis also affected her father's job:

> My father's job was declining. We did not have much money for school, taxes, and everything was becoming complicated. (Carmen)

The way which Carmen understands and describes these situations reveals the impact they had in her life. She was ten years old and had finished elementary school when these events happened. Her family's motives for returning relate to King's (2000) economic category.

Despite the 2010 economic crisis, her father remained in the US – this time in Texas. Although her family returned to Mexico, they still rely on the remittances sent by her father. Her experience demonstrates the effects of the 2010 economic crisis in the US and the impact it had on many families. Such factors may be considered as socio-economic and political which affect migrant families (Boehm, 2012; Fitzgerald, 2009; Lamy, 2013; Romo & Mogollon-Lopez, 2016).

In the US, Carmen attended a transitional bilingual elementary school. She mentioned that Spanish was spoken at first and second grades and once students reached third and fourth grades, little or no Spanish was spoken. Although this type of education may have its benefits for monolingual education, for bilingual students, it may be detrimental because while they are gaining one language, they face the possibility of losing the other. In Carmen's case, the effects of language shift may be seen when inserted into the Mexican educational system:

> there were some words that I thought meant something, but did not, […] they came in textbooks. […] Now they are easier because I understand them, but before I would confuse them and say, "What is this?" (Carmen)

In the previous excerpt, Carmen describes a gap in her linguistic knowledge that made it difficult to understand textbooks. She later discussed how her family paid for a private tutor to help her with the Spanish language and other content areas. Now, after receiving help from tutors, she describes her school in Mexico as:

> To be honest, it is a very good school. I have learned many things and they have helped me a lot. (Carmen)

Carmen's migratory experience is an example of how socio-economic factors have influenced transnational youth's academic trajectories. Her case also demonstrates how assimilationist approaches to the integration of youth may have negative effects on their level of bilingualism.

### Janet

Janet was sixteen years old student at the ENMS Silao. She was born in Los

Angeles, CA, where she lived for the first three years of her life. Her entire family then returned to Mexico. She studied kindergarten and elementary school in Mexico. When she finished elementary school (between 13 or 14 years old), her father encouraged her to go to the US, so that she could study middle and high school. She recalls her family's plan:

> [It] was to stay there all of middle school, finish high school and return to Mexico to study university. (Janet)

It is interesting to see that her parents' plans for her were to study basic education in the US and then continue with higher education in Mexico. A possible reason for such is that her parents saw the importance of her daughter learning or consolidating a second language as this would help her in the Mexican context. Her parents noticed that investing (Darvin & Norton, 2015; Norton Pierce, 1995; Norton & Gao, 2008) in the language would probably give her an upper hand at obtaining a better education or employment.

During this period, she lived with an aunt in Palmer – a town near Dallas, TX. She received financial support from her parents in Mexico. However, the expenses of her living in the US became too much of a burden on her family, as she states below:

> My father had problems supporting me economically over there [US]. (Janet)

At that time, she was thirteen years old. She recalls that she was unaware of her parents' plans to ask her to return to Mexico. It was not until Christmas break when she went to Mexico to spend the holiday that she found out.

> I was angry with my father. He had asked me if I wanted to return [to the US], and I had said "yes" because I had really liked it there. Then he told me "I cannot continue supporting you over there". (Janet)

Janet's forced return by her father parallels with Juanita's, presented above. She recalls feeling upset because she felt that her plans had been changed by her father. She was able to only spend four months in the US, and her return to Mexico seems to have evoked emotions other than anger.

> I could not go back again. I had just come here to spend Christmas with my family, and then I would return. The most difficult part was staying here because I wanted to return. (Janet)

She explains that the most difficult part of remaining in Mexico was that she could not return to the US on her own. The excerpt above shows her frustration of not being able to have a say in the situation. This change also brought fear:

> I was afraid to go to middle school here again. To introduce myself once again and to make new friends, leaving behind the friends I had made there [US]. (Janet)

She states having felt fear of making new friends and enrolling at a new school. She was also concerned with leaving behind the social network she had built in Texas. Janet's emotional return to Mexico reflects the lack of agency children have among transnational families (Boehm, 2012; Hamann, Zuñiga, & Sanchez-Garcia, 2006). She portrays her father as being the main source of support for her and does not mention her mother in the decision-making process.

**Discussion and conclusion**

From the semi-structured interviews, the transnational experiences of the participants demonstrated variety, but also many similitudes. One thing in common is that these experiences were not something they had planned, but rather it was their parents' decision to immigrate to the US to live the "American dream" or to return to Mexico. This influenced their world knowledge, their linguistic knowledge, and their academic trajectories.

Their migratory experiences are also aligned with Mexico-US migration trends. The participants all lived in states known for their high numbers in migrants, either documented or undocumented. The states that the participants mentioned were: Arizona, California, Florida, Illinois, and Texas. According to the Pew Research Center, these states are within the top ten receiving states of both documented and undocumented Mexican migrants (Passel & Cohn, 2014; Passel & Suro, 2005).

Gender, age, and family were dominating themes among the participants' transnational trajectories. In regard to gender, the roles of both male and female parents were portrayed in the transnational profiles of the student participants. In Norma and Juanita's profiles, their mothers were stakeholders in the choices made regarding their families' migration. In contrast, Carmen and Janet displayed a traditionalistic trend in migrant families in which the father is the decision maker. Also, it is interesting to note that all the participants were young women who had migrated alone or with family to the US. Their age also contributes to the new trends of transnational migration in which a younger population is involved in such a process. Finally, family was a centerpiece of the discussion, as most of the decisions revolved around family.

A difference among their experiences is the amount of years spent in the US. Carmen was the participant who spent the most time in the US- ten years, and Janet spent the least amount of years- three years and four months. This also signifies that the amount of time spent in the US educational system varies. Janet, for example, only spent four months in a US school. However, this does not mean that her experience is less valid than the rest. It simply serves to demonstrate the complexities of transnational academic trajectories.

Snapshots of translational youth's migratory and academic trajectories provided in this study demonstrate how children often lack agency in these processes. Their experiences show how transnational youth of Mexican descent navigate through two educational systems often designed under monolingual and monocultural norms and expectations. These systems see transnational bilingualism from a deficit perspective and view it as intrusive. However, what the stories of these participants call for is for an inclusive system which incorporates their linguistic and cultural knowledge. This would involve cooperation from the community and policy makers as well as teachers and administrators in schools. In Mexico, this is not an easy task as these students frequently go unnoticed.

## References

Anderson, B. (2006). Imagined communities: Reflections of origin and spread of nationalism. London, UK: Verso.

Boehm, D. A. (2012). Intimate migrations: Gender, family, and illegality among transnational Mexicans. New York, NY: New York University Press.

Bourdieu, P. (1991). Language and symbolic power. (G. Raymond & M. Adamson, Trans.). Cambridge, UK: Polity Press.

Brito-Rivera, L. F., Subero Tomas, D., & Esteban-Guitart, M. (2018). Fondos de conocimiento e identidad: Una vía sociocultural de continuidad educativa. Revista Educación, 42(1). doi: 10.15517/revedu.v42i1.23470.

Charteris, J., Thomas, E., & Masters, Y. (2018). Funds of identity in education: Acknowledging the life experiences of first year tertiary students. The Teacher Educator, 53(1), 6-20. doi: 10.1080/08878730.2017.1367057.

Coleman, J. S. (1988). Social capital in the creation of human capital. American Journal of Sociology, 94, 95-120. Retrieved from http://www.jstor.org/stable/2780243.

Consejo Nacional de la Población (CONAPO). (2015). *El retorno en el nuevo escenario de la migración entre México y Estados Unidos*. Mexico City, Mexico: Author.

Darvin, R., & Norton, B. (2015). Identity and a model of investment in applied linguistics. *Annual Review of Applied Linguistics, 25*, 36-56. doi: 10.1017/S0267190514000191.

de la Piedra, M. T. (2011). Tanto necesitamos de aquí como necesitamos de allá: Leer juntas among Mexican transnational mothers and daughters. Language and Education, 25(1), 65-78. doi: 10.1080/09500782.2010.535905.

Dörnyei, Z. (2007). Research methods in applied linguistics: Quantitative, qualitative, and mixed methodologies. Oxford, UK: Oxford University Press.

Durand, J. (1998). Nuevas regiones migratorias. In R. M. Zenteno (Ed.). *Población, desarrollo y globalización, V Reunión de Investigación Socio-Demográfica en México* (pp. 101-115). Mexico City, Mexico: El Colegio de la Frontera.

Durand, J. (2004). Ensayo teórico sobre la migración de retorno. El principio del rendimiento decreciente. *Cuadernos Geográficos, 35*(2), *103-116*.

Esteban-Guitart, M. (2014). Funds of identity. In T. Teo (Ed.), The Encyclopedia of Critical Psychology (pp. 752-757). New York, NY: Springer. doi: 10.1007/978-1-4614-5583-7_576.

Esteban-Guitart, M., & Moll, L. C. (2014a). Funds of identity: A new concept based on the funds of knowledge approach. Culture & Psychology, 20(1), 31-48. doi: 10.1177/1354067X13515934.

Esteban-Guitart, M., & Moll, L. C. (2014b). Lived experience, funds of identity and education. Culture & Psychology, 20(1), 70-81. doi: 10.1177/1354067X13515940.

Fitzgerald, D. (2009). *A nation of emigrants: How Mexico manages its migration.* Los Angeles, CA: University of California Press.

Frausto Hernández, I. (2017). Exploring transnationals and the borderlands: An interview with Mary Petron. MEXTESOL Journal, 41(3), 1-6. Retrieved from http://www.academiajournals.com/exploratoris/.

González, N., & Moll, L. C. (2002). Cruzando la frontera: Building bridges to funds of knowledge. Educational Policy, 16(4), 623-641. doi: 10.1177/0895904802016004009.

González, N., Moll, L. C., & Amanti, C. (2005). Funds of knowledge: Theorizing practices in households, communities, and classrooms. Mahwah, NJ: Lawrence Erlbaum.

Hamann, E. T., Zuñiga, V., & Sanchez-Garcia, J. (2006). Pensando en Cynthia y su hermana: Educational implications of United States-Mexico transnationalism for children. *Journal of Latinos and Education, 5*(4), 253-274. doi: 10.1207/s1532771xjle0504_3.

Hornberger, N. H. (2007). Biliteracy, transnationalism, multimodality, and identity: Trajectories across time and space. Linguistic Education, 18, 325-334. doi: 10.1016/j.linged.2007.10.001.

Instituto Nacional de Estadística y Geografía (INEGI). (2010). *Encuesta nacional de la dinámica demográfica (ENADID).* Mexico City, Mexico: Author.

Joves, P., Siques, C., & Esteban-Guitart, M. (2015). The incorporation of funds of knowledge and funds of identity of students and their families into educational practices. A case study from Catalonia, Spain. Teaching and Teacher Education, 49, 68-77. doi: 10.1016/j.tate.2015.03.001.

Kasun, G. S. (2014). Hidden knowing of working-class transnational Mexican families in schools: Bridge-building, Neplantlera knowers. Ethnography and Education, 9(3), 313-327. doi: 10.1080/17457823.2014.911664.

Kasun, G. S. (2015). The only Mexican in the room: Sobrevivencia as a way of knowing for Mexican transnational students and families. Anthropology & Education Quarterly, 46(3), 277-294. doi: 10.1111/aeq.12107

King, R. (2000). Generalizations from the history of return migration. In United Nations (Ed.) *Return migration: Journey of hope or despair?* (pp. 7-55). Geneva, Switzerland: United Nations, IOM.

Lamy, B. (2013). "¡Yo ya estuve en Estados Unidos!": Las consecuencias socioculturales de la migración. Caso del municipio de Ocampo, Guanajuato. In B. Lamy (Ed.), *Impactos socioculturales de la migración* (pp. 95-128). Mexico City, Mexico: Miguel Ángel Porrúa.

Moll, L. (2005). Reflection and possibilities. In N. González, L. C. Moll, & C. Amanti (Eds.), Funds of knowledge: Theorizing practices in households, communities and classrooms (pp. 275-287). New Jersey, NJ: Lawrence Erlbaum.

Moll, L. C., Amanti, C., Neff, D., & González, N. (1992). Funds of knowledge for teaching: Using a qualitative approach to connect homes and classrooms. Theory into Practice, 31(2), 132-141.

Moll, L. C., Velez-Ibañez, C., Greenberg, J., & Rivera, C. (1990). Community knowledge and classroom practice: Combining resources for literacy instruction. Tucson, AR: The University of Arizona.

Mora Pablo, I., Lengeling, M. M., & Basurto Santos, N. M. (2015). Crossing borders: Stories of transnationals becoming English language teachers in Mexico. *SIGNUM: Estudos da Linguagem, Londrina, 18*(2), 326-348. doi: 10.5433/2237-4876.2015v18n2p326.

Mora Pablo, I., Lengeling, M. M., Crawford, T., & Goodwin, D. (2015). La influencia de la familia en las decisiones profesionales de los migrantes de retorno. Academia Journals, November, 3856-3860.

Mora Pablo, I., Rivas Rivas, L., Lengeling, M., & Crawford, T. (2015). Transnationals becoming English teachers in Mexico: Effects of language brokering and identity formation. *Gist: Education and Learning Research Journal, 1*(10), 7-28.

Norton, B., & Gao, Y. (2008). Identity, investment, and Chinese learners of English. *Journal of Asian Pacific Communication, 18*(1), 109-120. doi 10.1075/japc.18.1.07nor.

Norton Pierce, B. (1995). Social identity, investment, and language learning. *TESOL Quarterly, 29*(1), 9-31.

Olmedo, I. M. (2004). Raising transnational issues in a multicultural curriculum project. Urban Education, 39(3), 241-265. doi: 10.1177/0042085904263061.

Passel, J. S., & Cohn, D. (2014). Unauthorized immigrant totals rise in 7 states, fall in 14: Decline in those from Mexico fuels most state decreases. Washington, D.C.: Pew Hispanic Research Center.

Passel, J. S., & Suro, R. (2005). *Rise, peak, and decline: Trends in U.S. immigration 1992-2004.* Washington, D.C.: Pew Hispanic Research Center.

Petrón, M. A. (2003). *I'm bien pocha: Transnational teachers of English in Mexico.* Retrieved from Dissertation Abstracts International.

Petrón, M. A., & Greybeck, B. (2014). Borderlands epistemologies and the transnational experience. *Gist Education and Learning Research Journal, 8*(1), 137-155.

Poole, A. (2017a). "I want to be a furious leopard with magical wings and super power": Developing an ethico-interpretive framework for detecting Chinese students' funds of identity. Cogent Education, 4, 1-20. doi: 10.1080/2331186X.2017.1316915.

Poole, A. (2017b). Funds of knowledge 2.0: Towards digital funds of identity. Learning, Culture and Social Interaction. doi: 10.1016/j.lcsi.2017.02.002.

Programa Educativo. (2010). Plan educativo 2010. Retrieved from http://www.enms-guanajuato.ugto.mx/.

Rios-Aguilar, C., Kiyama, J. M., Gravitt, M., & Moll, L. C. (2011). Funds of knowledge for the poor and forms of capital for the rich? A capital approach to examining funds of knowledge. Theory and Research in Education, 9(2), 163–184. doi: 10.1177/1477878511409776.

Romo, H. D., & Mogollon-Lopez, O. (2016). The role of elite women immigrants in maintaining language and Mexican identity. In H. D. Romo & O. Mogollon-Lopez (Eds.), *Mexican migration to the United States: Perspectives from both sides of the border* (pp. 184-211). Austin, TX: University of Texas Press.

Sanchez, P., & Kasun, G. S. (2012). Connecting transnationalism to the classroom and to theories of immigrant student adaptation. Berkeley Review of Education, 3(1), 71-93. Retrieved from: http://escholarship.org/uc/ucbgse_bre.

Saubich, X., & Esteban-Guitart, M. (2011). Bringing funds of family knowledge to school. The Living Morocco Project. Multidisciplinary Journal of Education Research, 1(1), 79-103. doi: 10.4452/remie.2011.04.

Serna Gutiérrez, J. I. O., & Mora-Pablo, I. (2017). Relatos de alumnos migrantes de retorno: Percepciones de inserción a los sistemas educativos de México y Estados Unidos. *Academia Journals, 9*(6), 6282-6286.

Smith, P. H. (2001a). Community language resources in dual language schooling. Bilingual Research Journal, 25(3), 375-404. doi: 10.1080/15235882.2001.10162799.

Smith, P. H. (2001b). Tendencias en el desarrollo de la planificación lingüística. MEXTESOL Journal, 25(1), 75-86.

Smith, P. H. (2006). Transnacionalismo, bilingüismo y planificación del lenguaje en contextos educativos mexicanos. In T. Roland & L. García Landa (Eds.). Los retos de la planificación del lenguaje en el siglo XXI (pp. 419-441). Mexico City, Mexico: Universidad Nacional Autónoma de México.

Subero, D., Vujasinovic, E., & Esteban-Guitart, M. (2016). Mobilising funds of identity in and out of school. Cambridge Journal of Education, 1, 1-17. doi: 10.1080/0305764X.2016.1148116.

Tacelosky, K. (2013). Community-based service-learning as a way to meet the linguistic needs of transnational students in Mexico. *Hispania, 96*(2), 328-341.

van Dijk Kocherthaler, S. C. (2013). Imaginarios sociales y personales de niños, niñas y adolescentes con y sin experiencias migratorias, que crecen en contextos altamente migratorios, en comunidades rurales y suburbanas del Estado de Guanajuato. In B. Lamy (Ed.), *Impactos socioculturales de la migración* (pp.65-93). Mexico City, Mexico: Miguel Ángel Porrúa.

Wenger, E. (1998). Communities of practice: Learning, meaning, and identity. Cambridge, UK: Cambridge University Press.

Wolf, E. R. (1966). Peasants. Englewood Cliffs, NJ: Prentice Hall.

# CHAPTER 9

# 'I AM PROUD AS A POLISH WOMAN, BUT I WOULD LIKE TO CHANGE MY 'NACIONALIDAD' – A CASE STUDY OF ACCULTURATION GAP BETWEEN POLISH TEENAGER LIVING IN SPAIN AND HER MOTHER

Paulina Szydłowska, Marisol Navas, Weronika Kałwak and Halina Grzymała-Moszczyńska

The group of Polish immigrants in Spain is relatively small – around 52.000 Polish people are living in Spain, including about 9.000 children and adolescents (INE, 2018). According to The Centre for the Development of Polish Education Abroad (2019) there are 24 Polish Saturday schools, where Polish children learn the language and study Polish culture during their school-free time. Polish masses are provided by some churches, as well as there are Polish associations (e.g., Ambar, Aguila Blanca or Krakus) that make up the visibility of attempts to maintain their own culture by this minority group. These actions constitute a part of an effort to acculturate in Spain by Polish migrants. The aim of this paper is to identify and describe what kind of behaviours and experiences of Polish migrants may be interpreted as a part of their specific perceptions and preferences of acculturation. Furthermore, it is interesting how, within families of migrants, do the perceptions and preferences of acculturation of parents and children interact with each other in different life areas (peripheral and central)?

To answer these questions, the case study of an adolescent girl and her mother was carried out. A case study methodological approach was implemented, since it allows to study deeply the phenomenon at hand and to take its contexts into account, on the way of using various perspectives and methods of data collection. Here, semi-structured individual interviews were conducted with a teenager and her mom. The interview guides were based on the Relative Acculturation Extended Model (RAEM) theoretical frame (Navas et. al. 2005). Finally, qualitative data from interviews and field notes were analyzed with a method of template analysis (Langridge, 2007), based on Interpretative Phenomenological Analysis (*IPA*, Pietkiewicz & Smith, 2014).

This chapter starts with a brief history of acculturation models, then it turns to describe the developmental context of acculturation. Next, the choice of methodological approach in the study is discussed and procedures presented. It ends with results – description and interpretation of the data. In the subsequent part, descriptions of teenager's and her mother's experiences are interpreted as specific perceptions (strategies) and preferences (attitudes) of acculturation using the frame of RAEM (Navas et al., 2005). In the conclusions, the limitations of the study and cues for further research are described.

**A brief history of acculturation models**

The rich acculturation research history begins with anthropological definitions created by Redfield, Linton and Herskovits (1936), according to which acculturation means the changes occurring as a result of intergroup contact. On that level, theories defined acculturation as a one-dimensional process (Gordon, 1964). Later on, Graves (1967) as the first author saw changes on the individual level as a result of contact with another culture. Berry's (1980) orthogonal model (based on the maintenance - or not - of the culture of origin, and the contact, or lack of contact, with host culture) divides acculturation strategies into integration, assimilation, separation and marginalization. As one of the most influential models, it serves as a basis for other, more complex models (e.g., Bourhis, Moïse, Perreault, & Senécal, 1997; Piontkowski, Florack, Hoelker, & Obdrzálek, 2000). A model that seems to deserve special attention here is the Relative Acculturation Extended Model (Navas et al., 2005), founded in the ethnically diverse Spanish context (especially Almeria, south of Spain). The purpose to develop such a model was to understand the inter-group relations in this region and design social interventions tailored to the needs of the local community (Navas & Rojas, 2010). RAEM is very complex but also flexible, which makes it helpful in covering various aspects of the acculturation process. It seems to be suitable for implementing the research of acculturation within the adolescent group because of several reasons:

- RAEM incorporates the strategies introduced by Berry – assimilation, integration, separation and marginalization – but, according to the model, life can be divided into peripheral and central areas. RAEM considers values, religion, family relations and social relations as central areas and economic, work, social welfare and politics as peripheral areas.

- RAEM was adapted to children and adolescents (López-Rodríguez et al., 2014; Mancini & Bottura, 2014). Adaptation of the model for adolescent's group considers values, religion, and family as central areas, and social relations, economy and school as peripheral areas. The social relations are on the border of central and peripheral areas of life.

- RAEM considers both the immigrants' and the host group's perspective and shows how do they interact with each other.

- According to RAEM, in each area, people can perceive (the strategies implemented by immigrants or perceived by the natives) and prefer (acculturation attitudes that both groups would prefer if they could choose) different acculturation options (integration, assimilation, separation and marginalization). They can, for example, perceive separation in one area (e.g., family) and assimilation in another one (e.g., work) and, at the same time, prefer assimilation in one area (e.g., work) and integration in another one (e.g., social relations).

- When using RAEM, researchers consider classic psychosocial variables in the field of intergroup relationships (such as intergroup attitudes, ingroup favouritism, perceived cultural enrichment, etc.) (e.g. Piontkowski et al., 2000). Usually, both with adolescents and with adults' model is implemented in quantitative approach (Cuadrado et al., 2018; López-Rodríguez et al., 2014; Navas et al., 2004, 2005; Navas & Rojas, 2010).
- Several studies with the use of RAEM in qualitative approach help to understand what do those strategies mean for participants of those studies (e.g., Pumares, Navas, & Sánchez, 2007).

**Why is it important to research acculturation in a group of adolescents and children?**

The phenomenon of acculturation is processual, and this process – involving individuals as well as families and groups – is strongly dependent on the natural context in which it occurs. Researchers claim that the process of cultural adaptation should be studied in the context of the development of the individual, not as a separate process (Sam & Oppedal, 2003), due to the fact that the child is functioning between two worlds: the world of the ethnic group 'at home' and the world of social majority group, that is, people from the country of settlement. Sam and Oppedal (2003) claim that acculturative changes can have an adaptive function as they serve to allow an adolescent growing up in the middle of multiple cultures. The beginning of the adolescence stage of development is set in literature at the age of 10-12 (Brzezińska, Appelt, & Ziółkowska, 2016). At this time, adolescents are going through a life span phase that is critical to personal and social identity development (Erikson, 1968; Marcia, 1980). This phase involves many tasks, like achieving emotional independence from parents, fulfilling the need for autonomy, and achieving personal independence (Brzezińska et al., 2016; Havighurst, 1981). Acculturation process, when it occurs simultaneously in this period, it may be an additional challenge for adolescents. At the same time, a question arises on inter-relations between the process of acculturation and life span phase specific challenges.

Moreover, when talking about children, the family context has to be taken into consideration since a child or adolescent still depends on his/her parents for most of the time. Berry et al. (2006) indicate that the challenges faced by migrant families include socialization of children living in the country of parents' emigration to the value of the parents' country of origin and country of emigration. Berry (1997) emphasizes that the greater the differences between these values, the more they can intensify the *intergenerational conflict* and result in greater stress during the cultural adaptation process. An additional factor strengthening the generational conflict may be the differences in the 'strategies' of cultural adaptation of parents and children (*acculturation gap*). In families where children are oriented towards adopting a new culture in the context of identity, attitudes and behaviour, but at the same time parents have expectations related to strategies of acculturation of separation, the intergenerational conflict intensifies (Berry et al., 2006). Kennedy's and MacNeela's (2014) meta-analysis of qualitative research of acculturation of youth adolescents shows similar paths. They claim that the family network, and parents, in particular, represent a strong link to the heritage culture, and often express traditional attitudes that are potentially incompatible with host culture expectations for personal independence of an adolescent. Children exist between expectations of parents, mostly based on the culture of the country of origin, and peer group, which partly represents the host culture.

Moreover, the meta-analysis points out that across the studies, adolescents described a distance between themselves and their host culture peers. They claim that it was attributed to conflicting values and differences in access to social capital, maintained by the motivation to preserve a strong in-group identity and intergroup boundaries. This result depended on competence in the host country's language, which is supposed to be one of the factors responsible for permeability of group boundaries. It can be assumed that the child or adolescent exists amid an acculturation gap between parents and him/her, but at the same time, she/he experiments conflict of values between 'home adopted values' and host peer group values.

Furthermore, research implemented by Berry et al. (2006) shows that, within adolescent immigrants living all over the world, preservation of one's own culture is a factor related to psychological adaptation. So probably children who report integration and separation strategies have better psychological adaptation. Alegria (2009) recalls unpublished data (Tamaki, Takeuchi, & Alegria), which shows that direct contact with the country of origin can provide a protective mechanism for immigrant health. Their results suggest that visiting the country of origin with some frequency appears to reduce the risk of depression by 50% among Asian immigrants. Authors suppose that maintaining the culture of origin by exposing children to the language and values, providing conditions for meeting members of the extended family are conducive for better health. It also shows that contextual factors such as socio-economic status or ability to travel back home are important and can influence the acculturation process. Kennedy and MacNeela (2014) comparing several articles dedicated to youth adolescents claim that acculturating adolescents achieved a connection with others through secure bonds with family and heritage culture peers.

Alegria (2009) claims that existing acculturation measures do not capture this interaction between context- and individual-level processes, nor do they examine which contextual factors lead one to select or retain certain aspects of culture. In many studies (e.g., Berry et al., 2006; Berry & Sabatier, 2010; Kunst & Sam, 2013; López-Rodríguez et al., 2014; Mancini & Bottura, 2014; Pfafferott & Brown, 2006), the domination of quantitative paradigm in acculturation research of adolescents has been observed. Alegria's argument is supported by Ward (2008) who claim that one of the most influential acculturation theories designed by Berry (1980) does not include information on what set of behaviours and experiences the respondent has in mind while assessing each of the spheres of acculturation. Ward (2008) emphasizes that Berry's orthogonal matrix does not allow to explore 'ways of reaching' specific cultural adaptation strategies and to examine whether acculturating individuals always experience these strategies in the same way. To support this idea, Rudmin, Wang and Castro (2016) claim that people who acculturate should be given a voice. Finally, Thelamour (2017), who was using RAEM in her research with the American population, highlights the need to apply more targeted RAEM-based qualitative questions to deem and justify the answers provided in the questionnaires. Moreover, the socio-economic status seems to be an important factor because low-income migrants are less likely to have access to resources to help them adjust to their new environment (Portes & Rumbaut, 2014). Therefore, the qualitative methodology seems to be the response for these challenges and the way to complement some gaps in knowledge on acculturation as, for example, the context and the meaning of specific behaviours related to acculturation.

## Methodology

For this chapter, the case study approach was chosen, with the implementation of a qualitative methodology for data collection and analysis. It is to allow to study the phenomenon deeply by the thorough investigation of the case, by considering its context and by using various perspectives and sources of data. The case presented in this chapter is one of a series since the whole project involved multiple case studies.

### Case characteristics and recruitment process

The case here is the adolescent (15 years old) and her mother (40 years old) - they are considered as a family system. However, they were interviewed separately, in view of the quality of data collection process. They were invited to the research through the Polish Saturday school headmaster. The mother moved to Spain when she was 20 years old with her Polish boyfriend (who is now her husband). She admits she comes from a family of medium or even low socioeconomic status. She experienced difficulties during her first few years in Spain because of the lack of ability to speak Spanish and discrimination at work.

She wanted to come back to Poland, but after giving born to her children, she realized that Spain is a good and friendly place to live for a family. Right now, she has three children: Krysia (15 years old), Henryk (11 years old) and Daria (6 years old).

Her oldest daughter, Krysia, was born in Spain, both of her parents are Polish. The girl attends a Roman Catholic school where she achieves very good results. Krysia describes herself as an ambitious person who did not like to have too much contact with other people in the past. She seems to have a very strong sense of belonging to Spain, to the extent that she formulates intention to change her nationality from Polish to Spanish. However, the reason for that may partially be the fact of her plan to study criminology and to work as a police officer. In Spain, Spanish nationality is mandatory to undertake such a service. For her, the dominant language is Spanish.

### Data-collection method

The semi-structured individual interviews were conducted separately with the adolescent and her mother. The interview guides were based on the RAEM. The additional methods of data collection were field notes and reflective notes in order to implement the triangulation of the data. The interviews took place at their home in the suburbs of Madrid (Spain). They were conducted in the Polish language, but participants sometimes switched to Spanish or used Spanish words. Before the interview, each participant was asked to sign informed consent. The interview with the mother lasted 77 minutes, and the one with the teenager was 67 minutes long. The interviews were audio-recorded and fully transcribed prior to the analysis. Names of the participants were changed in order to protect personal data.

### Data analysis method

Template analysis (Langridge, 2007), based on Interpretative Phenomenological Analysis (*IPA*, Pietkiewicz & Smith, 2014), was implemented as a method of qualitative data analysis. The RAEM (Navas et al., 2005) was used to design the interview guide, as well as to prepare the template for the analysis of data. In the same time, the analysis was not fully theory-guided, but exploratory themes were also allowed– e.g., behaviours and lived experiences introduced by participants and not provided by RAEM theory beforehand. Template analysis lets the researcher add some topics and themes, that are important for the respondent, as it assumes that the template is flexible. Triangulation of the data was incorporated to ensure the reliability of the results.

### Results: description and interpretation of the data

Krysia, 15-years-old adolescent, seems to be assimilated to the Spanish society to such extent that she claims that she would like to reject Polish nationality and become Spanish. One of the conditions, when you can apply for Spanish citizenship, is being born in Spain and having foreign parents. If you decide to change your citizenship into Spanish, you will lose Polish citizenship in Spain, but Polish law does not prohibit a Polish citizen from acquiring the citizenship of another country. So, in Poland, you will still be treated as a Polish person by law.

> I am not attracted to Poland; I don't like it. I told my family, and they are a little sorry. But if I come to them, they are happy. For now, I'm Polish, and I respect it, they have gone through a lot. I am proud as a Polish woman, but I would like to change 'nacionalidad'! [even though the interview was implemented in Polish, the girl used Spanish word]. I would like to be Spanish. (Krysia)

At the same time her mother, even though she has been living in Spain for 20 years, expresses signs of being separated and she scratches the picture of a possible return to her country of origin. In Poland, she finished high school of economics and she wanted to work as a police officer, but it never came true. She went to Spain at the moment when she could be recruited for the police school. She lost this opportunity, and she regrets it. Right now, she is a volunteer working with elderly people and taking care of her children.

> I do not want to change my citizenship, because I imagine my future probably in Poland. (Mom)

At first glance, what can be found here, within the mother-and-daughter dyad, are opposite acculturation attitudes of separation and assimilation. Thus, the acculturation gap is being encountered, which is defined as differences between perceived and preferred acculturation options of parents and their children. It is especially interesting here since literature suggests that acculturation gap may strengthen the generational conflict (Berry, 1997). What connects the experiences of migrant children and differentiates them from the host group is not only the knowledge about the country of origin of parents but also experiences such as discrimination based on the country of origin of parents. On the other hand, what makes them similar to a host group is the experience of a generational conflict between children and parents (Sam & Oppedal, 2003). What is natural in a relationship between parents and children in adolescent life span stage (at least in western context) are conflicts related to the need of autonomy of the child as leisure time, time spent on education. Children with migration experience or born in a foreign country in the adolescent period of life experience existence between two worlds of values – the world of home, core values very often related to values of parent's country of origin and the world of the host society, that is, peers' core values. This phenomenon is being observed in the case described here, in areas related to social relations and school/career defined by RAEM, and also plans for the future which are not directly a part of acculturation model but an additional factor which probably has a meaning in the context of school life and preparation for adult life.

RAEM (Navas et al., 2005, p. 28) defines *Social* area as 'formed by social relationships maintained outside of the family, fundamentally friendships' and the *Economic* area as 'sharing goods produced, economic transactions and consumer habits (items purchased, money spend and saved and ways of managing income)'. Those two areas were put together because they are related to each other in an adolescent's life. On the other hand, very often, Polish adult immigrants have friends from their group of origin, which can be related to participation in associations, church masses, Polish Saturday Schools (Stanek, Sobczak, 2007). Sometimes the church is a place, which gathers the Polish minority and gives the opportunity to meet not only during mass but also after the mass. On the other hand, cash savings are sometimes related with participating in Polish events organized by those associations but also maintaining contact with Polish friends and family in Poland (e.g., organizing trips to their country of origin). Analysis of the case shows that mother has some bad experiences related to Polish people and Spanish people, but she maintains the superficial contact with both groups, mostly with parents from Polish Saturday School and Spanish everyday school. Moreover, she wants her daughter to be in contact with Polish peers and, in order to achieve that goal, she forces her daughter to go to Polish Saturday School even though she is aware that it is against her will. On the other hand, the teenager verbally expresses a lack of will to have much in common with Poland and Polish peers. They, as a family, spend each summer holidays in Poland but she admits that she goes to Poland only to visit her family. It can be explained by the aspiration of fulfilling the need of pertaining to the Spanish group of friends. However, in order to realize this, she needs to be able to pertain in social life, which is mostly available on weekend evenings, when she is obliged to go to Polish Saturday school or to Polish masses in church. So, the acculturation preferences can be an additional source of the conflict or misunderstanding between a teenager and her mother:

> I respect that my mother keeps tradition. I know my mother would like to, but I will not always be Polish. (...) I want to have more earrings, but my parents do not like it. But they do not let me even though my friends have it. (...) I have to come back home at 10.00 p.m. because my mom is afraid of me. (...) On Friday I have a Polish school, a Polish mass and a Polish school again. It tires me a lot because I can only meet friends on Fridays. I do not want to go to a Polish Saturday school. I do not like Poland even a little bit. People are completely different; they think differently from me. (...) I do not say that my mom is bad, but sometimes I feel as if she did not understand me. (Krysia)

On the other hand, *School/Academic* area defined in RAEM questionnaire for children and adolescents as peripheral one related with 'study level, schedules, relationships with teachers, preparation for professional life, etc.' (unpublished research report). Some children with Polish origin and living abroad attend

Polish Saturday school, which is an additional one since they are obliged to implement an education program of the country of residence. Therefore, they go to regular Spanish school during weekdays, and they participate in the classes of the Polish language, history and geography during the weekend (on Friday evening or Saturday morning). For many children, this is an additional obligation after a whole week of studying in a Spanish school. It is even more difficult when children start secondary school in which they have more classes and homework, and they experience adolescents' life stage challenges as sleeping problems, sometimes even mood swings (Brzezińska et al., 2013). Most of the time, the decision of attending this school depends on parents. First of all, they have to register children and then probably bring them to school every week or every two weeks. So when this decision it is not consulted with a child can raise misunderstandings between children and parents as observed in the following case:

> They never wanted to go to a Polish school. For them, it is a punishment. I think they hate me very much for that. She [teenager] had such moments that she just got out of the car after I parked near the school, and she ran away saying that she would not enter school. Now she knows that it won't impress me. (Mom)

There are also many differences between the Polish educational system and Spanish one related with, for example, power distance described by the rules of communication between teachers and students (Hofstede, Hofstede, 2007). Sometimes it can be a deciding factor for the preference of Spanish school rather than Polish school. Other, interesting factor is language proficiency (Spanish as a first language), which can be an argument of planning future education or even job plans in Spain:

> K: I prefer a Spanish school. At Polish school, I don't trust people.
>
> P: And where do you have better contact with teachers?
>
> K: In Spanish one. Well, in a Polish school... I had a lot of problems last year. (...) In a Spanish school, we speak to teachers either Mrs/Miss or by name, and in a Polish school I once called the history teacher Janina, and she said: "I am not your friend". I do not know. If it bothers her, why doesn't she say "I don't want you to call me by my name". We respect the teacher's opinion. (Krysia)

This quotation leads us to central areas defined by RAEM adapted to adolescents (López-Rodríguez et al., 2014; Mancini & Bottura, 2014) as values, religious beliefs and practices, and family relations. Here it can be observed that respect for the older people is important for Krysia and that probably, nonverbally, she agrees with the norms and values related to the Polish educational system. Using the RAEM language, it can show a perception of maintaining the Polish culture in a school area. Even though the acculturation gap seems to be visible in the above results related to the peripheral areas after the deeper analysis, it can be considered as a more complex phenomenon. The girl claims directly that she does not like Poland but, on the other hand, some statements indirectly show a different direction. Some of them can be interpreted as maintenance of Polish culture but not verbally admitted by the girl.

Let's start with the *Values and Religion* areas (both central areas in the RAEM), which seem to be related in the case analyzed here. Values are defined in RAEM questionnaire for adolescents as 'friendship, companionship, respect for people elderly, equality between men and women, the role of religion in your life, etc.'; and Religion as 'beliefs and practices and personal compliance with obligations or prohibitions religious' (unpublished research report). Mom decided that her daughter would attend in Spanish religious school run by nuns since religion is a very important aspect of raising a child for her. She transmits religion as a value to her children:

> Our daughter was the first Polish child baptized in Polish church in Aluche [Aluche is a district of Madrid]. I've been there for so many years; we go there. Holy Communion, Confirmation, Every Sunday and Friday I am there. I try to always be there with the kids.
>
> (...) With Spanish friends, we have more or less the same approach of bringing up children, but I cannot force them to believe in God, but they respect me. I am never ashamed of my faith. (Mom)

Because of historical reasons, in Spain, religion is not as important as in the past. Since religion was used as an instrument to legitimize the Franco's dictatorship in the 20th century, it was associated with the regime. After Franco's death in 1975, the political system in Spain started to change, and political and social influence of Catholic Church declined gradually (Box, 2010) and finally resulted in secularization and diminished the practice of Catholicism in the country (Raquena & Stanek, 2013). According to Centro de Investigaciones Sociológicas (CIS, 2018) in 2017, only 27% of the population was defining themselves as 'practising Catholics'.

The situation in Poland was quite different, and the church during the communist regime was a symbol of the national unity and the fight against the oppression. After the political transition, which started in 1989, and the first democratic elections in 1990, the church also gradually started to lose the position but in a different way than experienced in Spain. It was not negatively associated with people's experiences during communism as in Spain. Raquena and Stanek (2013) claim that the decrease in Spain was happening mostly on cohort (group) level and in Poland at the individual level and that Polish people born during or after the fall of communism are much less religious than earlier generations. The mother interviewed in the following research was born before the fall of communism, she went to Spain in about 1997, and she was actively involved in Polish church before the migration started. She was using religion as a resource, which is a strategy mentioned in other research done with Polish migrant population (Ziarko, Sęk, Seński, & Lewandowska, 2014), as an element of life which was giving her hope and helped with coping with stress:

> I have always had a rosary, which is still with me today. I brought it from Poland. I have always had in my pocket. (Mom)

Furthermore, it can be observed that her daughter manifests similar behaviours related to religion and religious practices:

> I pray very often. When I forget something during exams, I always say ...'Jesus, I trust in you'. (Krysia)

Those differences between perceptions of the value of religion can create a gap between Spanish and Polish migrants for whom religion is important. As previous research showed, conflicting values and interests could hinder the process of interacting with members of other groups (Li, 2009). This 'value gap' according to respect for religion can influence on child's peer relations or out-group perception.

> P: Do you also have religion at school?
>
> K: But it's not the same, there is no *respeto* (respect) [even though the interview was implemented in Polish the girl used the Spanish word]
>
> P: What does respect mean for you?
>
> K: Spanish people are non-practising Catholics. In one year, half of my classmates will be 18 years old, and they don't believe in God and interrupt during the religion class. They don't have respect!. I don't like it. I think everyone can have his/her own opinion, but also can keep it for themselves. They don't have to speak aloud because I don't care what they think.

On the other hand, *Family* area is described in RAEM questionnaire as 'way of relating to parents, with the elderly people of the family, with your brothers and sisters, distribution of roles or functions, etc.' (unpublished research report). As Chao (1994) claims, parenting styles depend on values respected in a specific culture. There are many differences between parenting behaviours and upbringing strategies. Most of the research is based on differences between parenting strategies of Americans and Japanese (Matsumoto & Juang, 2007), but according to research parenting styles are related to developmental aims defined by the culture and can depend on economic situation of the family (Matsumoto & Juang, 2007). What until now was described mostly by Stanek (2007) about Polish population living in Spain shows that many families try to have contact with Polish culture by registering children in Polish Saturday school and attending Polish masses in the church. It is obvious that it does not represent all Polish minority members in Spain, but our participants belong to this group. It is hard to describe specific differences between Polish and Spanish developmental aims, but some of them can be illustrated by mother's observation:

> She goes to a religious school. We are very faithful, and her teachers appreciate the way I raise my child. She got the mobile when she was 13 years old (last one in the whole class)(...) when I saw these presents (at birthday parties) – football clothes, PlayStation, telephones. I do not understand this. And it annoys me in them, you know? They want to do everything for these children. (Mom)

To sum up, a girl's acculturation process is very complex and strategies perceived by her differ in different life domains as previously mentioned by various researchers (Lechuga, 2008; Nagata 1994). The other area emerging from the data are directly and verbally admitted perceptions and preferences of acculturation and indirectly admitted perceptions and preferences of acculturation. In the above mentioned case, focusing on girl's experience, some conflicting results related to school and social areas can be observed. It perhaps can be explained by the conflict of host country values and values related to the Polish culture transmitted to her by her mom:

> There are a lot of events here in Spain that last a long time. And the Poles ... are very hard-working, very and always ... I don't know. Poles are different from Spanish people, that Poles want to work, and Spaniards don't have to go to work.
>
> P: But tell me if ... you said you felt more Spanish than Polish...
>
> K: Yes.
>
> P: But you are hardworking...
>
> K: I am. (Krysia)

Even though a girl wants to change her nationality and to give up of being Polish, which can be interpreted as a preference of assimilation, the reason why she wants to do it may be related to some family values, a need of fulfilling her mother's unfulfilled wish of being a police officer what can be seen as a separation preference. This example shows how complex the acculturation process is and how entangled it is in the developmental processes, self-awareness, identity development and the influence of the family and the social context.

## Conclusion

The aim of this chapter was to illustrate what kind of behaviours and experiences of Polish migrants can be interpreted as part of specific perceptions and preferences of acculturation; how do these perceptions and preferences of acculturation of particular members of family, parents and children interact with each other in different life areas (peripheral and central), according to the Relative Acculturation Extended Model (Navas et al., 2005). Here the model was adapted to our qualitative approach, and the research question was answered drawing on a case study of a teenager and her mother. Moreover, the developmental context, intergenerational conflict and acculturation gap were taken into account (Berry et al., 2006).

According to Havighurst (1981), adolescents have to fulfil the need of autonomy, among others. Adolescents pay much attention to peer relations and the need for being accepted (Havighurst, 1981). So that may be the reason why the teenager interviewed here was trying, perhaps, to accomplish the autonomy from her mother by verbally rejecting the Polish culture. In this case study, we see that the acculturation gap (mostly in peripheral areas) strengthens generational conflict between the teenager and her mother, mainly in relation to school/academic and social areas. However, in the central areas, the opposite tendency was observed: the teenager was very committed to the values transmitted to her at home, and she has been observing, in a peer environment, some actions that were against her values, which she did not like and criticized. Therefore, both acculturation gap between the teenager and her mother and the 'values gap' between her and her peers exist simultaneously. Conflicting perceptions and preferences according to acculturation in different life areas can be related to the ongoing process of identity formation (Erikson, 1968; Marcia, 1980).

Furthermore, the meaning and the role of socio-economic status of the family (Portes & Rumbaut, 2014) should be considered for further analysis in future research, since it seems to influence the level of access to both 'host' and 'origin' culture. One of the ways to maintain contact with the culture of origin is the high frequency of visits to Poland, and this obviously depends on the opportunities available to the family. In the above mentioned case, contact with the family was relatively frequent and regular. This may be related to maintaining Polish culture in central areas of life. On the other hand, there are cultural differences between the attitudes of Polish and Spanish parents towards the way of upbringing children and spending leisure time, allowing children to own things like mobile phones, personal computers, etc. These aspects are also partially related to socio-economic possibilities, values and other aspects of intergenerational conflict.

It is worth mentioning that qualitative research on the acculturation process allows us to discover the complexity in acculturation perceptions and preferences in different life areas and observes how do those areas interact. Therefore, it enriches RAEM itself by offering a better understanding of the complexity of the model. Quantitative research on acculturation (e.g., using the orthogonal Berry's model) does not take into account information about what set of behaviours and experiences the participant has in mind when assessing each of the areas (Ward, 2008). By using a qualitative paradigm, not only 'the content' of acculturation perceptions and preferences (behaviours) is being observed, but also the experiences and circumstances, which shape the life context related to acculturation.

The acculturation process can enrich life. On the other hand, it can increase the misunderstandings between parents and children and children and peers. It is crucial to raise awareness of parents and teachers about the aspect that a migrant child is never 'monocultural' because he or she grows between worlds of different values and norms and sometimes can feel lost between those different worlds. Besides, this kind of awareness could enable parents to understand better the child's perspective and his/her behaviours related to acculturation.

Some important suggestions for teachers in Polish Saturday Schools abroad could also be drawn from this study. Teachers play a dual role as parents want to see them as guardians of Polishness of their children. Children see them first and foremost as teachers in a school setting. Therefore, they apply rules from regular school in the country of residence, to Polish Saturday Schools as well. It sometimes creates conflict. Lack of formal addressing of teacher and strong rebuttal of teacher -e.g. "I am not your friend"- is just an example. Such a reaction is counterproductive. Teachers need to recognize not only the bilingualism of their pupils but also their biculturalism. Therefore, they should serve as cultural brokers who help children to navigate in Polish culture, and who present usefulness rather than obligation to learn Polish, as a possibility to continue future education in Poland either within Erasmus programme or any other international programme (for example, Global Minds – a program sponsored by the EU).

## References

Alegria, M. (2009). The challenge of acculturation measures: what are we missing? A commentary on Thomson & Hoffman-Goetz. *Social science & medicine (1982)*, *69*(7), 996-998.

Berry, J. W. (1980). Acculturation as varieties of adaptation. In A.M. Padilla (Ed.), *Acculturation: Theory, models and some new findings* (pp. 9-25). Boulder, CO: Westview.

Berry, J. W. (1997). Immigration, Acculturation, and Adaptation. *Applied Psychology: An International Review*, *46*(1), 5–34.

Berry, J. W., Phinney, J. S., Sam, D. L., & Vedder, P. (2006). *Immigrant youth in cultural transition: Acculturation, identity, and adaptation across national contexts*. New Jersey: Lawrence Erlbaum Associates.

Berry, J.W. & Sabatier, C. (2010). Acculturation, discrimination, and adaptation among second generation immigrant youth in Montreal and Paris. *International Journal of Intercultural Relations*, *34*, 191-207. doi: 10.1016/j.ijintrel.2009.11.07

Bourhis, R.Y., Moïse, L.C., Perreault, S., & Senécal, S. (1997). Towards an Interactive Acculturation Model: A Social Psychological Approach. *International Journal of Psychology*, *32*(6), 369–386.

Box, Z. (2010). España, año cero. La construcción simbólica del franquismo. Madrid: Alianza Editorial.

Brzezińska, A.I., Appelt, K., Ziółkowska, B. (2016). *Psychologia Rozwoju Człowieka*. Sopot: GWP.

Chao, R. K. (1994). Beyond parental control and authoritarian parenting style: Understanding Chinese parenting through the cultural notion of training. *Child development*, *65*(4), 1111-1119.

Centro de Investigaciones Sociológicas (CIS) (2018).

Cuadrado, I., García-Ael, C., Molero, F., Recio, P., & Pérez-Garín, D. (2018). Acculturation process in Romanian immigrants in Spain: The role of social support and perceived discrimination. *Current Psychology*, 1-10.

Gordon, M.M. (1964). *Assimilation in American life*. Nueva York: Oxford University Press.

Graves, T.D. (1967). Psychological acculturation in a tri–ethnic community. *South–western Journal of Anthropology*, 23, 337–350.

Erikson, E. H. (1968). *Identity: Youth and crisis*. WW Norton & Company.

Havighurst, R.J. (1981). *Developmental tasks and education*. New York: Longman.

Hofstede G., Hofstede J. (2007). *Kultury i organizacje*. Warszawa: Polskie Wydawnictwo Ekonomiczne.

Instituto Nacional de Estadística (2018). Población extranjera por nacionalidad y sexo. Download from: http://www.ine.es/jaxi/Datos.htm?path=/t20/e245/p04/provi/l0/&file=0ccaa002.px.

Kennedy, L. A., & MacNeela, P. (2014). Adolescent acculturation experiences: A meta-ethnography of qualitative research. *International Journal of Intercultural Relations*, *40*, 126-140.

Kunst, J.R. & Sam, D.L. (2013). Relationship between acculturation expectations and Muslim minority youth's acculturation and adaptation. *International Journal of Intercultural Relations*, *37*(4), 477-490. doi: 10.1016/j.ijintrel.2013.04.007

Langdridge, D. (2007). Phenomenological psychology: Theory, research and method. Glasgow: Pearson Education.

Lechuga, J. (2008). Is acculturation a dynamic construct? The influence of method of priming culture on acculturation. *Hispanic Journal of Behavioral Sciences, 30*(3), 324–339

Li, J. (2009). Forging the future between two different worlds: Recent Chinese immigrant adolescents tell their cross-cultural experiences. *Journal of Adolescent Research, 24*, 477–504.

López-Rodríguez, L., Bottura, B., Navas, M.S., & Mancini, T. (2014). Acculturation strategies and attitudes in immigrant and host adolescents: The RAEM in different national contexts. *Psicologia Sociale, 2,* 133-158. doi: 10.1482/77473

Mancini, T. & Bottura, B. (2014). Acculturation processes and intercultural relations in peripheral and central domains among native Italian and migrant adolescents. An Application of The Relative Acculturation Extended Model (RAEM). *International Journal of Intercultural Relations*, *40*, 49-63. doi: 10.1016/j.ijintrel.2013.12.002

Marcia, J. E. (1980). Identity in adolescence. *Handbook of adolescent psychology, 9*(11), 159-187.

Matsumoto, D. & Juang, L. (2007). *Psychologia międzykulturowa*. Gdańsk: Gdańskie Wydawnictwo Psychologiczne.

Nagata, D. (1994). Assessing Asian American acculturation and ethnic identity: The need for a multidimensional framework. *Asian American and Pacific Islander Journal of Health, 2*(2), 108–124.

Navas, M., García, M. C., Sánchez, J., Rojas, A. J., Pumares, P., & Fernández, J. S. (2005). Relative Acculturation Extended Model (RAEM): New contributions with regard to the study of acculturation. *International Journal of Intercultural Relations*, *29*(1), 21-37.

Navas, M., Pumares, P., Sánchez, J., García, M. C., Rojas, A. J., Cuadrado, I., & Fernández, J. S. (2004). Estrategias y actitudes de aculturación: la perspectiva de los inmigrantes y de los autóctonos en Almería [Acculturation Strategies and Attitudes: the perspective of immigrants and natives in Almería]. Sevilla: Junta de Andalucía.

Navas, M. S., & Rojas, A. J. (2010). Aplicación del Modelo Ampliado de Aculturación Relativa (MAAR) a nuevos colectivos de inmigrantes en Andalucía: rumanos y ecuatorianos [Application of Relative Acculturation Extended Model (RAEM) to new collective of immigrants in Andalusia: Romanians and Ecuadorians]. Sevilla: Junta de Andalucía.

Pfafferott, I. & Brown, R. (2006). Acculturation preferences of majority and minority adolescents in Germany in the context of society and family. *International Journal of Intercultural Relations*,

*30*, 703-717. doi: 10.1016/j.ijintrel.2006.03.005

Pietkiewicz, I., & Smith, J. A. (2014). A practical guide to using interpretative phenomenological analysis in qualitative research psychology. *Psychological Journal, 20*(1), 7-14.

Piontkowski, U., Florack, A., Hoelker, P., & Obdrzálek, P. (2000). Predicting acculturation attitudes of dominant and non-dominant groups. *International Journal of Intercultural Relations, 24*, 1-26.

Portes, A. & Rumbaut, R. G. (2014). *Immigrant America: A portrait, updated and expanded.* Oakland: University of California Press (4ª ed.).

Pumares, P., Navas, M., & Sánchez, J. (2007). *Los agentes sociales ante la inmigración en Almería [Social agents facing immigration in Almería].* Almería: Servicio de Publicaciones Universidad de Almería.

Requena, M., & Stanek, M. (2013). Secularization in Poland and Spain after the democratic transition: A cohort analysis. *International Sociology, 28*(1), 84-101.

Redfield, R., Linton, R., & Herskovits, M. J. (1936). Memorandum for the study of acculturation. *American Anthropologist, 38*(1), 149-152.

Rudmin, F. W, Wang, B., & Castro, J. (2016) Acculturation Research Critiques and Alternative Research Designs. In Seth J. Schwartz & Jennifer Unger (Eds.), *The Oxford Handbook of Acculturation and Health.* London: Oxford University Press.

Stanek, M., & Sobczak, E. (2007). Polacy i Polonia w Hiszpanii na przełomie XX i XXI wieku. *Studia Polonijne, 28*, 215-241.

Sam, D. L. & Oppedal, B. (2003). Acculturation as a developmental pathway. *Online readings in psychology and culture, 8*(1). https://doi.org/10.9707/2307-0919.1072

Thelamour, B. (2017). Applying the Relative Acculturation Extended Model to examine Black Americans' perspectives on African immigrant acculturation. *Journal of Cross-Cultural Psychology, 48*(9), 1457-1471.

Ward, C. (2008). Thinking outside the Berry boxes: New perspectives on identity, acculturation and intercultural relations. *International Journal of Intercultural Relations, 32*(2), 105-114.

Ziarko, M., Sęk, H., Sieński, M., & Lewandowska, K. (2014). Coping with stress among Polish immigrants. *Health Psychology Report, 2*, 10-18. doi: 10.5114/hpr.2014.42784

## Internet resources:

http://www.orpeg.pl/index.php/szkolynaswiecie/szkolne-punkty-konsultacyjne

## CHAPTER 10

# A CASE FOR COSMOPOLITAN, PRAGMATIC SOCIOLOGY IN THE CONTEXT OF MIGRANT YOUTH INTEGRATION

Sirkka Komulainen

Migration has become increasingly political and urgent on a global scale (Cuomo, 2011; Castles, 2014). Europe (the primary focus of this paper) has witnessed unprecedented flows and moves of migrants a great deal of whom are young people and young adults. Public discourses on migration matters continue to be polarised, especially around the migrations of young men. Nations that may have previously expressed a great deal of solidarity towards immigration are growing reticent in their public accounts.

In times like this, a need arises for fresh approaches to migration within social theory. The need reflects a wider trend within social sciences calling for research and theory with more impact, especially when concerned with vulnerable groups living in precarious circumstances. Such vulnerability calls for ethically sound social scientific practices that involve both macro- and micro-perspectives.

A number of questions are posed regarding ethics. First, which ethics and values are at play within migration discourses and practices? These may, for instance, be humanist, solidarity, Christian, hospitality, cosmopolitan etc. approaches that may also co-exist and inform one another. Second, in terms of impact, what is the role of politics in social scientific accounts on migration? What is the role of social class and generation in the analysis? What does 'glocal' mean here regarding ethics and politics?

This chapter brings forth a Cosmopolitan framework. It looks especially into Beckian Cosmopolitics as it combines interests in macro-level politics and sociological research practice. The discussion highlights the heightened need for 'cosmopolitan realpolitik' in contemporary Europe to address global inequalities (Beck, 2003), social class inequalities and local concerns. Beckian concerns are brought into the present-day situation regarding today's younger generations and considerations for the future.

Third, a critical approach taken in this chapter comes from the contention that sociology has been rather a-political for some time (e.g. Szelenyi, 2015). It is argued that in the "Migration studies" context, this should no longer be the case. Alternative perspectives for social studies are sought for. There are approaches like Pragmatic sociology (Blokker, 2011), for instance, where one gets closer to questions of social action. Instead of separating sociological knowledge from moral and political philosophical considerations and notions of the common good, pragmatic sociology seeks to explore the moral dimensions of how people engage with the social world. There is an aim to reduce the gap between a supposedly neutral sociological enterprise and the normativity of social action (ibid). This is done in parallel with understanding the gaps between generations.

Finally, some practical recommendations will be suggested for migration scholars for the future. This involves the discussion on the role of the social scientist in the rapidly changing world. In terms of understanding contemporary migrations, one should not overlook the multiple and ever-developing cosmopolitan connections enabled by the internet and, e.g. the social media. This said, certain basic values still continue to affect human connections.

**Ethics and values – what's the problem?**

In discourses on migration, Europe or the EU are often talked about in terms of its norms, values and ethics (Bulley, 2017). Approaches to migrations may involve both hospitality and/or hostility. Recent political currents and debates in Europe have re-introduced the questions as to why immigrants should be received in host countries and how should solidarity be shared between the receiving countries.

We may ask a few questions about the values underlying solidarity. Is it borne out of sheer kindness and sympathy towards the stranger? Is it for peace-keeping and the common good? Is it for social justice and human rights? Is it because there are no alternatives or that there are threats? Apart from humanitarian concerns, there are also issues of security, religions and belief systems, social cohesion and economic considerations. There are specific concerns around the radicalization of the young and increasing inequalities.

For Bulley (2017: 27-8), practices of charity, aid, human rights promotion, humanitarianism and care often assume certain ethical qualities on the part of the 'giver'. These are typically associated with moral capacities, assuming that the 'Europeans proper' have these. Post-colonial and post-structural approaches have shown that, whether motivated by pity, compassion or responsibility, a hierarchical host-guest situation is being constructed. In Foucauldian terms, this hierarchy is then used to exercise further power, surveillance as well as financial and political governance within 'systems of domination' (Foucault, 1998:92). In sociological research, these can be examined regarding power practices as well as discursive claims to compassion, human rights, humanitarianism and obligation.

Hospitality as a quality of the host is different in this context as it seems to refer to equality between the host and the guest, *'the cosmopolitanism of a moment'* (Kristeva, 1991: 11; ibid). It is this very idea of 'cosmopolitanism' that merits further exploration. What is it, and what good does it do?

## Cosmopolitanism

In the everyday use of the word, a 'cosmopolite' is a well-travelled, affluent, liberal and educated citizen of the world. In philosophical and social sciences accounts as well as in the context of migrations that are regarded as problematic, 'cosmopolitanism' involves a range of (often interconnected and overlapping) meanings.

One may distinguish several different cosmopolitan paradigms in social science and philosophical literature. *Moral cosmopolitanism* may be associated, for instance, with the work of Martha Nussbaum who suggested a new cosmopolitan approach (to education) based on tolerance, openness and accepting of differences. *Political cosmopolitanism* draws on the Kantian tradition with a humanist advocating of human rights on a global level. It may also be associated with global citizenship, international relations, transnational theories and multiculturalism. *Cultural cosmopolitanism* (Kleingeld & Brown, 2014) embraces cultural relativism, i.e. multicultural settings and the rejection of nationalism. There is also economic cosmopolitanism that instead of capitalist globalization ambitions aims at poverty alleviation from the perspective of the 'capabilities approach' (e.g. Exarchou, 2016).

Cosmopolitanism[1] as a field of social scientific study consists of three dimensions: 1) it concerns empirical phenomena in the form of 'experience'; 2) the normative component of Cosmopolitanism is empirically grounded; 3) there are also meta-level scientific interpretations beyond personal experiences. Cosmopolitanism may be seen as a contested term; there is no uniform interpretation of it in the social science literature (Komulainen, 2017; Delanty, 2011: 7; Skey, 2012; Beck and Sznaider, 2010).

Further and in a much wider sense, cosmopolitanism as a humanist philosophy has a very long history, stemming from the ancient tradition of moral universalism (Delanty, 2012). Cosmopolitanism has stood for global justice and diversity as well as sameness. In Europe, it is very much associated with the Kantian thought (Brown & Held, 2010; Axtmann, 2011: 20-23). On a macro-level, cosmopolitanism as a term is similar to globalization (ibid). In political philosophy and theory, many authors have approached cosmopolitanism primarily as a normative theory (Krossa, 2012). Micro-level

[1] Cosmopolitanism in this text written with capital C refers to Cosmopolitan Studies paradigm in social sciences.

concerns related to cosmopolitanism are to do with everyday interactions between people and groups. Cosmopolitanism relates to concepts such as (inter)cultural competences and (inter)cultural capital (Delanty, 2012; Weenink, 2008; Bourdieu, 1986). Cosmopolitanism may not be a fixed category or an attitude of a person but a dimension of social life that must be actively constructed through practices of meaning-making in social situations (Komulainen, 2017; Skrbis and Woodward, 2007).

In public discourses in Europe, only some migrants deserve the status of a cosmopolite. There are the migrants/cosmopolites with the privilege of free movement and opportunities for life choices. Then there are those considered as 'intruding' immigrants subject to surveillance, governance and unwelcoming attitudes. Discursively, to the former, a migrant status is a privilege whereas for the latter it is a deficit and often this division may be associated with the migrants' social class and generational position (Chernilo, 2012:48; Komulainen, 2017). Today's European young may be less affluent than previous generations and face new kinds of risks in their lives. The ability to stay and not move may indeed be considered as a privilege.

For Chernilo (2012), here we may witness a scenario where estranged victims of globalisation have been uprooted by political processes and then subjected to nationalist integration processes (see also Komulainen, 2017 & 2013). There may also be so-called 'ordinary cosmopolitans' (Lamont & Aksartova, 2002), such as labour migrants, the 'disposables', who - in hegemonic nationalist discourses - are only needed when the low-paying jobs are not taken up by the natives and should leave the country as soon as the same jobs run out. When it comes to social class, inequalities and discrimination, one enters the realm of sociology. The next section looks particularly into Cosmopolitics as in the work of Ulrich Beck in terms of how sociological concerns may be connected to politics.

### Cosmopolitics and pragmatic interests

In the 2000s, Ulrich Beck developed a macro-sociological theory to overcome methodological nationalism in the ever-transforming world with new transnational and cosmopolitan connections and mobilities. Beck's (2006) methodological cosmopolitanism posed challenges to different levels of social research: a) to theory, in terms of conceptualizing the effects of cosmopolitanization; b) to comparative methods beyond the nation; c) to data generation, in terms of novel transnational forms of research; d) and to normative self-reflection regarding cosmopolitical agency (Komulainen, 2017).

Due to increasing levels of migrations (in Europe, but also globally), Beck and Sznaider (2010) called for a 'cosmopolitan turn' in social sciences. Beck and Sznaider thought of Cosmopolitanism as glocal. They saw it as having the potential to be practised in neighbourhoods, in global cities, in the management of multi-national co-operations or human rights organizations. In particular, they referred to reflexive Cosmopolitanism and Cosmopolitics as the way forward (see Komulainen, 2017).

Beck's contentions were not immediately accepted in his time. In terms of politics, possibly the most famous critic of Beck – Bruno Latour (2004) steered the attention towards the diplomatic role of the social scientist, somewhat away from political engagements. Contrary to Beck, for Latour, the important discussion on cosmopolitanism was actually not whether cosmopolitanism was a good and necessary thing at all, but a discussion was needed on what it meant in the first place.

Later on, other writers have been interested in Beck's and Latour's debate on Cosmopolitics. Saito (2015), for example, developed the perspectives further. He proposed a synthesis calling for a renewal of critical theory by making social scientists reflect on their involvement in Cosmopolitics. This would help social scientists explore how they can pragmatically support certain ideals of Cosmopolitics with their transnational subjects of study.

Beck and Sznaider (2010), however, did distinguish between the roles of social scientists and other actors. They considered it as naïve to think that a change in social scientific paradigm would inevitably and instantly lead to changes in the 'real world'. Thereby the actual task of social scientists in their micro-level work was to study the cosmopolitanisation of this very 'real world' (see Komulainen, 2017 paraphrased).

On macro-level, on the other hand, Beck developed a concept of cosmopolitan realpolitik to understand that national problems could only be addressed via transnational/national co-operation. The glocal means that national, localized perspective may obscure us from seeing vast global inequalities, even with the awareness of them. Beck argued that if there was no pragmatic realpolitik, macro-level issues were not solved (Beck, 2003: 457-460; Komulainen, 2017).

As with Saito's work, there has been a wider renewed interest in pragmatic approaches to studies of the social world, including Cosmopolitics. There is, for example, a paradigm called pragmatic sociology that may be understood as an attempt at a renewal of the social sciences. As in the debate between Latour and Beck, Pragmatic sociology involves a reassessment of the relationship between theoretical knowledge as elaborated by the social scientist and the forms of theoretical knowledge implicated in social practice (Blokker, 2011: 251).

Pragmatic sociology has attempted to situate itself between an emphasis on human agency and structural features of social life (ibid, 252). For instance, it involves a contrast to the critical sociology of Pierre Bourdieu. The problem is about matters relating to social action. One of the key moves in pragmatic sociology has been steering away from a structuralist approach, and abandoning ideas of overdetermined social action as well as that of the external position of the sociologist. Bourdieu talked about routine forms of individual behaviour on the basis of 'habitus' and the structuredness of the social world in general (in distinct fields). Instead, Pragmatic sociology sees human action as situation-bound, calling for interpretation by the observers. The approach is akin to critical realism in that "*it is possible for social science to refine and improve its knowledge about the real world over time, and to make claims about reality, which are relatively justified, while still being historical, contingent, and changing*" (Archer et al., 2016).

These ingredients, i.e. Beck's Cosmopolitics and related debates and pragmatic sociology, may be taken on and developed further to understand and work with Cosmopolitics. The idea is to imagine ways for glocal research and action that is cosmopolitical and likely to have an impact at least in the field of Education and youth work, but also on public discourses. This is to work towards social justice so that migrants themselves can see it taking place. Pragmatic, in this context, particularly means that the aim is to reach the general public as the audience. What could academics do? They also can do things and not only observe from the side-lines, leaving the hands-on work for others. The next section considers and weighs up a number of practical actions.

## Discussion and recommendations

Increasingly, in critical accounts, it is argued that academic (sociological) research tends to shy away from political concerns. For critics, after the golden years of sociology in the 1970s, the discipline has suffered from malaise. In the western world, economics and 'hard sciences' have taken the front stage whereas sociology has remained in the margins. The academia has not been an agent for social change for decades, but instead a greenhouse for growing conservatives. For Szelenyi (2015):

> If one today compares sociology with economics and political science our discipline appears to be in a triple crisis: it lost its political appeal (and radical mission); it could not find, so far, an appropriate response to the methodological challenge from economics and rational choice; and the discipline appears to be in utter confusion over whether it has a common theoretical core (which are the "great books" every sociologist should be familiar with), and even debates whether such a core would be desirable.

One of the reasons for such trends in academia is undoubtedly financing that does not encourage 'non-profit' type subjects like sociology. There is another problem, however, which has to do with scientific interests. Although knowledge production is valuable in itself and indeed the task for universities, the funders might wish to fund studies and projects that support decision making directly. Aligning sociological interests successfully with such funding will not happen unless there are some re-definitions as to what sociology is and what it can do. Such alignment requires uses of theories for pragmatic purposes.

In this chapter, Cosmopolitanism and Cosmopolitics are brought forward for this very reason.

The contention is that a benign radical form introducing hoped-for social change is the task for the young and the next generations. There are already signs that today's youth are politically active and take action, for example, regarding climate change. Similar kinds of mass movements could be organised around social solidarity and everyday cosmopolitanisms.

**Recommendations**

Everyday practical actions on social justice may and do utilize social media, which is a way for reaching wider audiences. To succeed, it will require some thought as it is not always easy to find the most appropriate format or wording for the messages. Understanding different ways and channels for influencing is helpful. It is important to master the etiquette of social media and take responsibility so as not to actually harm anyone in the process. Social theory may be utilized, once successfully translated into a day-to-day language the hoped-for readers use.

Due to advances in media technologies, there are and have been possibilities for increasing at-home global awareness. The least this could be similar to armchair travelling with an educational component. Cultural awareness and intercultural competences very much come under cosmopolitan auspices. They may be taught at school - starting from early education – but also incorporated in such pragmatic actions as youth work practice. It will work out the best when reciprocal, involving genuine as well as imagined encounters. It may work better when conflicts and problems are not swept under the carpet, but an atmosphere of openness is facilitated. The works of Nussbaum, Kant, Beck and others could well work as frames of reference for students as well as for the general public. Education may involve media literacy training, diversity training and 'connecting facts to values'-training, as with critical realist approaches (see also De Jaynes & Curmi, 2015; Duhn, 2014).

Literacy training may reveal, for instance, discriminatory types of sedentarism. These sedentarisms are suspicious of strangers and any kind of movement/mobilities. They aim to tie people to their native homelands like trees are planted in the ground (Malkki, 2012). From Kant and subsequently, Beck, however, one could borrow frameworks for having roots and wings at the same time (Komulainen, 2013). The traces of (white) colonialisms could be re-visited in connection with contemporary world events, such as Brexit in Europe or South-to-North migrations across the Mediterranean.

In higher education, possibilities for Cosmopolitics are numerous. Intercultural competences training programmes may be used. Besides, understanding conflicts, as well as the relations between citizenship and political bodies, may be among the additional topics to cover. It may be the case that students may not opt for intercultural competences courses. However, with the increasing need for such competences, such courses could be incorporated into compulsory training programmes.

## Conclusion

This paper has sought for greater transparency regarding ethics behind glocal immigration reception and integration practices. This has been done steering the attention towards potential uses of social theory. An attempt has been made to unpack as to what is meant by equality and diversity approaches, not so much by directly deconstructing these terms but pointing sociologically towards social class issues and generations as the key dimensions[2].

The paper has aimed to show that Cosmopolitanism as global awareness means understanding of unequal power structures. This also involves good ethnic relations and non-discriminatory practices in changing national and transnational circumstances. It should not be the same as naïve cultural relativism but also acknowledge possible conflicts (Fine and Boon 2007, 9). Cosmopolitan thought does not downplay the problems that sometimes emerge in cross-cultural encounters; neither will multiculturalism be idealized (Beck & Sznaider 2006; Latour 2004), especially not when taking social class inequalities into consideration. As for Beck, cosmopolitanism can be realpolitik but this requires pragmatic action in real life situations (Komulainen, 2017).

The scope of this short chapter has not been to exhaust the aforementioned issues. Instead, the focus has been on offering Cosmopolitanism and Beckian Cosmopolitics as potentially useful frameworks for both social theory and practice around migrations. To imagine how such practices might take place, a number of pragmatic recommendations have been sketched for (European) migration scholars and others to take further.

Cosmopolitan education seems especially important for today's European young. This chapter has suggested a number of practical actions, such as awareness-raising in the social media; increasing at-home global awareness; thinking of migrants as people with roots and wings, and teaching intercultural competences. They may be more than mere soft skills, aiming at counter-acting unnecessary fears and replacing them with healthy and benign forms of nationalism. The role of the social scientist is where intellectualism feeds into practice and is not divorced from everyday realities of human migrations.

## References

Archer, M., Decoteau, C., Gorski, P., Little, D., Porpora, D., Rutzou, T., Smith, C., Steinmetz, G., Vandenberghe, F. (2016). What is critical realism? *Perspectives, ASA Newsletter.* Retrieved

[2] The focus on social class in this paper is not to ignore issues of race, gender and other attributes for which individuals and groups face discrimination. Involving all the possible attributes would be beyond the scope of this paper.

from 23.12.2016, URL: http://www.asatheory.org/current-newsletter-online/what-is-critical-realism

Axtmann, R. (2011). Cosmopolitanism and globality: Kant, Arendt, and Beck on the global condition, *German Politics and Society,* 29(3), pp. 29-37

Beck & Sznaider (2010). Unpacking cosmopolitanism for the social sciences: a research agenda, *British Journal of Sociology*, 61:1, pp. 381–403.

Beck, U. (2006). *The cosmopolitan vision.* Cambridge: Polity.

Beck, U. (2003). Toward a new critical theory with a cosmopolitan intent. *Constellations* 10(4), pp. 453-468.

Blokker, P. (2011). Pragmatic sociology: Theoretical evolvement and empirical application *European Journal of Social Theory,* 14(3), pp. 251–261.

Brown, G.W. & Held, D. (2010). *The Cosmopolitanism Reader.* Cambridge: Polity Press.

Bourdieu, P. (1986). The forms of capital. In Richardson, J. Ed. *Handbook of Theory and Research for the Sociology of Education.*
Westport, CT: Greenwood, pp. 241–58.

Bulley, D. (2017). Migration, Ethics & Power. Spaces of Hospitality in International Politics. London: Sage.

Castles, S. (2014). International migration at a crossroads. *Citizenship Studies* 18(2), pp.190–207.

Chernilo, D. (2012) Cosmopolitanism in social theory: An ambivalent defence. In: Robertson, R. &

Krossa, A.S. Eds. (2012). *European Cosmopolitanism in Question.* London: Palgrave Macmillan, pp. 44-63.

Cuomo, C.J. (2011). Climate change, vulnerability, and responsibility. *Hypatia* 26(4), pp. 690-714.

De Jaynes, T. & Curmi, C. (2015) Youth as Cosmopolitan Intellectuals *English Journal* 104.3 (2015): 75–80.

Delanty, G. Ed. (2012). Routledge Handbook of Cosmopolitanism Studies. London: Routledge.

Duhn, I. (2014) Being and Becoming Cosmopolitan in Early Childhood Curriculum: 'roots', 'wings' and cosmopolitan citizenship *Global Studies of Childhood* 4(3): 224-234.

Exarchou, S. (2016). *Cosmopolitanism or Something Else? A comparative educational research on primary school policies between Greece and Europe.* Master's Degree Studies in International and Comparative Education, No. 38. University of Stockholm, Sweden.

Fine, R. & Boon, V. (2007). Introduction: Cosmopolitanism: Between past and future. *European Journal of Social Theory* 10(1): 5–16.

Foucault, M. (1998). *The Will to Knowledge: The History of Sexuality Volume 1*, (trans. Robert Hurley). London: Penguin.

Kleingeld, P. & Brown, E. (2014). Cosmopolitanism. *The Stanford Encyclopedia of Philosophy.* (Zalta, E.N. Ed., Fall 2014 Edition).

Komulainen, S. (2017). Ulrich Beck's cosmopolitanism for social sciences re-visited: overcoming dualisms towards pragmatic ends? In Caselli, M. & Gilardoni, G. Eds. *Globalization, Supranational Dynamics and Local Experiences.* Frankfurt: Palgrave Macmillan, pp. 109-125.

Komulainen, S. (2013). A chick cosmopolitan migrant condition. In: Lindberg, S. Ed. *The Migrant Novel in Quebec and Scandinavia. Performativity, Meaningful Conflicts and Creolization.* Frankfurt am Main: Peter Lang, pp. 161-180.

Kristeva, J. (1991). *Strangers to Ourselves.* (trans. Roudiez, L.S.). New York: Columbia University Press.

Krossa, A.S. (2012). Why 'European cosmopolitanism'? In: Robertson, R. & Krossa, A.S. Eds. *European cosmopolitanism in question.* London: Palgrave Macmillan, pp. 6-24.

Lamont, M. & Aksartova S. (2002). Ordinary Cosmopolitanisms: Strategies for Bridging Racial Boundaries among Working Class Men. *Theory, Culture and Society* 19 (4):1-25.

Latour, B. (2004). Whose cosmos, which cosmopolitics? Comments on the peace terms of Ulrich Beck. *Common Knowledge* 10(3), pp. 450-462.

Malkki, L. (2012). *Kulttuuri, Paikka ja Muuttoliike* (Culture, Place and Migration flows; SK translation). Tampere: Vastapaino.

Saito, H. (2015). Cosmopolitics: towards a new articulation of politics, science and critique. *The British Journal of Sociology* 66(3), pp. 441–459.

Skey, M. (2012). We Need to Talk about Cosmopolitanism: The Challenge of Studying Openness towards Other People *Cultural Sociology* 6, pp. 471-87.

Skrbis, Z. & Woodward, I. (2007). The ambivalence of ordinary cosmopolitanism: Investigating the limits of cosmopolitan openness. *The Sociological Review* 55(4), pp. 730-747.

Szelenyi, I. (2015). The triple crisis of sociology. *Contexts, Understanding people in their social worlds.* Retrieved from 20.4.2015 https://contexts.org/blog/the-triple-crisis-of-sociology/

Weenink, D. (2008). Cosmopolitanism as a form of capital: Parents preparing their children for a globalizing world. *Sociology* 42(6), pp. 1089-1106.

Made in the USA
Middletown, DE
15 June 2022